HOW
PHILOSOPHY
WORKS

HOW PHILOSOPHY WORKS

THE CONCEPTS visually explained

Consultant editor Marcus Weeks

DK | Penguin Random House

Senior editor	Andrew Szudek
Project editor	Sam Kennedy
US editor	Kayla Dugger
Project art editor	Renata Latipova
Editors	Richard Gilbert, Victoria Pyke, Laura Sandford, Alison Sturgeon
Designers	Laura Gardner, Vanessa Hamilton
Managing editor	Gareth Jones
Senior managing art editor	Lee Griffiths
Jackets designer	Tanya Mehrotra
Senior Jackets designer	Suhita Dharamjit
Managing jackets editor	Saloni Singh
Senior DTP designer	Harish Aggarwal
Jackets editorial coordinator	Priyanka Sharma
Publisher	Liz Wheeler
Publishing director	Jonathan Metcalf
Art director	Karen Self
Jacket designer	Surabhi Wadhwa-Gandhi
Jacket editor	Emma Dawson
Jacket design development manager	Sophia MTT
Pre-production producer	Robert Dunn
Senior producer	Rachel Ng

First American Edition, 2019
Published in the United States by DK Publishing
1450 Broadway, Suite 801, New York, NY 10018

Copyright © 2019 Dorling Kindersley Limited
DK, a Division of Penguin Random House LLC
19 20 21 22 23 10 9 8 7 6 5 4 3 2 1
001–312721–Aug/2019

A catalog record for this book
is available from the Library of Congress.
ISBN 978-1-4654-8222-8

Printed and bound in China

A WORLD OF IDEAS:
SEE ALL THERE IS TO KNOW

www.dk.com

CONTRIBUTORS

Marcus Weeks (consultant editor) studied Music and Philosophy at Sheffield University and worked as a teacher, piano restorer, and trombonist before settling into a career as an author. He has written and contributed to numerous books on philosophy, psychology, music, and the arts, including several titles in the Dorling Kindersley "Big Ideas" series.

Roxana Baiasu has taught philosophy to students from all around the world at universities including Oxford, Vienna, and Birmingham. She has published in the areas of European Philosophy, the philosophy of Ludwig Wittgenstein, feminist philosophy, and the philosophy of religion.

Robert Fletcher has written on political developments for journals such as *Talking Politics* and *Politics Review*. He has taught at Oxford University, and he currently specializes in the Philosophy of Mind, in which he is working toward a PhD.

Andrew Szudek is a writer and editor who studied philosophy at Cambridge University, where he specialized in Wittgenstein and the Philosophy of Mind. He has worked on numerous nonfiction titles, ranging from travel guides to military history.

Marianne Talbot has taught philosophy for the colleges of Oxford University for 32 years. Her philosophy podcasts have been downloaded more than 8 million times.

CONTENTS

CONTINENTAL PHILOSOPHY

PHILOSOPHY OF MIND

RIGHT AND WRONG

POLITICAL PHILOSOPHY

LOGIC

INTRODUCTION

Curiosity has been the driving force behind philosophy since its earliest beginnings in ancient civilizations. Rather than simply accept the way things are, we humans have a natural tendency to question the world around us, and our place in it, and attempt to satisfy our curiosity with rational explanations—to philosophize.

Philosophy emerged from the ponderings of people in the ancient world about the nature and structure of the universe. This is the branch of philosophy known as "metaphysics," and from it, centuries later, the natural sciences were born. However, philosophers also posed questions that science cannot answer. These were questions about the nature of existence itself—the field known as "ontology"—and about the nature and limits of knowledge—the field of "epistemology." Other, more practical questions became the subjects of moral and political philosophy: How should we live? What is good? What is bad? How should we organize society?

These fundamental questions are not only the foundations of philosophy, they are also the topics of conversation among ordinary people. In this book, you will find many different theories and suggestions that philosophers have offered in answer to these questions and their justifications for their views. Some will be familiar to you, or will agree with your own ideas, which will perhaps give you food for thought. Chapter 1 traces the history of metaphysics and epistemology from Thales to Nietzsche—that is, from the 6th century BCE until the end of the 19th century. Chapters 2 and 3 continue the story through the 20th century, focusing on the parallel developments of analytic and continental philosophy. Chapter 4 examines the philosophy of mind; Chapters 5 and 6 focus on ethics and political philosophy, respectively; and the final chapter, Chapter 7, covers logic.

FOUNDATIONS

In the beginning, philosophy was the same as science. Philosophers looked for natural explanations for the way things are. Crucially, however, they also asked: How do we know when our explanations are correct?

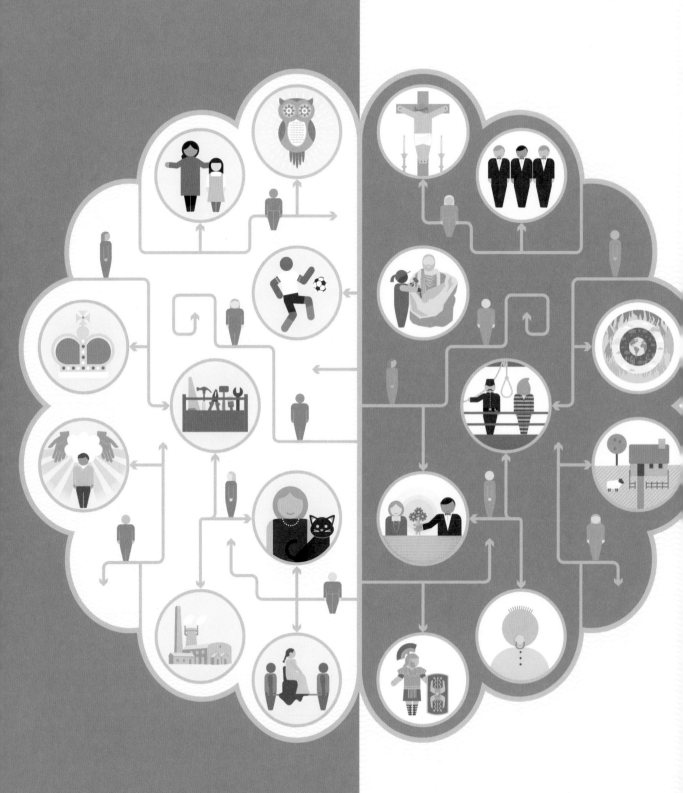

FOUNDATIONS

This chapter explores the central questions of metaphysics and epistemology, namely "What is the nature of things that exist?" and "What exactly is knowledge?" It examines how philosophers have answered these questions historically, taking the story up to the end of the 19th century. Chapters 2 and 3 complete the story, focusing on the "analytic" and "continental" schools of the 20th century.

The first Greek philosophers asked, "What is everything made of?", which is the fundamental question of metaphysics. This prompted further inquiries into the structure of the cosmos, and also raised more abstract questions about the nature of existence itself—the branch of metaphysics known as ontology. Over the centuries, philosophers have offered many different answers to these questions, inspiring different approaches and schools of thought. Some, for example, argued that the universe is made up of a single substance—a view known as "monism"—while others proposed that the universe has two component elements—a view known as "dualism." Similarly, some regarded the universe to be eternal and immutable, while others thought that it is constantly changing.

These contrasting views were the subject of philosophical debate, which gave rise to yet more questions: How can we know anything about the world? How do we acquire our knowledge? These questions are the topic of epistemology, or the theory of knowledge. According to some philosophers, known as "rationalists," knowledge comes primarily from our ability to think; for others, known as

"empiricists," our primary source of knowledge is observation. In turn, these theories raise questions about the nature of human understanding and even of thought itself.

Historically, the rationalist school can be traced back to Plato, who argued that our senses are unreliable, but that the truth can be arrived at through rational reflection. This idea was revived in the 17th century by René Descartes, Baruch Spinoza, and Gottfried Leibniz. Empiricism, on the other hand, can be traced back to Aristotle, who claimed that our senses alone can be trusted. In the modern age, this idea was revived by John Locke, George Berkeley, and David Hume—Hume even claiming that our belief in causation, for example, is unjustified. For Immanuel Kant, this took skepticism too far. He proposed instead that we gain knowledge through perception, but that the world we perceive is already shaped by concepts that we are born with. This synthesis of rationalism and empiricism inspired the idealism of Georg Hegel—a monist who argued that history is driven by the evolution of ideas.

Karl Marx, an admirer of Hegel's, subverted this idea, arguing that economic conditions rather than ideas are the driving force of history. At the same time, Friedrich Nietzsche argued a far more radical idea—that objective truth itself is an illusion. He claimed that the very idea of "the truth" is a hangover from our religious past, and that without it there are simply "perspectives," or individual points of view. His claim that "God is dead" left a challenge for subsequent philosophers: to search for new foundations or to learn to live without them.

The source of everything

The origins of Western philosophy lie in the ideas of the so-called Milesian school, a group of thinkers led by Thales of Miletus in the Greek province of Ionia (part of present-day Turkey).

Seeking rational explanations

Thales (c.624–c.546 BCE) and the other Ionian philosophers—including Anaximander (see pp.18–19) and Anaximenes (c.585–c.528/5 BCE)—were the first thinkers known to have questioned the previously accepted mythological explanations of the nature of the cosmos. Instead, they looked to nature itself, using reason and observation to fathom the natural world, thus paving the way for future scientific and philosophical thought.

Often referred to as the "first philosopher," Thales was also a celebrated astronomer, engineer, and statesman. His inquiries led him to believe that everything in the world, the whole of nature, is derived from a single source—what Aristotle later described as its *arche*, its fundamental nature or principle. This, he reasoned, must be a single material substance from which everything else in the cosmos is derived.

Thales eventually concluded that this single substance must be water. His argument was based on observations: water is a vital resource, necessary for all forms of life, and all living things are moist; it is capable of changing from liquid to solid to gas, so all matter must be water in some stage of transformation; the Earth (it seemed at the time) floats on a sea of water; and moist substances become air and earth as they dry out. While he is often cited as stating "everything is water," it would be more accurate to say that he held water to be the fundamental source of everything.

> **"Nothing is more active than thought, for it flies over the whole universe."**
> Thales of Miletus (6th century BCE)

PRACTICAL INQUIRIES

Gifted with a practical mind, Thales applied intellectual rigor to philosophy and geometry. He is credited with the discovery that the height of a pyramid can be determined by measuring its shadow. Once a day, a person's shadow is exactly the same length as their height. Thales noted that if a pyramid's shadow is also measured at this critical moment, the height of the pyramid is revealed.

The four elements

The ancient Greeks believed that the world was made of four elements—earth, water, air, and fire—to which Aristotle added a fifth, the "quintessence" (see p.43). These elements roughly correspond to our modern understanding of the four states of matter: solid, liquid, gas, and plasma. For Thales, water was primary and gave rise to the other elements. For Anaximenes, the primary element was air.

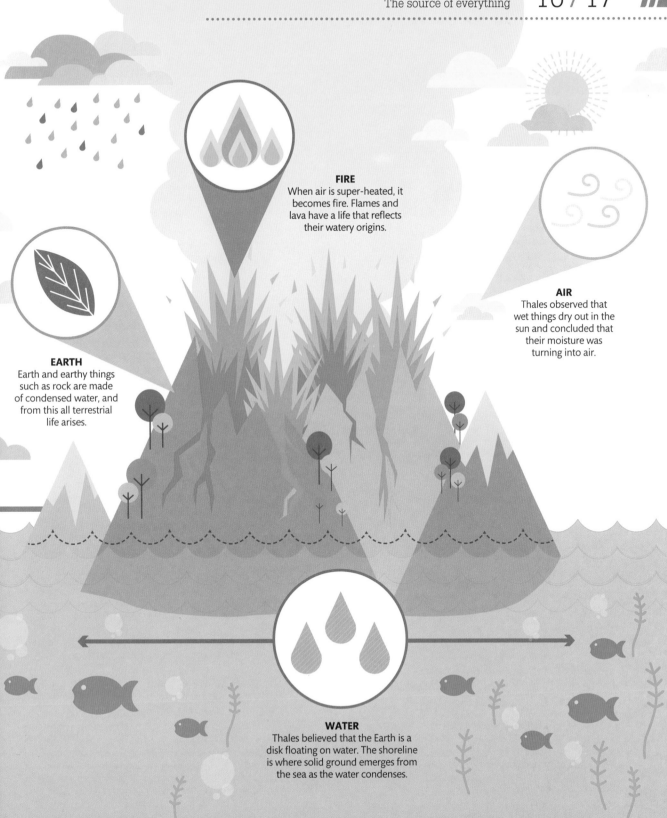

FIRE
When air is super-heated, it becomes fire. Flames and lava have a life that reflects their watery origins.

AIR
Thales observed that wet things dry out in the sun and concluded that their moisture was turning into air.

EARTH
Earth and earthy things such as rock are made of condensed water, and from this all terrestrial life arises.

WATER
Thales believed that the Earth is a disk floating on water. The shoreline is where solid ground emerges from the sea as the water condenses.

Cosmic origins

Anaximander, Thales' student, developed an innovative theory to explain the origin and structure of the cosmos. It was radically different from the ideas of his contemporaries in Miletus.

The Boundless

Born in the Greek city of Miletus, Anaximander (c.610–546 BCE) studied with Thales (see pp.16–17), but also traveled widely, learning from Babylonian and Egyptian scholars. From his travels, he gained a knowledge of geography and astronomy that helped him to develop a strikingly original explanation of how everything had come into being. Like the other early Greek philosophers, he believed that there is a fundamental underlying principle, an *arche*, which is the source of everything

The birth of the cosmos

Anaximander was the first thinker to offer a rational and comprehensive description of the origin of the cosmos. Based on observation, he proposed a theory that explained the behavior of the heavenly bodies, as well as the natural phenomena of the Earth.

APEIRON – – – – –➤ GERM

1 **IN THE BEGINNING**
A small "germ" separates itself from the *apeiron*. This contains all the essential ingredients of the universe, including the heavenly bodies and the space they inhabit.

HOT
VAPOR
COLD

MOON
RING

2 **THE SEPARATION OF OPPOSITES**
Within the "germ" that has separated from the *apeiron*, opposing forces, such as hot and cold and wet and dry, begin to emerge. A cold center forms, surrounded by vapor and an expanding sphere of fire.

3 **THE SUN, MOON, AND STARS**
As the ball of fire expands, it disintegrates into three concentric rings, or "wheels," with the Earth at their center. Light shining through holes in these opaque rings is observed as the Sun, the Moon, and the stars. The hole in the "Moon wheel" periodically closes, generating the phases of the Moon.

in the universe. However, he rejected the idea that this is a specific material substance, such as water (as Thales believed), and instead suggested the idea of the *apeiron* (meaning "the Boundless"), from which everything is derived, and that the universe itself originates from a small part of the *apeiron*.

Anaximander describes the process of the birth of the cosmos as one of the separation of opposites, especially hot and cold, to form three concentric rings of fire, which he likened to the rims of chariot wheels.

At the center of these rings is the Earth, which is drum-shaped, like the hub of a wheel. Anaximander's most remarkable insight is his conception of space: he realized that the heavenly bodies are not situated on a domed vault equidistant from the Earth, but that they circle the Earth at different positions in space. Perhaps even more remarkably, he reasoned that the Earth, because of its position at the center of the cosmos, is not supported by water or any other object, but is floating freely in space.

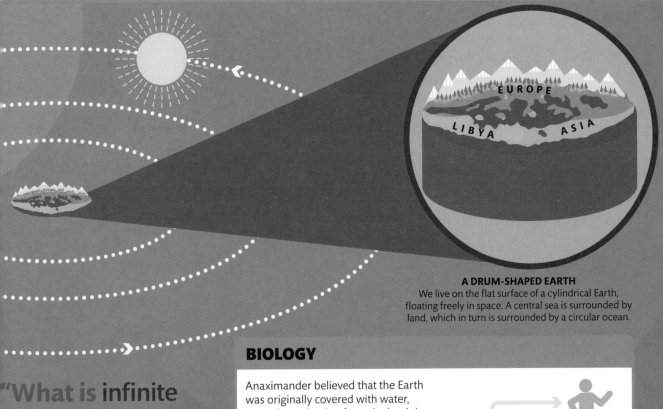

A DRUM-SHAPED EARTH
We live on the flat surface of a cylindrical Earth, floating freely in space. A central sea is surrounded by land, which in turn is surrounded by a circular ocean.

"What is infinite is something other than the elements, and from it the elements arise."
Anaximander of Miletus (6th century BCE)

BIOLOGY

Anaximander believed that the Earth was originally covered with water, which later dried to form the land due to the heat of the Sun. The first life forms were fishlike creatures with tough, thorny skins. This defensive covering provided a protective environment for their more vulnerable offspring, the first humans, who were generated to populate the land.

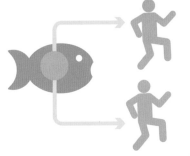

Sacred geometry

Perhaps the best known of the pre-Socratic philosophers, Pythagoras was a near-mythical figure who established a cultlike community devoted to the pursuit of science, mathematics, and mysticism.

A cosmos governed by numbers

Pythagoras (c.570–c.495 BCE) is remembered as the mathematician who gave his name to the theorem of right-angled triangles—that the square of the hypotenuse is equal to the sum of the squares of the other two sides. However, in his own time, he was better known for his belief in the transmigration (rebirth) of the soul. Little is known of what he

actually thought, since he left no written legacy and many of the ideas ascribed to him may very well be those of others. However, it is certain that he set up a community in southern Italy and trained his followers in philosophical and scientific inquiry. The "so-called Pythagoreans," as Aristotle later described them, studied astronomy and geometry and examined the link between numbers, mathematics, and the

Sacred numbers

Numbers took on a mystical significance for the Pythagoreans as they made links between mathematics and the natural world. The first four integers (whole numbers) were especially important: 1) the fundamental number associated with the origin of everything; 2) the material derived from it; 3) the beginning, middle, and end; and 4) the number of the elements. Together, they add up to 10—the "perfect number."

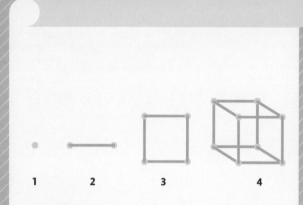

1   2   3   4

GEOMETRIC OBJECTS
Pythagoreans revered the number 1, from which they believed all numbers derive. For example, geometric figures can be created from a single point: connecting two points creates a line; connecting parallel lines forms a square; and connecting parallel squares creates a cube.

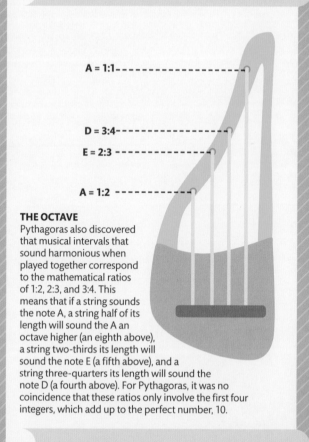

A = 1:1

D = 3:4

E = 2:3

A = 1:2

THE OCTAVE
Pythagoras also discovered that musical intervals that sound harmonious when played together correspond to the mathematical ratios of 1:2, 2:3, and 3:4. This means that if a string sounds the note A, a string half of its length will sound the A an octave higher (an eighth above), a string two-thirds its length will sound the note E (a fifth above), and a string three-quarters its length will sound the note D (a fourth above). For Pythagoras, it was no coincidence that these ratios only involve the first four integers, which add up to the perfect number, 10.

natural world. For example, the Pythagoreans—notably Philolaus—discovered that musical harmony is based on mathematical ratios using the first four whole numbers (see below).

Pythagoras is believed to have learned geometry from Thales (see pp.16–17). However, he was also familiar with the cosmological theories of the Milesian school, and Anaximander in particular, whose chief thesis was that the cosmos is formed from "the Boundless"—an inexhaustible, unobservable, life-giving substance (see pp.18–19). Pythagoras reasoned that the cosmos must have an underlying structure determined by the laws of mathematics, which imposes limits on the Boundless, giving form to the universe. For the Pythagoreans, the cosmos—and everything in it—is governed by numbers, so numbers have an almost divine significance.

> **"The Pythagoreans ... fancied that the principles of mathematics were the principles of all things."**
>
> Aristotle, *Metaphysics* (4th century BCE)

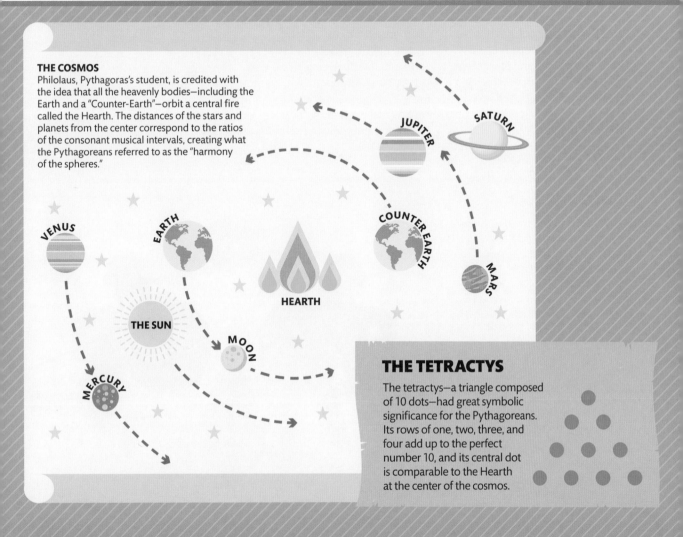

THE COSMOS

Philolaus, Pythagoras's student, is credited with the idea that all the heavenly bodies—including the Earth and a "Counter-Earth"—orbit a central fire called the Hearth. The distances of the stars and planets from the center correspond to the ratios of the consonant musical intervals, creating what the Pythagoreans referred to as the "harmony of the spheres."

SATURN

JUPITER

COUNTER EARTH

MARS

VENUS

EARTH

HEARTH

THE SUN

MOON

MERCURY

THE TETRACTYS

The tetractys—a triangle composed of 10 dots—had great symbolic significance for the Pythagoreans. Its rows of one, two, three, and four add up to the perfect number 10, and its central dot is comparable to the Hearth at the center of the cosmos.

All is flux

While other thinkers believed the *arche*—the fundamental principle underlying the cosmos—to be an immutable substance, Heraclitus thought that the universe is governed by perpetual change.

The *Logos*

Lying at the heart of Heraclitus's cosmology is what he calls the *Logos*—the reason or explanation for everything that exists. His definition of the *Logos* is somewhat cryptic, but it can be seen as something like the laws of nature or physics that we now know govern the universe.

Heraclitus (c.535–c.475 BCE) made a radical departure from the thinking of his contemporaries by viewing what governs the cosmos not in terms of a substance, but instead as an ongoing process of change. He observed that over time, nothing remains the same: day becomes night, seasons come and go, and living things are born and die. Everything, he concluded, is in a state of constant flux.

Heraclitus argued that it is the nature of everything to be in a process of change, and that this change is caused by a war that exists in all things. Everything is made of two contrary properties and is characterized by both; however, over time, one of those properties becomes dominant, upsetting the former balance. Life and death, for example, are in constant strife, but also depend on each other. Heraclitus saw fire as a symbol of the *Logos*—always changing, yet remaining uniquely itself.

THE SAME RIVER

Heraclitus is famously quoted as saying that "everything flows," likening the world to a river. The waters of a river are constantly shifting, so a person can never go into the same river twice. However, the river is also a single, unchanging entity: if its waters stop flowing, the river becomes a lake or dries up completely.

Constant war

Heraclitus stated that all things come into being in accordance with the *Logos* and consist of conflicting, opposite properties. Light and dark, life and death, hot and cold are constantly fighting for dominance. However, just as a path on a mountain is both the path up and the path down, opposites are not inherently harmful—indeed, their tension sustains the world. For this reason, Heraclitus claimed that "War is the father of all things."

All is one

Taking up a position diametrically opposed to the views of Heraclitus, Parmenides argued that the change we perceive in the world is an illusion, and that reality is eternal and unchanging.

The illusion of change

Unlike Heraclitus, Parmenides (c.515–c.445 BCE) based his ideas on logic alone as opposed to observation. Consequently, his inquiries were less concerned with what the universe is made of than the nature of being itself.

First, he claims that a thing either is or is not: it either does or does not exist. Second, he argues it cannot be said that nothing—a void—exists, for only a *thing* can exist. Third, he says that since there is no such thing as nothing, it is impossible for something either to come from nothing or to be reduced to nothing. From this, it follows that change is impossible, for change can only ever be a particular thing (such as a seed) becoming nothing as it turns into something else (a plant)—but nothing can be reduced to nothing. What *is*, then, must always have been, and will always be. Strictly speaking, nothing can be said to be *unlike* anything else.

In contrast to this rational account of reality, the world as we perceive it seems ever-changing and impermanent. Parmenides says that this is due to the deceptive nature of our senses, and that only reason can reveal the true nature of things: a single, changeless reality in which "all is one."

The way of truth

In his philosophical poem *On Nature*, Parmenides describes the world as we perceive it as the "way of opinion"—that is, the way we interpret the changes we see in the world. The "way of truth," however, explains how the changes we see are illusions: reality is an unchanging, timeless, singular entity.

I CANNOT HAVE MOVED
I must always have been *where* I am, since motion, being change, is impossible.

THERE   HERE

I CANNOT HAVE BEEN
I must *always* have been as I am, since the past cannot have been different.

THEN   NOW

I CANNOT NOT BE

I CANNOT BE UNLIKE OTHER THINGS
Difference is impossible, so nothing can be unlike anything else.

ME   IT

ALL THAT IS, IS ONE, UNCHANGING
What exists is one, and indivisible, like a perfect sphere.

✓ **NEED TO KNOW**

❯ **Parmenides** is sometimes called the "father" of ontology (the study of the nature of being, existence, and reality).

❯ **The idea** of two worlds—one of illusion and one of reality and truth—had a significant influence on Plato (see pp.36–37).

❯ **The view** that existence is a singular, unchanging entity is known as Parmenidean monism.

Zeno's paradoxes

As a student of Parmenides, Zeno of Elea believed that all forms of change are illusory. To prove it, he devised a series of arguments that apparently demonstrate the impossibility of motion.

An unchanging reality

Like his mentor Parmenides, Zeno of Elea (c.490–430 BCE) was a pioneer of the use of logical arguments to justify ideas, even when these flew in the face of how things appear to us (see p.23). The Parmenidean notion of an unchanging, eternal reality, for example, contradicts the evidence of our senses, but Zeno set out to show that the changes that seem to occur in the world are logically impossible and nothing but an illusion. He did this by presenting a number of paradoxes—logical arguments that lead to apparently absurd conclusions.

The most famous of Zeno's paradoxes are those that concern motion, which he regarded as a specific kind of change—that of an object's position from one place to another. In the dichotomy paradox, he shows how a simple walk covering a finite distance can become an impossibly infinite task, involving the completion of countless stages (see below). In the paradox of Achilles and the tortoise, he gives a step-by-step account of a race in which a fast runner can never catch up to a slower one, thereby ridiculing conventional ideas of speed and motion (see right).

A third paradox concerns the flight of an arrow and cleverly demonstrates that it is never actually moving. If we accept that an instant is a moment in time with no duration, then at any given instant, Zeno argues, the

1 **A HEAD START**
At the beginning of the race, the tortoise starts from a position some distance ahead of Achilles. As the tortoise slowly moves away from its starting point, Achilles rushes to catch up with it.

THE DICHOTOMY

In order to walk a certain distance, a person must first walk half of that distance. But before reaching that halfway point, they must get a quarter of the way, and before that an eighth, and so on without end. Walking any distance at all will therefore entail an infinite number of shorter stages, involving an infinite number of tasks, which will take an infinite amount of time to complete. The same is true for anything that apparently moves, proving that movement is in fact impossible.

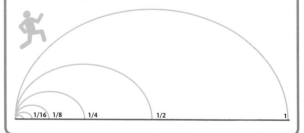

1/16 1/8   1/4   1/2   1

Achilles and the tortoise

Probably Zeno's best-known paradox tells of the race between the athletic warrior Achilles and a tortoise. To make the race fair, Achilles gives the tortoise a head start. Common sense suggests that Achilles will at some point overtake the tortoise, but Zeno succeeds in reasonably arguing that Achilles can do no more than narrow the gap between them.

flying arrow is in its present location and nowhere else. It occupies a static position in the air and is motionless. Time, he says, progresses through an infinite number of instants: if the arrow is motionless at every instant, it is never moving. Motion is therefore impossible, so our experience of motion must be an illusion.

Zeno's logic is apparently impeccable, and it is difficult to find any flaw in his arguments. Modern mathematical techniques, such as the calculus, have been used to resolve his paradoxes, but not to everyone's satisfaction. The philosopher Bertrand Russell considered the paradoxes "immeasurably subtle and profound," and Zeno a mathematical genius.

✓ NEED TO KNOW

❯ **A paradox** uses apparently sound logic to reach a conclusion that common sense suggests is ridiculous or contradictory.

❯ **A fallacy** is an error of reasoning, such as an invalid logical argument (see pp.246–47). Paradoxes are fallacies in which the flaws are difficult to identify.

❯ **Zeno's paradoxes** are examples of *reductio ad absurdum* reasoning that show the weaknesses of opposing arguments.

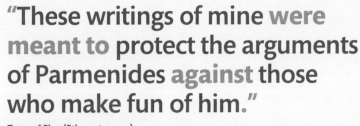

"These writings of mine were meant to protect the arguments of Parmenides against those who make fun of him."

Zeno of Elea (5th century BCE)

2 **NARROWING THE GAP**
By the time Achilles has reached the point where the tortoise began, the tortoise has moved on, so Achilles still has some distance to make up to draw level with it. The tortoise thus continues the next stage of the race with a head start, albeit a shorter one than before.

3 **STUCK IN SECOND PLACE**
When Achilles gets to the point that the tortoise had previously reached, the tortoise has again advanced to a position beyond it. At every stage in the race, Achilles can only reach the point where the tortoise has been, by which time the tortoise has moved farther along.

Elements and forces

In contrast to Parmenides's static view of the cosmos, Empedocles proposed a theory of a dynamic system composed of four elements driven by the forces of attraction and separation.

Cosmic building blocks

Although he accepted Parmenides's assertion that nothing comes from nothing, and that nothing can be destroyed, Empedocles (c.490–c.430 BCE) was uncomfortable with the idea of a singular and unchanging world (see p.23). The world as he saw it is marked by plurality and change. To reconcile the two ideas, he proposed a theory based on the four elements (or "roots," as he called them) that were identified by early philosophers: earth, water, air, and fire. These, he argued, are each immutable and eternal, satisfying the notion that nothing can be created or destroyed.

Empedocles described these elements as the "building blocks" of the cosmos, from which all matter is formed. The various material substances are made from combinations of these elements in different proportions. But, unlike the elements, the substances formed from them are not unchangeable.

In this way, Empedocles explains that change in the world is not an illusion: the elements can separate as substances disintegrate and recombine in different proportions to form new substances. He believed that there is a constant process of change and that the cosmos is a dynamic system characterized by the

Love and Strife

Empedocles suggests that the changing nature of the cosmos is driven by two opposing cosmic forces: Love and Strife. Love is the creative force of attraction, which causes the elements to combine in various forms. Strife is the destructive force of repulsion, which separates the elements from one another and therefore lies behind the decay of matter. The elements themselves are neither created nor destroyed, but constantly rearranged.

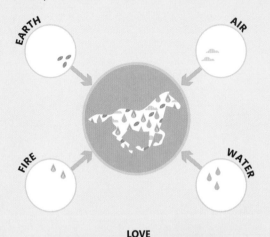

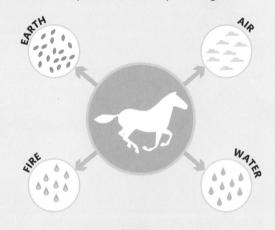

LOVE
The force of attraction, Love brings together the elements in various proportions and combinations to create the different material objects in the universe. The element of fire is what gives certain things life.

STRIFE
Material things are not permanent, but undergo a process of decay in which Strife, the force of repulsion, separates the elements. These elements can then reform in different combinations to make other things.

continual separation and combination of the four elements. To account for the behavior of the elements, Empedocles took an idea from Heraclitus: the action of opposing forces (see p.22). He argues that the cosmic forces of attraction and separation that underlie the formation of matter and even living things govern the ways in which the elements combine and disintegrate. The continual change inherent in the cosmos therefore results from the fluctuation in the balance or dominance of these opposing forces over time.

Cosmic cycle

The forces of Love and Strife are locked in a battle for dominance, creating an eternal cosmic cycle. When Love completely overcomes Strife, the elements cannot be separated from one another to form the various substances of the cosmos. In conflict with Strife, the elements separate and matter and life can be created. However, when Strife prevails, all that was created dissolves into separate elements, until the influence of Love brings them together again.

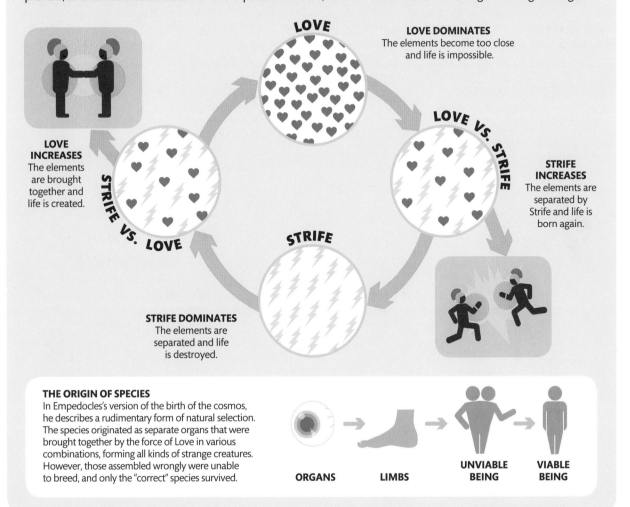

LOVE

LOVE DOMINATES
The elements become too close and life is impossible.

LOVE VS. STRIFE

STRIFE INCREASES
The elements are separated by Strife and life is born again.

LOVE INCREASES
The elements are brought together and life is created.

STRIFE VS. LOVE

STRIFE

STRIFE DOMINATES
The elements are separated and life is destroyed.

THE ORIGIN OF SPECIES
In Empedocles's version of the birth of the cosmos, he describes a rudimentary form of natural selection. The species originated as separate organs that were brought together by the force of Love in various combinations, forming all kinds of strange creatures. However, those assembled wrongly were unable to breed, and only the "correct" species survived.

ORGANS → **LIMBS** → **UNVIABLE BEING** → **VIABLE BEING**

Immortal seeds

In his novel theory of the cosmos, Anaxagoras suggested that, as it derives from a single original substance, everything in the physical universe contains a portion of everything else.

Everything in everything

Like most philosophers of his time, Anaxagoras (c. 510–c. 428 BCE) accepted Parmenides's arguments for the eternal nature of the universe (see p.23), but argued that there could also be change and diversity. According to Anaxagoras, the cosmos originates from a "mass" or unity consisting of inextricably linked particles that are eternal and indestructible. These are the "seeds" of all physical matter, but in this primordial state they are indistinguishable from one another and have not yet assumed distinct forms.

The "mass" from which the cosmos began was at some point prompted to start spinning. This motion acted like a centrifuge, separating the particles and arranging them into different substances. Each separate substance, like the unity it derives from, is a mixture of these infinitely small primary particles. While one particular type of seed might predominate to give the substance its distinct characteristics, every physical thing also contains seeds of every different type of matter. And so everything contains a portion of everything else.

The cosmic mind

According to Anaxagoras, the primordial, unified mass of all substances was set into motion by *nous*, the cosmic mind, the fundamental force and governing principle of the universe. As well as initiating the birth of the cosmos, *nous* determines the way that the "seeds" of physical substances are arranged to form distinct entities.

Controlling force
The *nous*, or mind, both initiates the revolution at the origin of the cosmos and shapes the way things grow.

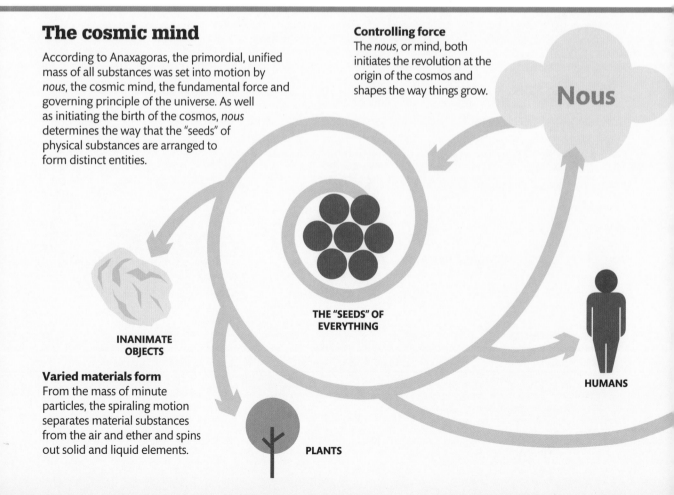

Nous

THE "SEEDS" OF EVERYTHING

HUMANS

INANIMATE OBJECTS

Varied materials form
From the mass of minute particles, the spiraling motion separates material substances from the air and ether and spins out solid and liquid elements.

PLANTS

INFINITELY DIVISIBLE

According to Anaxagoras, each and every thing is characterized by the proportion of the substances that it contains. When divided in two, the proportion of substances remains the same in each half; the halves themselves can also be divided repeatedly, and each piece will still have the same consistency.

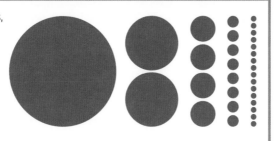

SUBSTANCE STAYS THE SAME
If the separate pieces of something are substantially the same, then, regardless of their size, they remain the same substance, even when divided into infinitesimally small pieces.

✓ NEED TO KNOW

> **The Greek word *nous*** in Anaxagoras's writings is often translated as "mind," but it also means "reason" or "thought."

> **Anaxagoras is credited** with bringing philosophy to Athens in around 460 BCE, and inspiring Socrates, Plato, and Aristotle.

> **In later life**, Anaxagoras left Athens for his own safety. According to some accounts, his unorthodox views led to him being charged with impiety.

"The seed of everything is in everything else."

Anaxagoras (5th century BCE)

FOOD BECOMES FLESH

ANIMALS

The nature of food
Anaxagoras noted that animals often feed on substances that bear no resemblance to the animals themselves. The leaves that a goat eats, for example, bear no resemblance to the goat.

From foliage to fur
A goat eats nothing but leaves, which contain no visible traces of muscle, bone, or fur. However, the goat's muscles, bones, and fur are constantly replenished by the leaves.

Portions of substances
For Anaxagoras, the leaves that the goat eats contain muscle, bone, and fur, albeit in minute quantities. The goat stays healthy if it regularly eats these minute quantities of muscle, bone, and fur.

Atomic theory

In the 5th century BCE, the philosopher Leucippus and his pupil Democritus proposed the revolutionary notion that everything is composed of indestructible particles moving in empty space.

Atoms and empty space

Like many other philosophers, the Atomists—as they were later known—attempted to explain the reality of motion and change. Parmenides had said that these are mere illusions, since motion requires the existence of a void, which he deemed a logical impossibility (see p.23).

Atomists turned this argument on its head, however, suggesting that since motion is patently possible, the void must exist, and matter must be free to move within it. Because the movement of matter takes place at a microscopic level, it is not visible. Matter is formed of minute particles that Leucippus called "atoms," which exist in empty space, and the changes that can be observed in the cosmos are due to the motion of these atoms in the void. Each atom is an eternal and unchanging entity, both indestructible and indivisible, but capable of joining with others to form different substances and objects.

Where Parmenides posited eternal, immutable unity, the Atomists proposed an infinite diversity of eternal particles that gives rise to an ever-changing cosmos.

Building blocks

According to the Atomists, the atom is the basic unit of every material substance. These building blocks of matter are constantly in motion in the void and react with each other, being either mutually repelled or attracted. There are countless kinds of atoms that join together in different combinations to form the huge variety of substances. They then separate as those substances decay. The atoms themselves are immortal and remain intact. They continue their movement through the void, continually and ceaselessly combining, separating, and reforming.

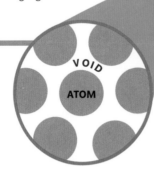

VOID

ATOM

Indivisible atoms
An object such as a tree can be divided into its constituent parts, and the parts cut into pieces. But these parts are not infinitely divisible—at a fundamental level, the atoms themselves are indestructible.

✓ **NEED TO KNOW**

❯ **The void** described by the Atomists is more than empty space—it is an absolute absence of matter, akin to a vacuum.

❯ **The word "atom"** comes from the Greek *atomon*, meaning "uncuttable" or "indivisible."

KINDS OF ATOMS

Democritus suggested that atoms come in a range of sizes and shapes, their properties determining the characteristics of different substances. He proposed that the atoms of liquids are smooth and can move freely past one another, while solids have more rigid atoms that move less and can connect with other atoms.

AIR
Air atoms are light and wispy, and move freely and independently.

WATER
The smooth, round atoms of water give it its flowing, liquid character.

IRON
Atoms of iron have hooks that interlock to give the metal its solidity.

SALT
The taste of salt is caused by its jagged atoms acting on the tongue.

"Nothing exists except atoms and empty space; everything else is opinion."

Democritus (5th century BCE)

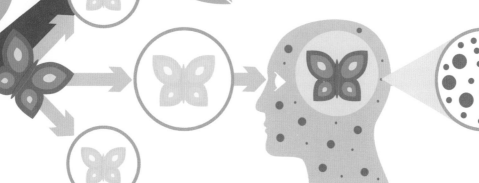

Object
All objects emanate "image particles" of themselves, which enable them to be perceived.

Image
These image particles, which Democritus called "idols," travel through the air in all directions.

Sensation
An image makes an impression on the atoms of the sense organs, creating a sensation.

Psyche
The *psyche* (soul) is made of "fire atoms," which interpret the sensations received by the senses.

Examining ideas

Socrates was a familiar sight in the marketplace in Athens, where he would engage citizens and students in philosophical discussion, challenging their preconceived ideas in his pursuit of knowledge.

The dialectic

Socrates (469–399 BCE) left no written record of his ideas and famously declared that all he knew for certain was that he knew nothing. Much of what is known of his thinking comes from his student Plato, who wrote a series of texts featuring Socrates as the protagonist, extracting and analyzing ideas in a masterful way. It is his method of eliciting and examining an argument—*elenchus* in Greek, meaning cross-examination or inquiry—that earned him his place as one of the foremost Athenian philosophers.

According to Plato, Socrates described himself as a sort of intellectual "midwife," helping to give birth to ideas. His method was simple, using a process of question and answer known as "the dialectic"— a dialogue between opposing views—that digs gradually deeper into the topic of discussion. The opening question is often a deceptively simple one, in which Socrates typically asks for a definition of a concept, such as "What is courage?" or "What is virtue?" He then examines the answer, pointing out any inconsistencies or contradictions in it, asking for an elaboration of the answer to account for them. This method gradually highlights any assumptions and preconceptions, uncovering the deeper meaning of the topic and taking it back to first principles.

Socrates then sifts out opinions and arguments that can be refuted, leaving only that which he knows to be true. From this, he uses the dialectic to construct a better-informed argument. Although such discussions often end without reaching a conclusive answer, Socrates' key contributions were to provide a new way of examining existence, and extending philosophy to include morality and justice, not just the physical world.

> "An unexamined life is not worth living."
> Socrates (5th century BCE)

SOCRATES' LEGACY

As well as pioneering the dialectic, Socrates distinguished between knowledge that is gained through reflection and knowledge that is gained via the senses. Although he placed little emphasis on the distinction, it was one that his successors developed into the rival schools of rationalism and empiricism.

An early form of rationalism was held by Socrates' most famous student, Plato, who believed that our experience of the world is deceptive and that true knowledge can be gained through rational reflection alone (see pp.34–37). Plato's own most brilliant student, Aristotle (see pp.38–45), argued the opposite idea—that knowledge is arrived at by observation only. The latter idea became the central tenet of empiricism. In modern times, rationalism was revived by René Descartes (see pp.52–55), and empiricism by John Locke (see pp.60–61).

Socratic irony

According to legend, Socrates began a campaign of inquiry after he learned that the oracle at Delphi had pronounced him the wisest man in the world. Socrates set out to prove the oracle wrong but discovered that most people in fact knew less than he did. Socrates feigned ignorance of a subject in order to start his discussions, but as he pointed out the inconsistencies in the replies, it became apparent that he knew more than he admitted. Claiming ignorance to elicit a response in this way has since become known as "Socratic irony."

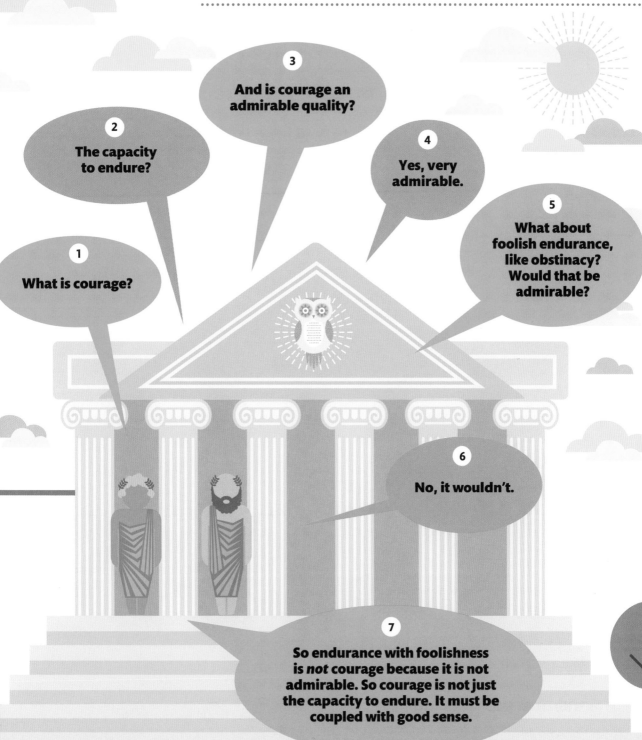

Platonic realms

At the heart of Plato's philosophy is the notion that the world we live in is deceptive and that our senses cannot be trusted. Indeed, for Plato, our world is merely a shadow cast by a higher realm of the Forms.

A world of Forms

Plato, like many philosophers before and since, was an accomplished mathematician and was fascinated by geometry. He observed that there are many instances of things that are, for example, circular in the world around us, and that we recognize them as instances

of a circle. We can do this, he argued, because we have an idea in our minds of what a circle is—what he called the "Idea" or "Form" of a circle—and unlike the particular instances of circular things, this Form is an ideal circle, with no imperfections. Indeed, everything we experience—from horses to acts

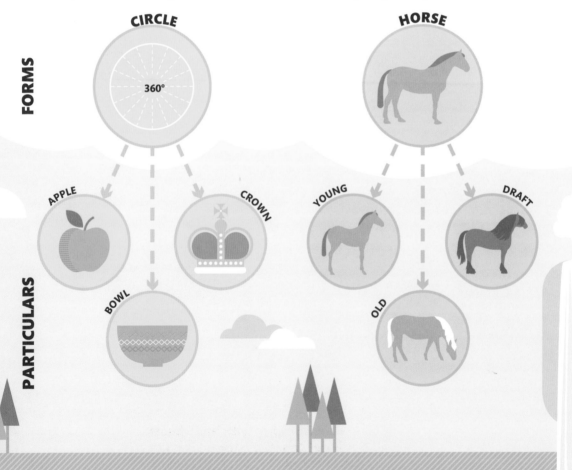

FORMS

CIRCLE — 360°   HORSE

PARTICULARS

APPLE   CROWN   YOUNG   DRAFT

BOWL   OLD

Forms and particulars

According to Plato, only imperfect, particular things exist in our world. The ideal circle, for example, exists only in the world of the Forms. The Forms are like blueprints from which particular things are made.

Material objects

There are many kinds of horses, but all are recognizably horses because they conform to the ideal Form of a horse. All our ideas of "horsiness" are derived from the ideal Form.

of justice—are particular things that we recognize by comparing them to their relative Forms in our minds. Moreover, Plato claimed that since we cannot perceive these Forms, they must exist in a realm beyond our senses—one that we recognize with our *psyche*, or intellect. This process of recognition is largely instinctual, but Plato argued that philosophers are needed to comprehend certain Forms. Indeed, for Plato, philosophers ought to be kings: they should organize society and advise on ethical matters (see pp.200–201).

THE GOOD

JUSTICE

BEAUTY

TRUTH

$2 + 2 = 4$

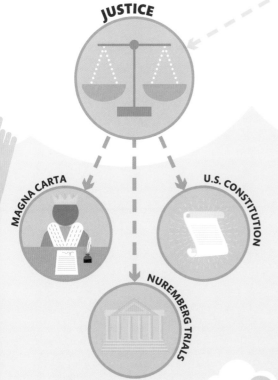

MAGNA CARTA

U.S. CONSTITUTION

NUREMBERG TRIALS

> "If particulars are to have meaning, there must be universals."
>
> Plato, *Republic* (4th century BCE)

Abstract concepts
There are also Forms of abstract concepts, such as truth, beauty, and virtue. Instances of justice in the earthly realm, for example, are reflections of the ideal Form of the concept of justice.

DUALISM

In Plato's dualistic universe, the two worlds he describes are perceived in different ways. The earthly realm is experienced by our bodily senses; the ideal realm is understood by the *psyche*— our mind or intellect.

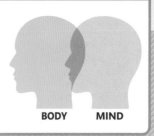

BODY   **MIND**

Plato's allegory of the cave

In the *Republic*, Plato presented an allegory to show how our knowledge of reality is restricted by the deceptive information provided by our senses.

A world of shadows

Plato asks us to imagine a cave in which some prisoners are held captive. They are shackled to face the back wall of the cave and are unable to turn their heads. Their field of view is restricted to the wall in front of them, across which they can see images moving.

The captives are unaware that behind them, hidden by a low wall, another group of people are parading a variety of objects in front of a fire. It is the shadows of these objects that the prisoners can see in front of them.

Because the prisoners can only see the shadows, this is the only reality of which they are aware. They know nothing of the objects casting the shadows and would not believe it if they were told about them. They are literally being kept in the dark about the true nature of the world that they inhabit. The point that Plato is making is that our own perception of the world is similarly restricted, and that the things we believe to be real are merely "shadows" of the things that exist in the ideal realm of the Forms (see pp.34–35).

Escaping the cave

Suppose that a prisoner in the cave is freed from her chains. As she looks behind her, she would be dazzled by the light of the fire, but would slowly make out the objects whose shadows she had mistaken for reality. She might then be persuaded to leave the cave and, after initially being blinded by the sunlight, she would see that there is more to reality than the world inside the cave. However, if she returned to the cave, she would find it difficult to convince the other captives of her discovery that their reality is an illusion.

2 ILLUSORY IMAGES
The prisoners see images of things on the wall, which, as they have experience of nothing else, they assume to be reality. What they cannot know, because they cannot turn around to see it, is that these are only the shadows cast by other objects.

1 RESTRICTED EXPERIENCE
All that the prisoners can see, and have ever seen, is the back wall of the cave. What they view there is the limit of their experience of the world.

"Earthly knowledge is but a shadow."

Plato, *Republic* (4th century BCE)

6 A SUPERIOR WORLD
The world she discovers is reality. For Plato, the philosopher's role is to encourage people to leave the cave—that is, to comprehend the limits of their experience.

5 EMERGING FROM THE DARK
If the prisoner is led out of the cave, once her eyes are accustomed to the sunlight, she sees things that she never knew existed.

4 SEEING THE LIGHT
At first she is dazzled by the light of the fire, but then observes the objects and how they are responsible for casting the shadows.

3 REALIZING THE DECEPTION
A freed prisoner can see behind her and realize that she has been deceived: there is more to the world than the images projected onto the wall.

INNATE KNOWLEDGE

Plato believed that our knowledge of the Forms is something we are born with, not something we acquire through experience. Rather, we use our reason to access the Forms, in whose realm we lived before we were born. For Plato, philosophers are like midwives: their role is to bring to light what we innately already know.

FORMS

One world only

Plato's most brilliant student, Aristotle, did not agree with his mentor's theory of Forms. Instead, he proposed that we learn about the world through experience alone.

Empiricism

Aristotle could not accept the idea of a separate world of ideal Forms (see pp.34–37). Plato had argued that the Forms—the qualities of being circular, good, or just, for instance—exist in a separate realm. Aristotle believed that there is only one cosmos, which we learn about through our experience of it. Although he accepted that "universal" qualities (such as redness) exist, he did not believe that they do so in a separate dimension. Rather, he said, they exist in each particular instance in this world.

For example, the idea of a "circle" is general: we have in our minds an idea of what constitutes a perfect circle. He explains that this is not because we have innate knowledge of the perfect (Form of a) circle, but because we experience circular things, and then generalize about them, having seen what they have in common. For Aristotle, we gather information about the world through our senses and make sense of it by using our intellect or reason. In this way, we build up ideas, apply labels to them, and make distinctions. As a philosophical stance, this is known as "empiricism," as opposed to Plato's "rationalism."

Using experience

Aristotle argued that we learn general concepts by experiencing particular instances: our idea of a cat is built from our experiences of many different cats. We use reason to grasp the general idea "Cat."

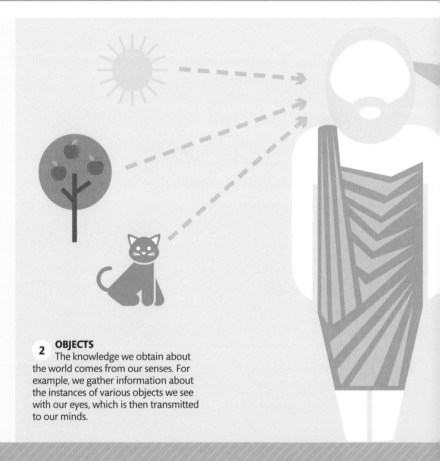

1 UNSCRIBED TABLET
According to Aristotle, we have no innate knowledge. When we are born, our minds are like "unscribed tablets" waiting to be written on. We build up our knowledge by learning from our experiences.

2 OBJECTS
The knowledge we obtain about the world comes from our senses. For example, we gather information about the instances of various objects we see with our eyes, which is then transmitted to our minds.

ESSENTIAL AND ACCIDENTAL PROPERTIES

Aristotle argued that all things have two kinds of properties. An essential property is what makes a thing what it is. Its other properties are "accidental" properties.

❯ An apple's accidental properties include its color, shape, and weight. It is an apple whether it is green or red, round or oval, large or small.

❯ The apple's essential property is the substance that it is made from.

❯ The essential property of a ball, however, is its shape; the substance it is made of is an accidental property.

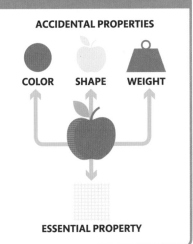

ACCIDENTAL PROPERTIES

COLOR   SHAPE   WEIGHT

ESSENTIAL PROPERTY

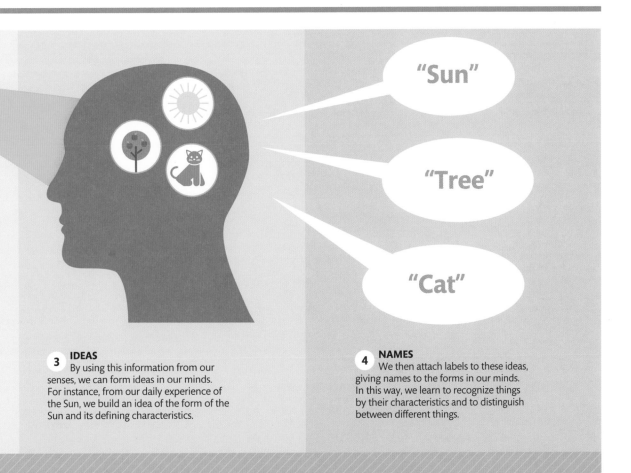

"Sun"

"Tree"

"Cat"

3 IDEAS
By using this information from our senses, we can form ideas in our minds. For instance, from our daily experience of the Sun, we build an idea of the form of the Sun and its defining characteristics.

4 NAMES
We then attach labels to these ideas, giving names to the forms in our minds. In this way, we learn to recognize things by their characteristics and to distinguish between different things.

Form is function

Aristotle argued that to understand a thing is to know four things about it: what it is made of, how it came into being, its design, and what function it performs.

Matter and form

In their efforts to understand the nature of things, the pre-Socratic philosophers focused on the "stuff" that things are made of—the matter of the cosmos.

Aristotle, however, noted that there is more to a thing than its physical make-up. For him, to know a thing is not only to know what it is made of, but also what processes brought it into being, what shape (or design) it takes, and what purpose it serves. Aristotle called these the "four causes," and argued that we only understand a thing when we know its four causes. This radically departed from the teachings of the Atomists, for example, who rejected the notion

that there are purposes in nature, favoring what Aristotle called "efficient causes" only (see below).

For Aristotle, clay can be used to make bricks, crockery, drainpipes, and even statues. All of these share the same matter, but each has its own form. The form of a statue, for instance, is different from that of a bowl because the function of a bowl (to contain food) is different from that of a statue (to honor a person). However, even unformed clay has a function, and that is to become those various forms. For Aristotle, matter without form cannot exist. What he calls "prime" matter is pure potential: it has yet to unfold into the various forms it can take.

 NEED TO KNOW

❯ **Aristotle's four causes** are not causes in the modern sense, but explanations or reasons for things coming into being. For Aristotle, all things have a purpose and are fully known by understanding their four causes (see pp.44–45).

❯ **"Form" in Aristotle's ontology** refers to what makes a thing specifically what it is—its essence—and is different from Plato's idea of a perfect Form on which a thing is modeled (see pp.34–35).

❯ **Aristotle's idea** that a substance is a combination of matter and form is known as "hylomorphism."

The four causes

Aristotle explained the nature of a thing in terms of its physical make-up, its design, the circumstances that brought it into being, and its purpose or function. Together, these four causes tell us all we need to know about a thing and go far beyond the Atomists' claim that a cause is simply a physical event that brings a thing into being (see pp.30–31). The Atomists' view came back into vogue with Galileo, who saw "efficient causes" as the only causes relevant to modern science (see pp.50–51).

1 MATERIAL CAUSE
The material cause of a thing is the matter from which it is made. In the case of a sculpture, the material cause is a slab of stone.

2 FORMAL CAUSE
The formal cause of a thing is its physical design. The formal cause of a sculpture is the blueprint prepared by its maker.

THE SUBSTANCE OF THINGS

According to Aristotle, the substance of a thing—that which makes it what it is—is more than simply the material from which it is made. All sorts of things can be made from clay, and it is the form of the clay that makes it, for example, a bowl. The substance of a thing is therefore its matter and its form. Later philosophers argued that because the substance of a thing underlies its physical nature, transubstantiation is also possible (see p.48).

 = +

Substance
The substance of a bowl is what makes it what it is—a vessel for containing food.

Matter
The matter of the bowl is the material from which it is made—clay.

Form
The form of the bowl is its shape, which enables it to contain food.

"The aim of art is to represent not the outward appearance of things, but their inward significance."

Aristotle, *Poetics* (4th century BCE)

3 **EFFICIENT CAUSE**
The efficient cause of a thing is the physical process that brings it into being. The efficient cause of a sculpture is its sculptor.

4 **FINAL CAUSE**
The final cause of a thing is the purpose for which it has come into being. A statue of Aristotle, for example, serves to honor the man it depicts.

An Earth-centered cosmos

Aristotle's concept of a cosmos with the Earth at its center, surrounded by heavenly spheres, was the model for astronomy for almost 1,900 years.

The Earth and the heavens

Aristotle believed that the Earth and the heavens are distinct regions, with a boundary between them marked by the orbit of the Moon. In the terrestrial, or sublunary, region, the matter from which everything is made consists of the four elements: earth, water, air, and fire. According to Aristotle, these elements have a tendency to move up or down, seeking their natural place of rest. The earth element tends to move downward, toward the center of the Earth; water is inclined to settle on the Earth's surface; above that floats the air; and finally, there is fire, which rises to the top.

The heavenly spheres

In line with his contemporaries, Aristotle believed that the circle was the perfect geometric figure. For this reason, he naturally thought that the heavenly bodies beyond the Moon moved in circular orbits. This model of a perfect, eternal, geocentric cosmos was accepted for almost all subsequent astronomical thought until Nicolaus Copernicus championed the idea of a heliocentric universe in 1543 (see pp.49–51).

FIRE

AIR

WATER

EARTH

KINDS OF SOULS

According to Aristotle, everything consists of both matter and form. The matter of living things is made up of the elements, but their form is the *psyche*, or soul, which gives them life. Different kinds of souls determine the natures of plants, animals, and humans.

VEGETATIVE
Plants have only a vegetative soul with the ability to grow and reproduce.

SENSITIVE
Animals have sensitive souls. They can move and experience sensations.

RATIONAL
Unique to living beings, humans have rational souls, which can think and reason.

The geocentric universe

Outside the orbit of the Moon lies the celestial region in which the Sun, the planets, and the stars move in orbits at various distances from the Earth. Unlike the sublunary region, the celestial region is made from an incorruptible substance, which Aristotle calls the "quintessence," or fifth element. According to Aristotle, the natural movement of the earthly elements is up or down, toward or away from the center of the Earth. By contrast, the natural movement of things in the celestial region is circular. What's more, earthly elements tend toward a position of rest, while celestial movement is unceasing. Thus, Aristotle reasoned that the stationary Earth, although imperfect, is at the center of the cosmos.

Beyond the Moon's orbit, Aristotle identified 55 concentric spheres to which the celestial objects are attached. As they radiate away from the Earth, the outer spheres draw closer toward perfection, stretching into spiritual realms that have no material existence. The universe, for Aristotle, is a perfect form and cannot have come into being at any one time: it is eternal, unchanging.

THE MOON

THE SUN

COMPOUND BEINGS

For Aristotle, everything in the terrestrial region is a combination of the four elements in varying proportions, giving beings their distinctive characteristics. The natural tendency of the elements to seek an appropriate level exerts an upward or downward force: rooting plants to the Earth or giving animals their mobility.

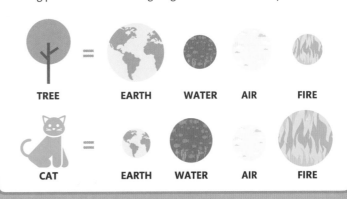

| TREE | = | EARTH | WATER | AIR | FIRE |

| CAT | = | EARTH | WATER | AIR | FIRE |

Purposes in nature

According to Aristotle, everything that exists has a final cause or purpose—what in Greek is called a *telos*. In other words, everything in nature exists to fulfill a goal.

Teleology

Explaining things in terms of their purposes was not unusual among classical Greek philosophers, but today it stands at odds with our modern, scientific understanding of the world (see pp.50–51). To our modern eyes, it is pretty normal to describe a man-made object, such as a tool, in terms of its function or purpose. A hammer, for example, exists for the purpose of pounding in nails. But this is an extrinsic purpose, one that is imposed upon it from the outside. What Aristotle proposed was that everything, including everything in the natural world, has an intrinsic purpose: that is, each thing exists in order to achieve its own ends—its internal purpose. For example, a seed's purpose is to germinate and become a plant, and trees exist in order to produce fruit.

For Aristotle, it is not only living things that exist for a purpose. Rain falls in order to moisten the ground and enable plants to grow. It is the rain's *telos* to water the earth and the plants' *telos* to grow. Their purpose or goal is the reason they have come into being.

More in line with our modern thinking is the Atomists' assertion that natural things do not have an intrinsic purpose or "final cause" (see pp.30–31): instead, their existence is the cause of other things. Rain does not fall in order to water the plants; rather, the plants use the moisture that happens to have been provided by the rainfall.

1 EFFICIENT CAUSE
The efficient cause in this example is the woman who pushes the rock. The rock moves because of her actions.

THE UNFOLDING WORLD

For Aristotle, the essential property of a seed is its ability to grow. That is also its intrinsic purpose: it exists to become a plant, which, in turn, exists in order to produce seeds. Living things are therefore characterized by their tendency to move or change and to reproduce. And, because all terrestrial things are imperfect and impermanent, beings not only grow, but also eventually perish and decay.

Causation

Aristotle's theory of causation is based on his idea that everything has four causes (see pp.40–41). What we usually think of as a cause—that which makes a thing happen—is what Aristotle calls an "efficient cause." For example, a person who pushes a rock downhill is the efficient cause of the rock's movement. The purpose, or "final cause," of its movement—why it goes downward instead of up or sideways—is that it is seeking the center of the Earth (see pp.42–43). The final cause of the *action* of pushing the rock is to see how far it will roll. The rock's movement is also determined by formal and material causes.

"It is [...] necessary always to investigate the supreme cause of every thing."

Aristotle, *Physics* (4th century BCE)

THE UNMOVED MOVER

Aristotle's universe had no beginning, but Aristotle believed that something must have set the heavenly bodies in motion, since everything is caused by something else. However, this raises two questions: What caused that cause, and what moved the mover of the universe? Aristotle proposed the idea of a first cause, an "unmoved mover," responsible for all the motion in the universe.

FIRST CAUSE

FIRE
The element fire rises to take its position above the air. A volcano's purpose is to enable the fire to escape from the Earth.

2 MATERIAL CAUSE
The material cause is the rock's physical composition. The rock is made of earth, so, because earthy things seek the center of the Earth, it moves downward.

RAIN
Water in the air, in the form of clouds, has a downward tendency and falls to settle on the Earth, moistening it.

My purpose is to think!

3 FORMAL CAUSE
The formal cause—the shape of the rock's trajectory— is determined by the landscape. The rock's rolling and bouncing are caused by the slopes and bumps of the hill.

4 FINAL CAUSE
The rock comes to rest when it reaches the closest it can get to the center of the Earth—the bottom of the hill.

TREE
The nature of trees, determined by their vegetative souls, is to grow in order to produce fruit to reproduce.

Scholastic philosophy

Medieval European culture was dominated by the Catholic Church, and the classical philosophy of Plato and Aristotle was only gradually assimilated into Christian teaching.

Catholic theology

The establishment of the Christian Church marked the end of the period of classical antiquity. Philosophy was regarded with some suspicion by early Christians, who considered its basis in reason, rather than faith, as incompatible with Christian doctrine. There were some, such as Augustine of Hippo (354–430 CE) and Boethius (c.477–524), who found ways to reconcile the idealist philosophy of Plato with their faith, but for several centuries, the Church's monopoly on learning prevented the spread of classical philosophy in Europe. This changed in the 12th century, when medieval scholars rediscovered and translated the classical Greek texts. Many of these had been preserved by Islamic scholars, who had translated them into Arabic.

Although it was relatively simple to incorporate Plato's idealist and sometimes mystical ideas, Aristotle's texts seemed at first to be contrary to Catholic dogma. His systematic reasoning, however, inspired a new approach to teaching, which became known as scholasticism. Education spread from the monasteries to newly founded universities in cities across Europe, where Aristotelian logic and dialectical reasoning were taught as a method for examining theological arguments, and to provide rational justification for the various pillars of Christian faith.

Although the first translations of Greek philosophers originated in southern Europe, with its links to the Islamic world, scholasticism arose in the scholarly work of Christian philosophers, such as John Scotus Eriugena in Ireland in the 9th century. By the 12th century, the scholastic tradition was flourishing across Europe. Among its most influential philosophers were Anselm of Canterbury (1033/4–1109), Peter Abelard (1079–1142), Duns Scotus (c.1266–1308), William of Ockham (c.1287–1347), and, a major figure in medieval European philosophy, Thomas Aquinas (1225–1274).

The schools that were established to provide scholastic education thrived for several centuries, and many still exist today. However, with the arrival of the Renaissance, scholasticism's emphasis on theology was replaced by scientific and humanist ideas.

CREATING ETERNITY

A major stumbling block for Christian philosophers trying to integrate Aristotle into Catholic doctrine was Aristotle's assertion that the universe has no end and no beginning, contradicting the Biblical description of God's creation of the world. Thomas Aquinas, however, believed that since human reason and Christian doctrine are both gifts from God, they cannot be contradictory. Using his God-given reason, he argued that Aristotle was not mistaken in his concept of an eternal universe, but that God was indeed its creator: in the beginning, God created the universe, but could have also created a universe that is eternal.

The ontological argument

In attempting to reconcile faith and reason, a problem for scholastic philosophers was to provide a rational argument for the existence of God. Probably the first of the Christian philosophers to present such an argument was Anselm of Canterbury. His reasoning, known as the ontological argument, defines God as "that than which nothing greater can be thought." From that premise, he methodically shows that if God exists in our imagination, then an even greater God is possible: one that exists in reality. Thomas Aquinas later identified four other arguments for the existence of God, derived from Aristotle's idea of an "unmoved mover" or first cause (see p.45).

"For I do not seek to understand in order to believe, but I believe in order to understand."

Anselm of Canterbury (11th century)

6 THEREFORE, GOD MUST EXIST IN REALITY

5 IF GOD EXISTS ONLY IN OUR IMAGINATIONS, HE WOULDN'T BE THE GREATEST THING CONCEIVABLE, BECAUSE GOD IN REALITY WOULD BE BETTER

4 THINGS THAT EXIST IN REALITY ARE ALWAYS BETTER THAN THINGS THAT EXIST ONLY IN OUR MINDS

3 THINGS CAN EXIST ONLY IN OUR MINDS OR THEY CAN EXIST IN REALITY

2 GOD EXISTS AS AN IDEA IN THE MIND

1 GOD IS THE GREATEST THING WE CAN THINK OF

Transubstantiation

Using the Aristotelian notions of substance, matter, and form, Thomas Aquinas argued that, in the Catholic Mass, bread and wine actually become the body and blood of Jesus.

Changing form

One of the most important philosophers of the scholastic tradition (see pp.46–47), Aquinas (1225–1274) was largely responsible for incorporating Aristotelian ideas into Christian theology. The down-to-Earth philosophy of Aristotle (see pp.38–45) appeared to be at odds with several tenets of Christian dogma—not least that God created the universe—but Aquinas saw that it was not only compatible with Catholic doctrine, but actually helped to explain it.

A particularly tricky problem was how to provide a rational, philosophical justification for belief in transubstantiation—the actual changing of bread and wine into the body and blood of Christ, which the Catholic Church claimed took place. To do this, Aquinas turned to Aristotle, whose ideas were only gradually gaining acceptance by Christian philosophers.

In true scholastic fashion, Aquinas rigorously applied rational argument to what seemed to be simply an article of faith. According to Aristotle, substance is a mixture of both matter and form (see p.41). Transubstantiation is a transformation of one substance into another: specifically from bread and wine into flesh and blood. And so, Aquinas reasoned that it is not the matter of the bread and wine, the physical materials they are made of, that undergo this change, but their form. He argued that the consecration of the bread and wine changes their function or purpose—as food and drink—into a sacred offering. And, therefore, by changing their essential properties, the substance (the combination of both matter and form) of the bread and wine is transformed into the flesh and blood of Christ.

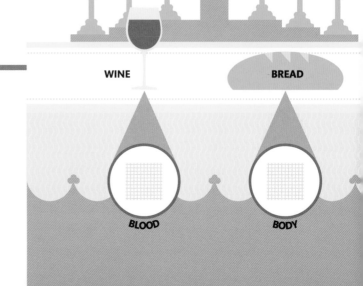

CHRIST CRUCIFIED

WINE

BREAD

BLOOD

BODY

"Reason in man is rather like God in the world."

St. Thomas Aquinas (13th century)

Substances

According to Catholic doctrine, the bread and wine consumed by the congregation in the Mass are transformed by the prayers said by the priest into the body and blood of Christ. However, in Aristotelian terms, it is not their matter that is altered, but their form—the function that they serve and their essential properties. Their physical, or "accidental" properties (see p.39), remain the same.

Occam's razor

William of Ockham was both a Franciscan friar and a scholastic theologian. His most famous idea, known as Occam's razor, was that given two competing hypotheses, we should choose the simplest.

Shaving away irrelevance

In a nutshell, the principle of "Occam's razor" states that one should "shave away" all unnecessary assumptions when constructing or assessing the validity of an argument. In Ockham's own words: "plurality should not be posited unnecessarily."

The premises of any argument have to be accepted as true, but the fewer assumptions that are made, the better. When there are alternative explanations for something, all things being equal, the one with the fewest variables is most likely to be correct. In practice, this principle has come to be adopted in the form of "the simplest solution tends to be the right one." However, Ockham's notion is rather more subtle: the more assumptions that are made, the less convincing the argument, so it is easier to decide between alternative hypotheses if irrelevant or fanciful assumptions are removed.

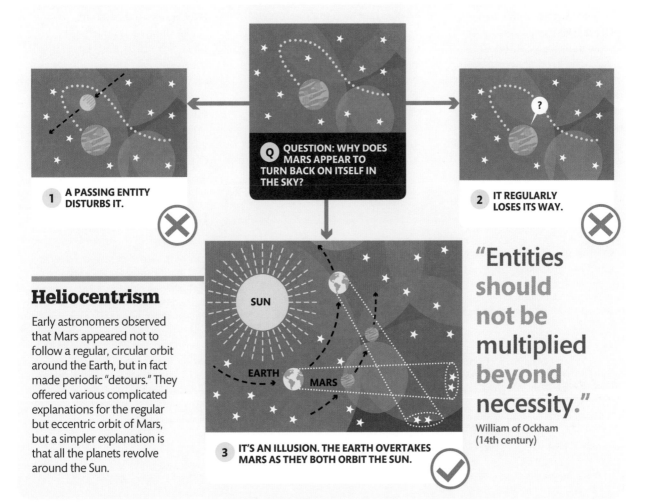

QUESTION: WHY DOES MARS APPEAR TO TURN BACK ON ITSELF IN THE SKY?

1 A PASSING ENTITY DISTURBS IT.

2 IT REGULARLY LOSES ITS WAY.

Heliocentrism

Early astronomers observed that Mars appeared not to follow a regular, circular orbit around the Earth, but in fact made periodic "detours." They offered various complicated explanations for the regular but eccentric orbit of Mars, but a simpler explanation is that all the planets revolve around the Sun.

SUN

EARTH MARS

3 IT'S AN ILLUSION. THE EARTH OVERTAKES MARS AS THEY BOTH ORBIT THE SUN.

"Entities should not be multiplied beyond necessity."

William of Ockham (14th century)

The Scientific Revolution

Although the Renaissance was primarily an artistic and cultural movement, its emphasis on free thinking challenged the authority of religion and paved the way for an unprecedented age of scientific discovery.

Tradition undermined

The scientific revolution began with the publication in 1543 of Nicolaus Copernicus's *De revolutionibus orbium coelestium* (*On the Revolutions of the Celestial Spheres*), which presented evidence contradicting the notion of a geocentric universe (see pp.42–43). That same year, Andreas Vesalius published *De humani corporis fabrica* (*On the Fabric of the Human Body*), which overturned many orthodox ideas in anatomy and medicine. What followed was a profound change in the approach to inquiry into the natural world.

Conventional wisdom, including the dogma of the Catholic Church, was no longer blindly accepted, but challenged. Even the work of Aristotle, who had initiated the idea of natural philosophy based on methodical observation, was subjected to scientific scrutiny.

At the forefront of this scientific revolution were philosophers such as Francis Bacon, whose *Novum Organum* (*New Instrument*) proposed a new method for the study of natural philosophy—systematically gathering evidence through observation, from which the laws of nature could be inferred.

But there was also a new class of thinkers and scientists, including Nicolaus Copernicus, Johannes Kepler, and Galileo Galilei. Galileo challenged dogma more than most by proving that the Earth orbits the Sun, and fell afoul of the Church for his efforts.

The discoveries made by these scientists, and the methods they used, laid the foundations for the work of Isaac Newton in the following century, and also influenced philosophers such as Descartes, Spinoza, and Leibniz, who helped to shape the ideas of the Age of Enlightenment.

ONE CAUSE ONLY

Central to Aristotle's philosophy was the concept of the "four causes" (see pp.40–41). The new scientific methods of the 16th and 17th centuries rejected these, especially the concept of a "final cause," or purpose. Instead, it was proposed that there are only "efficient causes" in nature—in other words, physical causal triggers. Although this is closer to the modern idea of cause and effect, the idea had first been proposed by the Atomists some 2,000 years earlier (see pp.30–31).

MATERIAL

EFFICIENT

FORMAL

FINAL

Laws of nature

The theories of Copernicus and his contemporaries heralded a new era of scientific discovery. Religious authority was undermined, but so, too, was the orthodox concept of the laws that governed the universe, which were based on Aristotelian cosmology and physics. In this new atmosphere of scientific inquiry, conventional assumptions were replaced with laws of nature derived from empirical evidence of observation and experiment.

> "... the things of this world **cannot** be made known without a knowledge of mathematics."
>
> Francis Bacon, *New Instrument* (1620)

THE NEW METHOD

Induction

Bacon described a method of scientific inquiry using the process of induction, inferring a general rule from particular instances. For example, the rule that water boils at 212°F (100°C) can be inferred because this is the case in every instance.

Experimentation

Often it is not enough simply to observe in order to come to a scientific conclusion. The scientific method pioneered by Islamic philosophers involves conducting controlled experiments to get reproducible results.

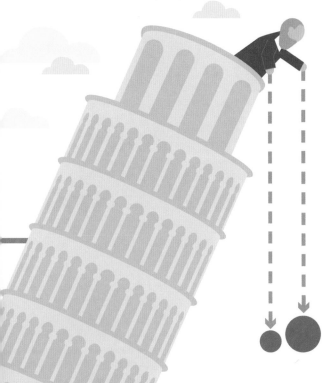

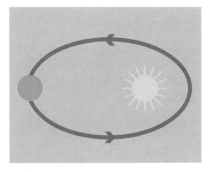

Sunspots

The detailed study of sunspots made by Galileo and others showed that these are inherent features of the Sun. These observations contradicted the Aristotelian idea of the perfection of objects in the heavenly spheres.

Gravity

Although it may only have been a thought experiment, Galileo dropped two balls of different weights from the Tower of Pisa to show that they fell at the same speed. This refuted Aristotle's assertion that heavy objects fall faster than lighter ones.

Elliptical orbits

Once it was proven that the Earth orbits the Sun, the orbits of the planets could then be explained. Kepler discovered that the orbit of Mars was not circular, but an ellipse, and concluded that all the planets had elliptical orbits.

Doubting the world

With probably the best known statement in Western philosophy, René Descartes ushered in a new approach to philosophical inquiry that would come to be known as rationalism.

I am thinking, therefore I am

Inspired by the Scientific Revolution of the 16th and 17th centuries (see pp.50–51), philosophers looked for a method for reliably acquiring and testing scientific knowledge. Francis Bacon, for example, advocated a method of observation, experiment, and inductive reasoning. Descartes, however, was uncomfortable with this approach. Instead, he proposed a reflective method, the aim of which was to find rational principles to serve as foundations for knowledge gained through observation and experiment. He argued that our senses are unreliable, and that we can doubt everything that they tell us. However, if we doubt everything, there must at least be something that doubts—an "I" that experiences doubt. As Descartes put it: "*Cogito, ergo sum*"—"I am thinking, therefore I exist."

The primacy of reason

This was the necessary truth that Descartes was looking for, and it came not from his senses, but from his intellect. From this insight, he developed a theory of knowledge that dismissed sensory experience as unreliable and instead proposed that knowledge is primarily acquired by deductive reasoning.

> "This proposition, I am, I exist, is necessarily true."
>
> René Descartes, *Discourse on the Method* (1637)

The method of doubt

Descartes' method of doubt is presented in his *Discourse on the Method* (1637). His goal was to show both that certainty can be gained through deductive logic alone and that science and reason are compatible with the Christian faith. His argument laid the foundations of modern rationalism—the belief that knowledge comes primarily from reason rather than experience. This view became popular in Europe and stood in contrast to the British tradition of empiricism, as exemplified by John Locke (see pp.60–61).

1 I cannot trust my senses
My senses can be deceived by things such as optical illusions—for instance, a straw "bending" in water. Therefore, they are not reliable sources of information about the world.

2 I may be dreaming
When I am dreaming, what I experience often seems to be real. Therefore, I cannot be sure that what I am experiencing now is not a dream.

5 God accounts for me
I necessarily exist, but I have not created myself; therefore, there must be something greater than me that created me: God.

6 God is good
God has provided me with senses and intellect. Because He is benevolent, He does not want me to be deceived, so I have faith in what my senses tell me about the world.

4 *Cogito, ergo sum*
If my body could be an illusion, there must be something other than my body that suspects this. Therefore, that thinking thing—which is me—must necessarily exist.

3 A demon may be tricking me
Although unlikely, it is even possible that an evil demon is playing tricks on me, making me believe things that are not real. Even my body may be an illusion.

THE DISEMBODIED SELF

Descartes dismissed sensory perception as unreliable: the only thing that he could be sure of was his own existence as a thinking thing. The essential self is therefore the mind, and is distinct from and independent of the physical body.

Mind and body

By drawing a distinction between the mind and the body and prioritizing reason over observation, René Descartes laid the foundations for modern rationalist philosophy.

Cartesian dualism

Descartes regarded the ability to reason as the defining feature of human beings. He believed that we have this ability because we possess a mind, or soul, which he saw as distinct from the physical body. He distinguished the mind from the body while engaged in his "method of doubt," which was his unique method of philosophical inquiry (see pp.52–53).

This method of doubt was a skeptical approach and led Descartes to conclude that our senses are far from reliable. Truth, he decided, can only be arrived at through reason. His claim "*Cogito ergo sum*" ("I am thinking, therefore I exist") expressed his realization that the only thing that he could be certain of was that he existed—that in order to think at all, he must exist. In addition, he realized that he was a *thing* that thinks—but not a physical thing, for he could doubt that his physical body was real. He concluded that there were two distinct parts of his existence—an unthinking, physical body and a thinking, nonphysical mind.

This led Descartes to conclude that there are two different types of substances—one material and one immaterial—in the universe. This view became known as Cartesian dualism. It raised the question of how the two substances interact, which is still debated today (see pp.142–163). Descartes claimed mind and body "commingle" in the pineal gland of the brain (see box), but he failed to show how they do so, and for many, including Thomas Hobbes (see pp.56–57), this failure undermined Descartes' theory.

In Descartes' day, sophisticated machines were being constructed—some even behaved like living things—and scientists believed that the world was mechanical, too: animals, the weather, and the stars were seen as machines whose movements could in principle be predicted (see pp.162–163). Descartes shared this view about everything except human beings: he claimed that we alone have the God-given attribute of reason.

THE PINEAL GLAND

Descartes believed that the mind and the body are two distinct entities, but conceded that there had to be some interaction between the two. In particular, he thought that the mind exercises control over the body. Indeed, our rational freedom—our ability to choose how to act—is a definingly human characteristic. However, there must then be a place where our minds interact with our bodies. Descartes suggested this is the pineal gland, which is located in the center of the brain. He described it as "the principal seat of the soul, and the place in which all our thoughts are formed."

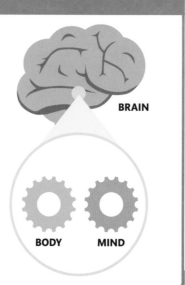

BRAIN

BODY   MIND

✓ NEED TO KNOW

❯ **An influential mathematician** as well as philosopher, Descartes invented the system of Cartesian coordinates and established the field of analytical geometry.

❯ **According to Descartes**, the mind, or soul, is unique to human beings. Other animals are purely physical beings and behave in predetermined ways.

❯ **Descartes' mind-body dualism** is regarded as the foundation of modern Western philosophy. However, in the 19th and 20th centuries, materialism increasingly became the norm (see pp.56–57).

MIND AND SOUL

Mind

For Descartes, the mind is the immaterial part of our being—the thinking thing that has the ability to have ideas. It is not located in space and can doubt everything that it perceives—even the reality of the eyes through which it sees.

Soul

According to Descartes, because the mind is immaterial, it is not subject to physical decay. It is therefore eternal and synonymous with the immortal soul or spirit. For Descartes, dualism was compatible with religious faith.

"With me, everything turns into mathematics."

René Descartes, in a letter to Marin Mersenne (1640)

The immaterial world

For Descartes, the immaterial world is the world of ideas, thoughts, and the spirit. It is composed of an immaterial substance that cannot be experienced by the senses, but which we have access to through reason, or rational thought.

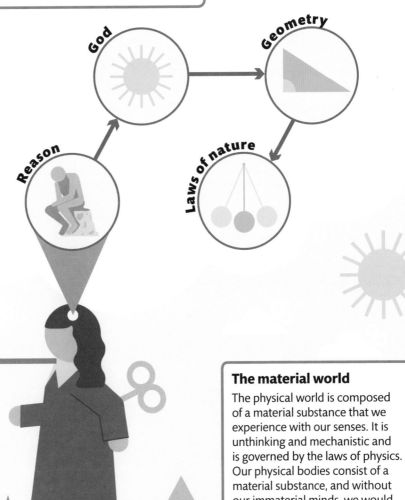

Reason

God

Geometry

Laws of nature

Two worlds

Descartes accepted the prevailing scientific view that all material things are mechanical. However, he believed that the immaterial mind is a uniquely human, God-given attribute, and that its ability to reason enables us to gain knowledge of immaterial things such as God, mathematics, and various physical laws.

The material world

The physical world is composed of a material substance that we experience with our senses. It is unthinking and mechanistic and is governed by the laws of physics. Our physical bodies consist of a material substance, and without our immaterial minds, we would simply be unthinking machines.

The body as a machine

René Descartes' mind-body dualism (see pp.54–55) sparked a debate that continued through the 17th and 18th centuries. Foremost among those who rejected Descartes' theory was a British philosopher, Thomas Hobbes.

Physicalism

Thomas Hobbes (1588–1679) was a contemporary of Descartes' and corresponded with him about mathematics. However, he differed from Descartes on the subject of dualism. He did not accept Descartes' idea of an immaterial substance, which he considered a contradiction in terms: a substance by its nature must be material. Following that belief, he argued that if there are no immaterial substances, then everything must be material—a view that has since become known as physicalism.

Hobbes took a particular interest in the natural sciences and was influenced by the ideas of Galileo (see pp.50–51). Like many other thinkers of the time, he thought that the universe behaves like a machine, so it is subject to physical laws. The movements of the planets and other heavenly bodies are explained by these laws, which apply to all physical objects. If, as Hobbes believed, humans are purely physical, then we, too, follow the same laws and are effectively biological machines. Even our minds, Hobbes argued, are

physical: our thoughts and intentions are not evidence of some immaterial substance, but the result of physical processes in our brains.

Hobbes's concept of a purely physical universe was a radical departure from conventional thinking at the time, especially since it denied the existence of an immaterial God. However, it provided a counterargument to rationalism (see pp.52–55) and paved the way for a distinctively British empiricist approach to philosophy (see pp.60–61).

MIND-BRAIN IDENTITY

Hobbes did not distinguish between the substances of mind and body: he argued that there is only physical substance, so the mind and the brain are one and the same thing. This means that the thoughts and feelings that we experience are physical events in the brain, which are prompted by information provided by our senses. These thoughts and feelings are not made of some form of immaterial substance, but can be understood in terms of physical processes. This idea was reformulated in the 20th century as the mind-brain identity theory (see pp.152–153).

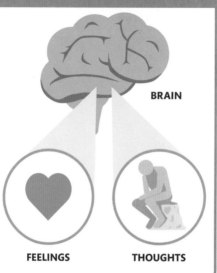

BRAIN

FEELINGS   THOUGHTS

Cogs in the machine

For Hobbes, physical laws govern the universe, which is made of many component parts, each of which has its own function, and is governed by physical laws. The natural world forms one such part of the universe, and within it, plants, animals, and humans each play their part. Humans have organized themselves into societies, and these in turn are governed by laws. Biologically, each human being is a complex machine composed of numerous functioning parts, all of which are controlled by physical processes within the brain. The brain itself is controlled by internal and external stimuli.

SOCIETY

INTENTION

ARM

HAND

NATURE

Society

Hobbes believed that humans are selfish and exist only to satisfy their individual physical needs. To avoid chaos, we organize ourselves into societies and submit to the rule of law, which serves as a kind of personal protection agency (see pp.202–203).

The body

Our bodies are biological machines and are governed by physical laws. We have physical needs, which prompt "vital" movements, such as the beating of our hearts. However, even our most "voluntary" movements are physically predetermined.

Nature

According to Hobbes, the universe is purely physical and operates like clockwork according to natural laws of motion. The natural world we live in is a part of that universe, and it and its component parts are similarly machinelike. Everything is predetermined, leaving no room for free will, nor for the mind as anything other than the operation of the brain.

"Understanding being nothing else, but conception caused by Speech."

Thomas Hobbes, *Leviathan* (1651)

The one substance

One solution to Descartes' mind-body problem (see pp.54–55) came from the Dutch philosopher Baruch Spinoza. He proposed that reality is a single substance that has both mental and physical attributes.

Substance and attributes

Spinoza (1632–1677) explained his concept of a single universal substance—an idea known as substance monism—in his posthumously published work, *Ethics*. In his formative years, Spinoza had followed Descartes' view that the physical and mental aspects of the universe were the activities of two substances— the material and the immaterial. However, he rejected this idea later in his life.

In *Ethics*, Spinoza describes the whole of reality as being composed of one substance, of which both the material and the immaterial are attributes. The human mind is what he calls a modification of this substance conceived under the "attribute of thought," whereas the human brain is a modification of the substance conceived under the "attribute of extension." In this way, he avoids the mind-body problem: the two attributes work

Thought and extension

Spinoza contended that God and nature are identical. He claimed that there is no separate, transcendent creator, but instead that the divine is everything in reality. God manifests in an infinite number of attributes, but only two of these are expressed in our universe: thought (mind) and extension (matter). These are the physical and mental attributes that make up our world, and through them we live and come to understand our nature. They are predetermined and work like clockwork, both being driven by God. These are only two of God's attributes—others are manifested in worlds beyond our own.

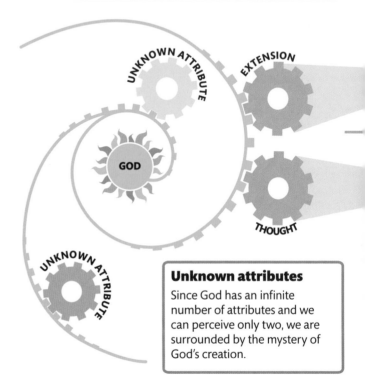

God

For Spinoza, God is immanent in everything and has an infinite number of attributes. Two of those attributes constitute our universe: extension (matter) and thought (mind).

Unknown attributes

Since God has an infinite number of attributes and we can perceive only two, we are surrounded by the mystery of God's creation.

ACCUSATIONS OF HERESY

Spinoza was brought up as a practicing Jew, but as he grew up, he increasingly challenged the authority of Judaism and was eventually banned from the synagogue. His pantheistic claim that God is immanent in everything was later seen as heretical by the Catholic Church, and his works were banned. Although he was often branded an atheist, Spinoza later influenced numerous Christian philosophers, including Søren Kierkegaard.

in parallel and have no interaction at all. For Spinoza, matter and mind are like the shape and taste of an apple: neither gives rise to the other, but each is an attribute of something greater than itself. Interestingly, Spinoza believed that everything in nature has both physical and mental attributes, so even rocks have a form of thought.

More controversially, Spinoza argued that God and substance are identical. Indeed, he uses the words "God" and "nature" interchangeably, and both as synonyms for "substance." He shared Hobbes's view that everything is predetermined (see pp.56–57), but for Spinoza, this included God. This is because freedom of choice is a *human* need, and God—being everything and lacking nothing—has no need for choice. For these and other ideas, Spinoza's work was widely condemned, but it also laid the foundations for much of modern philosophy (see box, right).

✓ NEED TO KNOW

❯ **Spinoza's view** is often seen as a form of "property dualism," which states that the world is composed of just one substance that has both physical and mental properties (see pp.146–147).

❯ **Pantheism** is the belief that God is not distinct and separate from the world, but identical to everything that exists in the universe (see pp.160–161).

Extension

The first attribute of substance that makes up our universe is extension, or matter. This is the world of physical things, including their aspects of height, length, and breadth. Matter is like a gear engaged with God but not engaged with mind, which has a parallel existence to it.

Thought

The second attribute of substance that makes up our universe is thought, or mind. This enables us to understand the world in terms of ideas and concepts, and it is shared by all other things in the natural world, including rocks and trees. Thought is also engaged with God and works in parallel with matter.

"I say that all things are in God and move in God."

Baruch Spinoza, *Ethics* (1677)

The blank slate

In *An Essay Concerning Human Understanding*, John Locke rebutted the rationalists' argument that we are born with innate ideas (see pp.52–55), which laid the foundations for modern empiricist thought.

British empiricism

Central to the philosophy of John Locke (1632–1704) is the idea that there is no such thing as innate knowledge: at birth, the mind is what he called a *tabula rasa*, or "blank slate." When we observe newborn babies, he said, it is clear that they do not bring ideas into the world with them. It is only as we go through life that ideas come into our minds, and these ideas are derived from our experience of the world around us. This idea stood in marked contrast to a lot of contemporary thinking, particularly the ideas of Descartes (see pp.52–55) and Leibniz (see pp.62–63), who argued that we are born with innate ideas and that our reason, rather than our experience, is our primary means of acquiring knowledge.

Locke's idea was not new—it had been defended by Francis Bacon (see pp.50–51) and Thomas Hobbes (see pp.56–57), and even went back to Aristotle (see pp.38–45). However, Locke was the first philosopher to give a comprehensive defense of empiricism—the idea that experience is our principal source of knowledge. That is not to say, however, that Locke dismissed the importance of reasoning in our acquisition of knowledge. Indeed, he believed that each of us is born with a capacity for reasoning, and that the right education is critical to a child's intellectual development.

> "No man's knowledge here can go beyond his experience."
>
> John Locke, *An Essay Concerning Human Understanding* (1689)

Learning the world

Locke claimed that there are two kinds of ideas—ideas of sensation and ideas of reflection—and that the latter are made out of the former. In Locke's words, the objects of the world "cause" ideas of sensation to form in our minds. We then organize these ideas into ideas of reflection.

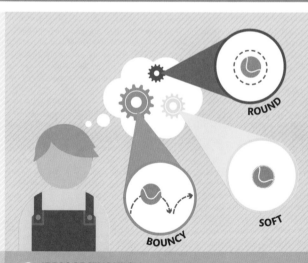

ROUND

BOUNCY

SOFT

1 BLANK SLATE
At birth, a baby brings no ideas into the world; its mind is completely blank. This means that everything that it will know will come from the world around it. For this reason, Locke claimed that the child should be exposed to the best ideas possible.

2 IDEAS OF SENSATION
According to Locke, the objects of the world cause ideas of sensation in the infant's mind. These simple impressions form in the way that light forms images on photographic film: it is a mechanical process that requires no effort on the child's behalf.

PRIMARY AND SECONDARY QUALITIES

According to Locke, we can only receive information about the world through our senses. This information, he claimed, is of two kinds and concerns what he called the primary and secondary qualities. An object's primary qualities, such as its height or mass, are objective and exist independently of whoever is observing it. However, its secondary qualities, such as its color or taste, may differ between observers. A ball, for example, may appear gray or multicolored to two different observers, but both will agree on its size.

PRIMARY QUALITIES
For Locke, the primary qualities of a thing are its length, breadth, height, weight, location, motion, and overall design.

SECONDARY QUALITIES
The secondary qualities of a thing are its color, taste, texture, smell, and sound. These qualities depend on the perceiver's senses.

3 IDEAS OF REFLECTION
As the child grows older, it builds ideas of reflection out of its ideas of sensation. From its interactions with other people and its simple understanding of the qualities of a ball, for example, it can create the idea of "soccer." From that and other simple ideas, it forms the more complex ideas of "teamwork" and "competition."

✓ NEED TO KNOW

> **Although Locke denied** the existence of innate ideas, he claimed that we have innate capacities for perception and reasoning.

> **In the 19th century**, the notion of innate ideas resurfaced. Scholars questioned whether behavioral traits come from "nature or nurture."

> **In the 20th century**, Noam Chomsky (see pp.162–163) extended Locke's idea that we have an innate capacity for reasoning. Chomsky claimed that all humans have an innate ability to acquire language.

An infinity of minds

In his book *Monadology*, Gottfried Leibniz presented a radical alternative to Descartes' dualism (see pp.52–55). He argued that the universe is made up of an infinite number of mindlike substances, which he called "monads."

Monads

Like Descartes, Leibniz (1646–1716) was a rationalist and believed that knowledge comes primarily from reasoning rather than experience. He argued that the universe is composed of an infinite number of mindlike monads, each of which contains a complete representation of the universe in its past, present, and future states—and that the human mind is one such monad. According to Leibniz, our minds contain every imaginable fact about the universe, so in theory we should be able to know everything—even the temperature on Mars—through rational reflection alone. We are unable to do this, however, because our rational faculties

Properties of monads

Leibniz believed that the fundamental building blocks of the universe had to be indivisible. However, he also argued that since all physical things are divisible, then the true elements of the universe must be nonphysical. For Leibniz, these monads are eternal and unchanging and have no "windows" through which to communicate with each other. Because monads do not exist in physical space, they are similar to the immaterial mind, or soul, that Descartes identified in his dualist theory of the universe.

MONADS ARE ...
INDIVISIBLE

WINDOWLESS

are too limited, and so, Leibniz argues, we have to "discover" such facts empirically—by doing scientific experiments, for example.

Leibniz distinguished "truths of reasoning" from "truths of fact," defining the former as truths that we know, if only to a limited extent, through rational reflection alone: these include mathematical truths, such as "two plus two equals four." Truths of fact, on the other hand, are those that we discover through experience, such as the nature of the weather on Mars.

> ✓ **NEED TO KNOW**
>
> ❯ **The word "monad"** is derived from the Greek word *monás*, meaning "unit," which Leibniz borrowed to describe the fundamental units of existence.
>
> ❯ **Like Descartes**, Leibniz was an accomplished mathematician. He invented calculus (which Isaac Newton also invented independently) and various mechanical calculating devices.
>
> ❯ **Leibniz** is often characterized as an optimistic philosopher. He believed that God is supremely perfect, and that ours is the best possible world—one in which the monads exist in harmony.

IMMATERIAL

SOUL-LIKE

INDEPENDENT

ETERNAL

UNIQUE

Facts and ideas

Like John Locke before him, David Hume believed that our knowledge derives primarily from experience. However, he also argued that we can never know anything about the world with certainty.

Natural assumptions

David Hume (1711–1776) was primarily interested in epistemology (the nature of knowledge) rather than metaphysics (the nature of the universe). In *An Enquiry Concerning Human Understanding*, he set out to examine the way that human psychology determines what we can and cannot know, and in particular what we can and cannot know for certain.

Although an empiricist—that is, he believed that experience is our primary source of knowledge—Hume conceded that many propositions, such as

mathematical axioms, can be arrived at by reason alone and cannot be doubted: to doubt that 2 + 2 = 4 is to fail to understand its meaning. However, he argued that such truths tell us nothing about the world: they simply express relationships between ideas. To gain knowledge about the world, we need experience, but Hume argues that such knowledge can never be certain. We are therefore caught on the tines of a fork: on the one hand, we have certainty about things that tell us nothing about the world; on the other hand, our knowledge about the world is never certain.

"THE ANGLES OF A TRIANGLE = 180°."

180°

"2 MEN + 2 WOMEN = 4 PEOPLE."

"IT IS SNOWING."

Relations of ideas

Statements of this kind are necessary truths, which means that they cannot be contradicted logically. For example, it is not possible to say that the angles of a triangle do not add up to 180°, or that 2 plus 2 does not equal 4. We can be certain of such truths, but they tell us nothing about the world; they merely express relationships between ideas.

Hume's fork

For Hume, there are two kinds of truth: "relations of ideas" and "matters of fact." The former are true by definition, while the latter depend on the facts. Philosophers call this distinction "Hume's fork."

Hume argues that it is human nature to make assumptions about the world, especially that it is predictable and uniform. We assume, for example, that when we throw a brick at a window, the brick "causes" the window to smash. However, Hume argues that all we know for certain is that throwing a brick at a window is regularly followed by the window smashing. We never perceive causes, he says, but only a "constant conjunction" of events—that is, the regular occurrence of certain events following others. We only imagine a "link" between them.

Hume is not saying that we are wrong to make assumptions—life would be impossible without them. Rather, he is suggesting that we should recognize the extent to which assumptions govern our lives and not confuse them with the truth.

✔ NEED TO KNOW

❯ **According to Hume**, the difference between mathematics and the natural sciences is that mathematical truths are what he calls "relations of ideas," or necessary truths, whereas scientific truths are contingent, or conditional, "matters of fact."

❯ **Half a century before Hume**, Gottfried Leibniz (see pp.62–63) made a similar distinction between truths of reasoning and truths of fact.

❯ **Immanuel Kant** (see pp.66–69) and later philosophers distinguished between analytic statements, whose truth can be established by reasoning alone, and synthetic statements, which are verified by reference to the facts.

"I HAVE A CAT."

Matters of fact

Statements of this kind are contingent, which means that their truth or falsity depend on whether or not they represent the facts. For example, it is not illogical to deny the statements "It is snowing" or "I have a cat." Their truth depends simply on the current state of the weather and whether or not I own a cat.

"Custom, then, is the great guide of human life."

David Hume, *An Enquiry Concerning Human Understanding* (1748)

THE PROBLEM OF INDUCTION

Hume argued that general statements such as "The Sun rises in the east" are logically unjustified because we cannot prove that the Sun will not rise in the west tomorrow. This also means that scientific claims, such as "The Moon orbits the Earth," are unjustified because we may discover, for example, that the Moon behaves in a different way tomorrow. Such statements are known as "inductions," because they use the inductive method of reasoning—that is, they make general claims based on a limited number of particular cases (see pp.244–245).

FOR HUME, we cannot be certain that a croquet ball will behave in the same way as it has in the past.

Shaping the world with the mind

Immanuel Kant recognized that while rationalism (see pp.52–55) and empiricism (see pp.60–61) presented opposing claims, both contained elements of truth. He argued that while we know the world through our senses, it is shaped by our minds.

Representations of things

Kant (1724–1804) sought to establish the limits of what we can know about the world. Unlike his predecessor John Locke, he argued that experience alone was unreliable: not only are we limited to our particular sense organs, when we do perceive something, we only perceive a "representation" of that thing in our minds, rather than see the thing in itself. A rose, for example, may appear red or gray to different animals, so it is only ever seen indirectly, as a construct of our senses.

Kant also argued that our psychological make-up shapes the world we perceive. Our minds are so constructed, he said, that we perceive things in terms of space and time, and that anything outside these parameters is beyond our understanding. He claimed that, in a sense, we project the concepts of space and time onto the world, then perceive the world accordingly. A child, for example, learns the concepts "here" and "there" through experience, but it only does so because it innately understands the concept "space." Likewise, the child learns the concepts "then" and "now" because it has an innate understanding of the concept "time."

Transcendental idealism

Kant argued that innate concepts are what make experience possible, and he identified 14 such concepts in all (see right). They are like lenses through which we both project and view the world. Kant was therefore neither a rationalist nor an empiricist—that is, he saw neither reason nor experience as our primary source of knowledge. He described his position as "transcendental idealism."

BUTTERFLY IN THE WORLD

THE NOUMENAL WORLD

Kant compared the way we perceive things to the way a painter presents an image of something. A painting may portray every detail of a scene, but it remains merely a representation of that scene, not the scene itself. In the same way, our perception of an object is a mental representation, not the object as it actually is. We experience only the "phenomenal" world, which is accessible through our senses, but can never have direct access to what he called the "noumenal" world of things-in-themselves.

THING-IN-ITSELF

Categories of understanding

According to Kant, when we perceive an object, we shape it with our innate ideas of space and time: we project these ideas onto the object and then interpret it in those terms. He described space and time as innate "intuitions" and distinguished a further 12 concepts, or "categories," which he also claimed we understand innately and project onto what we perceive. He classified these into the four divisions of quantity, quality, relation, and modality.

"Thoughts **without** content **are** empty, intuitions **without** concepts **are** blind."

Immanuel Kant, *Critique of Pure Reason* (1781)

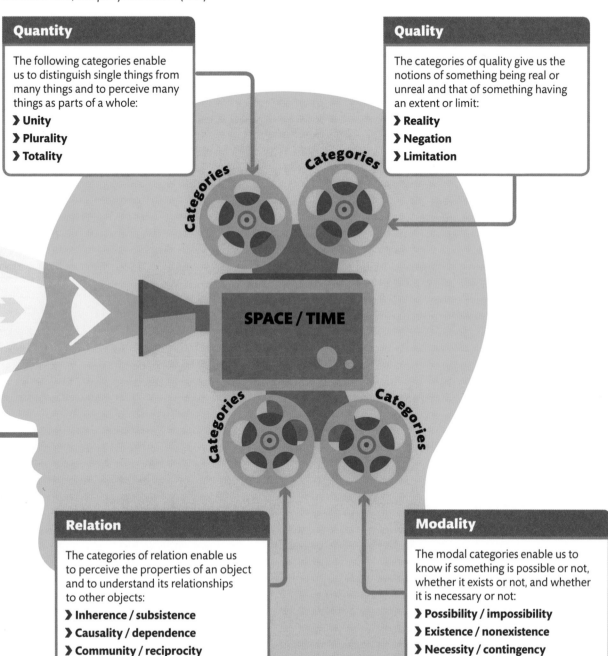

Quantity

The following categories enable us to distinguish single things from many things and to perceive many things as parts of a whole:

> Unity
> Plurality
> Totality

Quality

The categories of quality give us the notions of something being real or unreal and that of something having an extent or limit:

> Reality
> Negation
> Limitation

Categories

Categories

SPACE / TIME

Categories

Categories

Relation

The categories of relation enable us to perceive the properties of an object and to understand its relationships to other objects:

> Inherence / subsistence
> Causality / dependence
> Community / reciprocity

Modality

The modal categories enable us to know if something is possible or not, whether it exists or not, and whether it is necessary or not:

> Possibility / impossibility
> Existence / nonexistence
> Necessity / contingency

Kinds of truth

At the heart of Kant's transcendental idealism (see pp.66–67) is the idea that it is possible to have knowledge of the world independently of empirical evidence or experience.

A priori and a posteriori knowledge

Before Kant, many philosophers had realized that there are two kinds of truth: necessary truth and contingent truth. A necessary truth, such as "Circles are round," is one that is true by definition, so it cannot be denied without contradiction. A contingent truth, such as "The sky is blue," is either true or false according to the facts. Kant introduced two similar distinctions: first between analytic and synthetic statements, and second between a priori and a posteriori knowledge.

Types of statements

An analytic statement is one that is necessarily true, or true by definition, whereas a synthetic statement is one that is either true or false according to the facts. The distinction between a priori and a posteriori knowledge, however, concerns how we come to know the truth—whether by reasoning alone or by reference to the facts.

"All bachelors are happy."

SYNTHETIC
The statement "All bachelors are happy" is synthetic, since being happy is not contained in the definition of "bachelor."

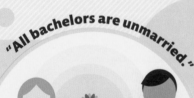

"All bachelors are unmarried."

ANALYTIC
The statement "All bachelors are unmarried" is analytic, since the term "unmarried" is contained in the definition of "bachelor."

"2+2=4"

A PRIORI
A priori knowledge is independent of experience and includes analytic statements, but also mathematical propositions, such as "2 + 2 = 4."

"Water is H_2O."

A POSTERIORI
A posteriori statements are dependent on empirical evidence, or experience, and cannot be arrived at through rational reflection.

An analytic statement, like any proposition, consists of a subject and predicate, but its predicate is implicit in its subject. For example, the statement "A square has four sides" is analytic because its predicate ("four sides") is implicit in its subject ("square"), so it is true by definition. Synthetic statements, however, have informative predicates, which tell us something new about the world. For example, "This square is red" is synthetic, because its predicate ("red") is not contained in its subject ("square").

Kant also identified two different kinds of knowledge: *a priori* knowledge, which is known independently of experience, and *a posteriori* knowledge, which is known through experience only. These two kinds of knowledge are expressed in analytic and synthetic statements respectively.

However, Kant also claimed that there is a third kind of knowledge: synthetic *a priori* knowledge (see below), which is both necessarily true (*a priori*) and informative (synthetic).

Synthetic *a priori* truths

Before Kant, it was assumed that all *a priori* knowledge must be analytic—that is, if it is known without any empirical evidence, then it cannot tell us anything new about the world. However, Kant claimed that from *a priori* statements, we can make deductions that are synthetic, which tell us something about the world.

"A triangle is a three-sided shape."

ANALYTIC *A PRIORI*
The statement "A triangle is a three-sided shape" is analytic: the definition of its subject, "triangle," is a shape with three sides. It is also an *a priori* truth, since we understand it without empirical evidence.

"The interior angles of a triangle add up to 180°"

SYNTHETIC *A PRIORI*
This statement tells us something about a triangle that is not implicit in its definition and is therefore synthetic. However, it is also an *a priori* truth, since, for Kant, it can be arrived at through rational reflection.

Synthetic *a priori* judgements

According to Kant, we are born with no knowledge of the world, but we do have innate concepts that enable us to experience the world intelligibly (see pp.66–67). For example, we have *a priori* knowledge of the concepts of space, time, and causality, and these enable us to arrive at scientific and mathematical truths that are both synthetic (informative) and *a priori* (necessary). For Kant, the statement "3 + 3 = 6" is a synthetic *a priori* truth, because it is informative (it says more than "3 + 3 = 3 + 3") and can be arrived at through reason alone.

3 PLUS 3 …

… EQUALS 6

Reality as a process

In the early 19th century, German philosophy was dominated by Georg Wilhelm Friedrich Hegel, who regarded reality not only as nonmaterial, but as an ever-changing, dynamic process.

Hegel's dialectic

Following Kant (see pp.66–69), many philosophers adopted the view that reality is ultimately nonmaterial. This view, known as idealism, became a feature of German philosophy in the 19th century and was keenly embraced by Hegel (1770–1831).

For Hegel, since reality is a single entity, the object of philosophical inquiry (the world) and the subject doing the thinking (consciousness) are one and the same thing. This entity is what Hegel calls *Geist* ("Spirit"). He argues that this *Geist* is not static, but is constantly evolving—unfolding into ever more sophisticated forms of itself. One example of this process is our own understanding of reality—for since we are *Geist*, advances in our understanding are *Geist*'s increasing insight into itself.

According to Hegel, this process of *Geist*'s evolution is dialectical—that is, one in which contradictions appear and vie with each other and find resolutions that in turn create further contradictions. Every thing (such as anarchy) contains its own opposite (such as tyranny), which combine to form a resolution (such as law) in a process that drives historical progress.

Hegel called these aspects of the dialectic the thesis, antithesis, and synthesis respectively—the synthesis being a new, richer phenomenon made up of the other aspects. However, this synthesis contains its own contradiction, or antithesis, so it becomes a new thesis, which resolves itself in a new, more sophisticated synthesis. For Hegel, the whole of history is such a dialectical process—one that is driven by *Geist* returning to itself, having "emptied" itself into time (see box).

The dialectic

The progress of our ideas follows a dialectical pattern, as thinkers become ever more conscious of the nature of *Geist*. From naive ideas about the substance of the universe, through various explanations of the nature of reality, our ideas evolve until the Absolute is reached and *Geist* becomes conscious of itself as the ultimate reality. According to Hegel, his own discovery of *Geist* is proof that the Absolute is near.

BEING AND BECOMING

For Hegel, no idea or phenomenon exists in isolation: everything, including human history, is bound up in a dynamic process of becoming. Even reality itself is a process. Hegel explains this by asking us to consider the concept of Being: it is impossible to imagine Being without its opposite, Nonbeing, which helps to define it. However, Being and Nonbeing are not merely opposites—they attain their full meaning in the concept of Becoming, which is a synthesis of Being and Nonbeing.

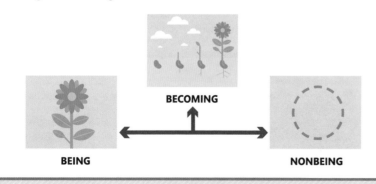

BECOMING

BEING

NONBEING

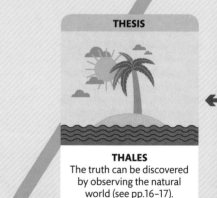

THESIS

THALES
The truth can be discovered by observing the natural world (see pp.16–17).

ABSOLUTE

SYNTHESIS

HEGEL
Reason and observation show that everything is *Geist*, and that *Geist* is evolving.

GEIST AND HISTORY

For Hegel, reality is a process of becoming (see box, left), although he rejects the notion that the world is made up of matter only (see pp.50–51). On the contrary, he argues that reality is fundamentally spirit, or *Geist*, and that matter and mind are aspects of this single, fundamental thing. History, then, is the history of *Geist*, which is simultaneously evolving and heading toward an end point. This end point is what he calls the Absolute: the time when all the contradictions in *Geist* are resolved and the dialectic comes to an end. At that time, *Geist* is as it was at the beginning of the dialectic—when, as Hegel puts it, it "emptied out into time."

SYNTHESIS / THESIS

ARISTOTLE
Observation shows that there is only one realm, which is evolving (see pp.38–45).

SYNTHESIS / ANTITHESIS

KANT
Knowledge derives from both reason and observation (see pp.66–69).

ANTITHESIS

PLATO
The natural world is the shadow cast by a higher realm (see pp.34–37).

THESIS

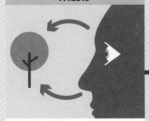

DESCARTES
Our primary source of knowledge is reason, not observation (see pp.52–55).

ANTITHESIS

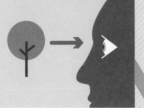

HUME
Our primary source of knowledge is observation, not reason (see pp.64–65).

The end of history

Having defined reality as an evolving process—one that is driven by the principles of thesis, antithesis, and synthesis (see pp.70–71)—Hegel then argued that history is the evolution of freedom.

Increasing harmony

According to Hegel, reality consists of *Geist* ("Spirit"), which has emptied itself into time, and history is the process of *Geist* returning to itself (see p.71). Because humans are aspects of *Geist*, human history is also *Geist*'s history, and so our progress from ignorance to knowledge, and from tyranny to freedom, are *Geist*'s own evolution. This evolution is characterized by increases in human freedom—because *Geist* is fundamentally free, and history is the process of *Geist* manifesting itself.

Because *Geist* evolves through a dialectical process, so, too, does human society. At any one time, the tensions within society are caused by a thesis (the status quo) vying with a contradictory position—one that promises to deliver more liberty for the people. This tension is resolved in a synthesis, which is the next stage in human history.

In Hegel's view, the purpose of history is thus the realization of human freedom—a social manifestation of the Absolute, when *Geist* achieves complete self-awareness and everything exists in harmony.

Historical progress

Hegel argued that because reality is not static, but follows a dialectical progression in which *Geist* becomes more self-aware, history develops in a similar way. He traced the development of history from ancient times, pointing out that in each age, conflicting notions of society have produced a synthesis in which there is an increased consciousness of freedom. From the tyrannies that existed in ancient civilizations, through the evolving systems of government in Classical times, to the overthrow of unjust aristocracies, the process has been toward fairer, more liberal societies. These have culminated in the ideal society—which, according to Hegel, is the Prussian state itself.

"The history of the world is none other than the progress of the consciousness of freedom."

Georg Hegel, *Lectures on the Philosophy of History* (1822)

Rome
Tensions between the Greek and Persian systems lead to the emergence of Rome as the dominant power that gives rights to its citizens.

Persia
Ancient Persia is ruled by an absolute monarch, who oversees a strictly hierarchical and authoritarian state, with little concession to individual liberty.

Tyranny

Prussian state

The synthesis of aristocracy and revolution emerges in the form of the Prussian constitutional monarchy. The monarch presides over a form of liberal democracy—an ideal state in which freedom is maximized.

The end of history

Reformation

Corruption in the Catholic Church and the Holy Roman Empire prompt reforms that create new nation states ruled by the aristocracy.

Revolution

With the power of the Church diminished, the divine right to rule is challenged and the aristocracy is ousted to give power to the people.

Christianity

In contrast to the Roman system, Christianity offers a society based on individual morality and compassion. It is governed by the institution of the Church.

Greece

New forms of society emerge with the establishment of Greek city–states, granting rights to their citizens and even a form of democracy.

THE *ZEITGEIST*

For Hegel, the process of history is a step-by-step procedure rather than a smooth progression and has distinct periods or ages. At each stage of historical development, *Geist* carries within it the antithesis that will provoke change, but until that emerges, the thesis is the dominant notion. Hegel called this the *Zeitgeist*, the "Spirit of the Age," which is characterized by its own distinctive ideas, conventions, and institutions.

Class conflict in history

As much an economist and sociologist as he was a philosopher, Karl Marx approached the idea of historical progress in terms of the relationship between people and their material conditions.

Materialism and the dialectic

Marx (1818–1883) agreed with Hegel's idea that history is a dialectical process (see pp.70–73). However, he was uncomfortable with the idealism on which Hegel's philosophy was based and eventually dismissed the whole idea of metaphysics. He particularly disliked Hegel's notion of *Geist*, and focused instead on the socioeconomic conditions within societies at each stage in their development. Marx's dialectic was a materialist one: the prevailing economic structure of each society contains within it its antithesis, and from the tension between the two a synthesis, or different form of society, emerges. Marx saw in this process a means of bringing about change that would eventually resolve all of society's contradictions. He believed that the perfect society was genuinely possible.

The class struggle

According to Marx, it is not *Geist* or even the desire for freedom that drives the historical process, but economic forces—specifically, the tension between those who control wealth and those who do not. Marx claimed that this struggle between the classes has always existed, and that the difference between the master/slave relationships of ancient times and those between what he called the bourgeoisie and the proletariat (see right) is only one of degree. Nevertheless, through the dialectical process, fairer societies have emerged over time. The end-point of history will be the creation of a classless, "communist" society, in which wealth is distributed fairly.

> "The history of all hitherto existing society is the history of class struggles."
>
> Karl Marx, *The Manifesto of the Communist Party* (1848)

Lords
In feudal society, the wealth consisted of agricultural land, which was owned by the lords but farmed by a class of serfs.

Nobles
In ancient civilizations, power and wealth lay in the hands of a ruling nobility, who owned slaves to carry out the necessary labor.

Prehistory

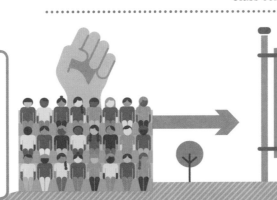

Socialism
One day, the workers will rise up and take control of the means of production (see pp.220–21). In the ensuing "socialist" society, the state ensures that the workers receive a fair share of the fruits of their labor.

Communism
Eventually, the state withers away, leaving a classless, "communist" society.

Bourgeoisie
The new ruling class in industrialized society, the bourgeoisie are the capitalist owners of the means of production. They profit from the sale of goods produced by the workers.

Proletariat
The proletariat, or workers, labor in the factories to produce goods for the bourgeoisie's profit. However, they receive only a minimal wage rather than a proportional share of the fruits of their labor.

Serfs
Although not owned as slaves, the serfs tended the land for the lords in return for a small proportion of the produce.

Slaves
The antithesis of the ruling nobility was the class of slaves. They were the property of the nobles but had no property of their own.

CAPITALISM
At the time when Marx was writing, the Industrial Revolution had created the conditions for a new class, the bourgeoisie—the industrialists and owners of capital. The economic theory of the time was based on Adam Smith's idea of enlightened self-interest, or capitalism. While Marx acknowledged that this was a driver of innovation and growth, he also pointed out its inherent weaknesses, and offered socialism as an alternative.

Useful truths

As the United States began to assert its cultural identity in the second half of the 19th century, American philosophers developed a distinctively practical school of thought, which became known as pragmatism.

Pragmatism

The pioneer of this American pragmatism was a mathematician and logician, Charles Sanders Peirce (1839–1914). Looking at philosophical inquiry from the point of view of a scientist, he was struck by how little practical application it had. Much of philosophy seemed to be a debate about abstract concepts with no connection to the world we live in. To counter this tendency, Peirce proposed a pragmatic maxim: "Consider the practical effects of the objects of your conception. Then, your conception of those effects is the whole of your conception of the object."

Peirce suggested that to understand the meaning of a proposition, we should consider what happens if we accept it and act upon it—in other words, whether it makes any practical difference. From this starting

Belief and action

James notes that we often have no evidence for our beliefs, but act on them anyway to discover if they are true. For example, if someone is lost in a forest and he comes across a path, there may be no evidence that the path will take him to safety, but it is vital that he believes that it does. The example gets to the heart of James's philosophy: that our beliefs are born of necessity, and their truth depends on how much they improve our lives.

2 A ROAD TO SAFETY
If the traveler believes that the path leads to safety, then he should take it.

1 LOST IN A FOREST
If a traveler, lost in a forest, comes across a path, he needs to decide whether or not to take it: it could lead to safety, or it could lead nowhere at all.

3 A ROAD TO RUIN
If the traveler believes that the path leads nowhere, then there is no point in him taking it.

point, he deduced that knowledge consists not of certainties, but of ideas that are valid for as long as they are useful. Science, for example, generates useful ideas that are abandoned or refined when better ones are conceived.

The "cash value" of truth

Peirce's friend and colleague William James (1842–1910) adopted and developed this pragmatic approach. Truths, he argued, are different from facts, which merely state what is or is not the case. For James, facts are not true in themselves: truth is what emerges if believing them to be true has a "cash value," or makes

a practical difference in our lives. Beliefs are not mental entities that are either true or false depending on how well they represent the world: the world is an unpredictable place, and our beliefs are true if they help us to make our way through it. James was a great admirer of Charles Darwin, whose *On the Origin of Species* (1859) was published when James was still a teenager. Darwin had argued that only the fittest of species survived and that they did so thanks to their development of superior biological characteristics. For James, something similar can be said about our beliefs—that they become true if they help us to survive, and become false if they have no utility.

JUSTIFIED BELIEF
4 If the traveler takes the path and finds safety, then his decision was justified: his belief has become true.

VALUELESS BELIEF
5 If the traveler stays in the forest, he dies. The truth as he saw it had no value at all.

> "**Truth** happens **to an idea. It** becomes **true, is** made true **by events. Its verity is in fact** an event, a process."

William James, *Pragmatism: A New Name for Some Old Ways of Thinking* (1907)

RELIGIOUS BELIEFS

Broadly speaking, pragmatism is the view that a belief is true if it works in practice—if it is useful and makes a positive difference in our lives. However, it could be argued that by that standard anything could be true, so long as it improves our lives to believe it. Religious beliefs, for example, are seldom held for rational or commonsense reasons: many people are religious because their faith gives them comfort and moral guidance, which are nothing if not "useful truths."

The pragmatist neither denies nor confirms the objective truth of, for example, the existence of God or the power of prayer, but rather defends the right of the believer to claim it as truth. William James stressed that in examining religious belief, it is important to consider the experience of the individual rather than the claims of religious institutions, for it is only the individual who can account for the importance of their beliefs—that is, what use they have in their lives.

The value of truth

With the decline of the Church's influence in modern industrial society, Friedrich Nietzsche saw the opportunity for a radical reexamination of the basis of truth and morality.

Beyond good and evil

In the 19th century, philosophers inclined increasingly toward a materialist view of the world (see pp.56–57). This was accompanied by an increasing secularism in society, with a growing number of thinkers openly expressing their atheism. Friedrich Nietzsche (1844–1900) lost his Christian faith as a young man, and this colored much of his subsequent thinking. In particular, he identified a problem for modern society: it had inherited the morals imposed by religion, but these now lacked a source that could lend them authority. He felt that moral philosophers and democratic governments were also at fault, since they proposed a morality that applied to everyone alike and failed to accommodate the perspective of the individual.

For Nietzsche, such general systems of morality prevent the individual from living authentically, according to their own standards. He was especially critical of Christian morality, saying that it turns nature on its head by valuing the weak over the strong—advocating humility as a virtue while threatening vengeful punishment on those who transgress. He called Christianity a "slave morality"—one that equates power with evil and weakness with good—and claimed that we should instead adopt the morality of the "master," who sees the world not in terms of good and evil, but in terms of what can either help or hinder us in living life to the full. To move "beyond good and evil" is to abandon Christian ideas, which for Nietzsche are based on the slave's need to exact revenge on the master: unable to do so in life, the slave invents an

The will to power

For Nietzsche, our conscious beliefs have little to do with the truth, but function as masks that hide our unconscious needs and desires. These desires are manifestations of what Nietzsche called the "will to power." The belief in free will, for example, is a mask that hides our need to hold people accountable for their actions: there is no "truth" as to whether or not they are in fact free.

GUILTY VERDICT
The judge and the society he represents hold people responsible in order to exercise control, not because the accused has freely made a choice to do something. The idea of free will is used to justify and facilitate punishment of transgressions.

✓ **NEED TO KNOW**

❯ **Standing above the superstitions of society** is an ideal individual—an *Übermensch* ("Superman")—who Nietzsche described in *Thus Spake Zarathustra* (1883).

❯ **In *On the Genealogy of Morals* (1887)**, Nietzsche argued that the moral values of the major religions, and in particular of Judaism and Christianity, are forms of "slave" morality, which venerate weakness and compliance as virtues.

❯ **Much of Nietzsche's** moral philosophy, such as the idea of the will to power and the concept of the *Übermensch*, was hijacked by totalitarian leaders who misconstrued it for their own ends.

afterlife in which the powerful receive their punishment. For Nietzsche, the notion of "free will" has its origin in this desire for revenge. Indeed, all claims to "truth" are shaped in some way by the "will to power"—an instinct that drives us to better our condition (see below).

Nietzsche claimed that Christianity should be replaced by a life-affirming morality, and that it should be seen as virtuous for each individual to achieve their full potential. This in turn affects our attitude toward truth, which Nietzsche said depends on perspective. Perspectivism, as he called it, frees the individual to choose which truths to believe, which ones they consider to be life-affirming, and which to ignore.

"GOD IS DEAD"

When Nietzsche announced that God is dead and that "we have killed him," he was referring to the rapid secularization of society that started in the 19th century. It was not so much God that had been killed, but religion, which had become increasing irrelevant in modern society.

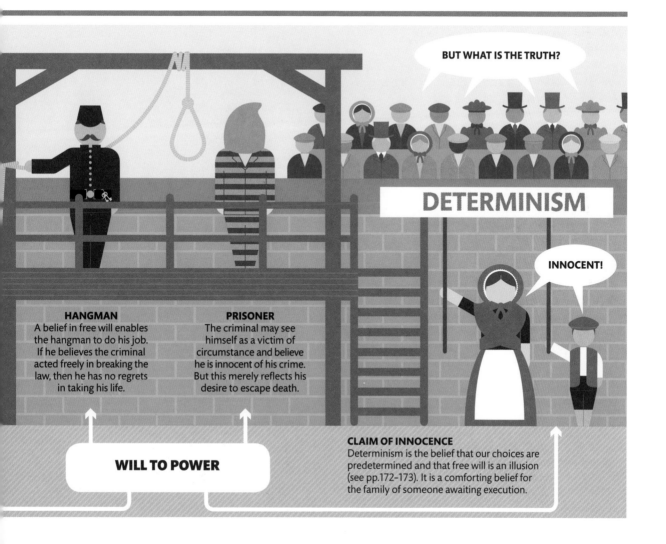

BUT WHAT IS THE TRUTH?

DETERMINISM

INNOCENT!

HANGMAN
A belief in free will enables the hangman to do his job. If he believes the criminal acted freely in breaking the law, then he has no regrets in taking his life.

PRISONER
The criminal may see himself as a victim of circumstance and believe he is innocent of his crime. But this merely reflects his desire to escape death.

WILL TO POWER

CLAIM OF INNOCENCE
Determinism is the belief that our choices are predetermined and that free will is an illusion (see pp.172–173). It is a comforting belief for the family of someone awaiting execution.

Ideas as tools

American thinker John Dewey (1859–1952) belonged to the pragmatic school of philosophy (see pp.76–77). He argued that ideas are neither true nor false, but are tools that either help or hinder us in our lives.

Naturalism

Like the pragmatist C. S. Peirce before him, John Dewey was influenced by the ideas of Charles Darwin, who argued that human beings have evolved through a process of natural selection in the same way as other species. In this sense, Dewey was a "naturalist," in that he believed that our ability to reason is bound up with our instinct for survival—that we think in order to solve practical problems, rather than to speculate about metaphysical issues. He was also influenced by Hegel (see pp.72–75), who argued that all human activities—including science, art, and philosophy—are shaped by history, so they can only be understood in their particular historical contexts.

Instrumentalism

Dewey sometimes referred to his position as "instrumentalism," by which he meant that ideas should be seen as tools and should be judged according to how useful they are at solving specific problems. He contrasted this with the idea that

DEWEY AND DEMOCRACY

Dewey was a passionate believer in democracy. He argued that democracy is only possible in a society in which people are properly educated, but felt that too many schools did little more than raise children to fit in with the social order. Instead, he proposed that schools should enable children to discover their own talents and to find their own unique place in the world. Only then, he argued, could children grow up and truly participate in democracy, for only then could their opinion be said to be fully informed. Effectively, he thought that schools should teach children how to live.

Dewey also supported women's emancipation and racial equality. As he wrote in *Democracy and Education* (1916): "If democracy has a moral and ideal meaning, it is that a social return be demanded from all and that opportunity for development of distinctive capacities be afforded all."

Useful thinking

Dewey rejected the traditional "correspondence" theory of truth, according to which an idea is true if it corresponds to reality. Instead, he argued that ideas are tools that we use to help us live our lives. He redefined "truths" as "warranted assertions," arguing that we hold them for as long as they are helpful.

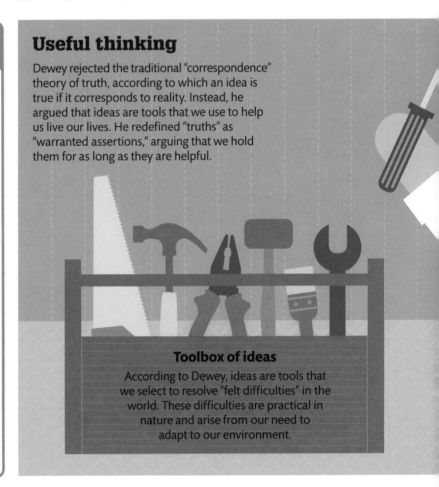

Toolbox of ideas

According to Dewey, ideas are tools that we select to resolve "felt difficulties" in the world. These difficulties are practical in nature and arise from our need to adapt to our environment.

thoughts are representations of the world. Additionally, Dewey believed that just as humans evolved by adapting to changing environments, the same is true of ideas. He argued that theories are neither true nor false, but only efficient or inefficient at explaining and predicting phenomena. Like his fellow pragmatists, he thought that the important question when assessing an idea is not "Is this the way things are?" but "What are the practical implications of this perspective?"

The process of inquiry

Dewey's view broke away from centuries of thinking about the nature of knowledge. Since Descartes (see pp.52–55), rationalists had argued that we are born with innate ideas, and since Locke (see pp.60–61), empiricists had argued that ideas are copies of impressions generated by experience. Dewey believed that both traditions were wrong and had failed to appreciate that our ideas serve to manipulate the world. He rejected the phrase "theory of knowledge," preferring "theory of inquiry" instead—inquiry being an active, human practice.

Dewey distinguished three phases of inquiry: first, we encounter a problem and react to it by instinct; second, we isolate the information that is relevant to the problem; and third, we imagine solutions to the problem and then act on our favored option. For Dewey, philosophers had wrongly isolated the third stage of this process, imagining that ideas can be separated from the world in which problems arise. Instead, he claimed that knowledge is functional and is only valid as a basis for human action.

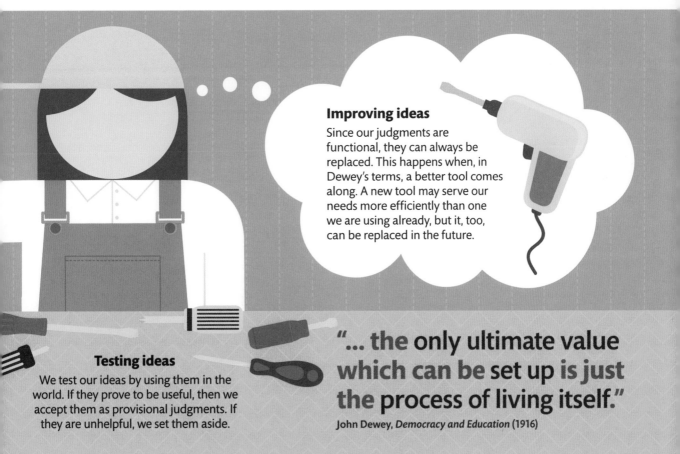

Improving ideas

Since our judgments are functional, they can always be replaced. This happens when, in Dewey's terms, a better tool comes along. A new tool may serve our needs more efficiently than one we are using already, but it, too, can be replaced in the future.

Testing ideas

We test our ideas by using them in the world. If they prove to be useful, then we accept them as provisional judgments. If they are unhelpful, we set them aside.

"... the **only ultimate value** which can be **set up is just** the **process of living itself.**"

John Dewey, *Democracy and Education* (1916)

ANALYTIC PHILOSOPHY

In the 20th century, a school of thought arose that challenged traditional thinking. Known as "analytic philosophy," it sought to solve philosophical problems by logically analyzing language.

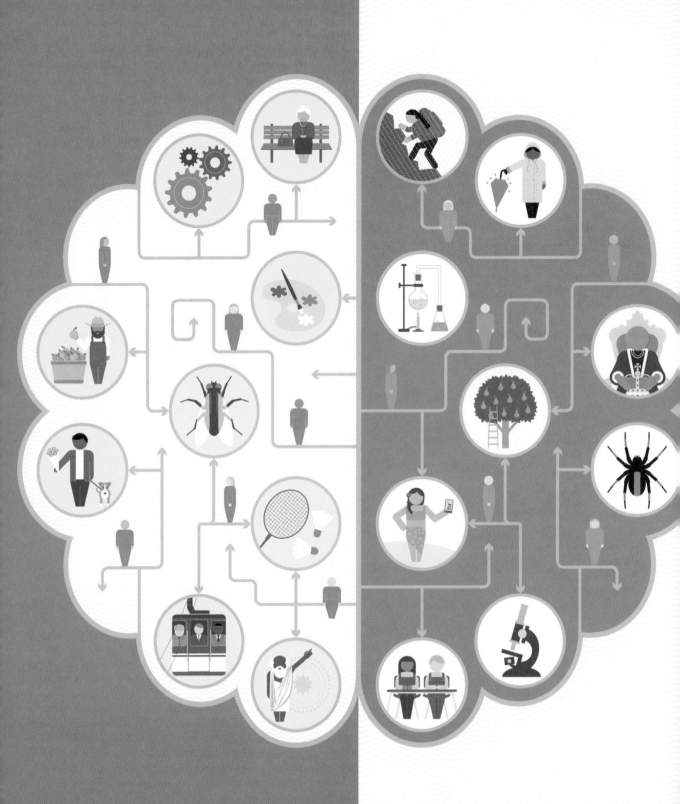

ANALYTIC PHILOSOPHY

Since its beginnings in the 17th century, modern philosophy developed along two different lines—one in mainland Europe and one in Britain. While European philosophers generally followed the example of Descartes' rationalism, British philosophers were predominantly empiricists.

In the 19th century, philosophy was dominated by German idealism, which flowed from the thinking of Immanuel Kant. However, at the turn of the 20th century, a new approach emerged in Britain that revived the distinction between British and "continental" philosophy. This was sparked by the work of Bertrand Russell on the link between mathematics and logic. What Russell (and the German mathematician Gottlob Frege, independently) established was that logic, like mathematics, is not a human invention: it is not merely a method that we have devised to present arguments, but is instead a system of rules that are universally valid, regardless of human experience. As such, logic can provide us with a means of establishing the validity of statements and arguments.

The implications of Russell's discovery were profound. The link between logic and mathematics provided new methods of logical analysis and opened up a whole new field of philosophy known as "analytic philosophy." At the time, many philosophers were skeptical of traditional metaphysical philosophy, which, they argued, made claims that could be neither proved nor disproved. Now, they believed, they had the logical tools with which to examine arguments rigorously. According to Russell, the problem with traditional philosophy was that arguments had been presented in ordinary language rather than in logical form, and this had led to ambiguity, inaccuracy, and confusion. In order to examine an argument properly, he claimed, it needed to be "translated" into the language of logic before being analyzed. This revealed that many philosophical statements had no logical meaning, even if they made perfect grammatical sense.

One of Russell's protégés, Ludwig Wittgenstein, went on to develop his own theory of meaning. In his *Tractatus Logico-Philosophicus*, he dismissed as nonsense any statement that failed to "picture" something in the world. This idea was embraced by the "logical positivist" school, which argued that philosophers should analyze scientific claims only, leaving metaphysics to theologians. At the same time, advances in the natural sciences led many philosophers to examine science itself, raising questions over the nature of scientific truth. Wittgenstein, however, changed his mind about the nature of philosophy and presented a second, radically different theory of language—one that abandoned the idea that words are pictures of objects. Others, too, rejected the constraints of strict analytic philosophy, recognizing that ordinary language also has a place in philosophical inquiry.

What does a word mean?

Widely regarded as the founder of analytical philosophy, the German philosopher Gottlob Frege greatly advanced the philosophy of language by distinguishing between the "sense" and "reference" of a word.

Sense and reference

Frege (1848–1925) noted that when we look at the sky just before sunrise and just after sunset, we see a bright star in each case. Traditionally, these stars have been known as the Morning Star and the Evening Star respectively, but astronomers have shown that they are in fact the same object: the planet Venus.

For Frege, this raised an interesting question: If the meaning of a word is an object it refers to (a theory that had been popular for centuries), then how is it that the names "Morning Star" and "Evening Star" have two different meanings when they refer to the same object?

Frege argued that the example shows that we need to distinguish between the sense of a word and its reference—that is, between the meaning it carries and the object it refers to. He did not claim that the reference of a word is irrelevant to its meaning—in fact, it may be vitally important—but rather that it does not exhaust the entire meaning of a word.

Pioneering logic

According to Frege, the difference between the names "Morning Star" and "Evening Star" lies in their "mode of presentation"—that is, that each carries a different sense, or way of thinking about the object they refer to. We think differently about Venus in the two cases: namely, as "the bright star visible before sunrise" and "the bright star visible before sunset." Even the times of day convey different moods—one of being early and one of being late. In other words, it is only in the context of whole sentences that words have a definite meaning.

Frege also showed that the statement "The Morning Star is the Morning Star" tells us nothing, whereas "The Morning Star is the Evening Star" not only states a truth, but expresses knowledge that has been established by astronomers. Neither of these would be possible if the meaning of a word were simply its reference.

NAMES AND MEANINGS

For centuries, philosophers believed that the meaning of a word is an object it refers to. However, Frege argued that this cannot be the case, and that we need to distinguish between a word's reference (the object it refers to) and its sense (the meaning it has within the context of a sentence). Even the word "Aristotle" is not merely the name of a certain person who lived at a certain time: it is a word that has a whole host of meanings, including "the Greek thinker who pioneered philosophical logic."

"ARISTOTLE" is a word that has many senses, but a single, real-world reference.

> "We let a sign express its sense and designate its denotation."
>
> Gottlob Frege,
> *On Sense and Reference* (1892)

The Morning Star

The phrase "Morning Star" refers to Venus as it looks in the morning.

The Evening Star

The phrase "Evening Star" refers to Venus as it looks in the evening.

Observing Venus

Frege argued that words have two aspects: their "reference," or the object that they describe, and their "sense," or the overall meaning that they convey. The expressions "Morning Star" and "Evening Star" have two different senses but share the same reference: the planet Venus.

Venus

Although it looks like a star, Venus is in fact a planet. It is visible in the morning or the evening, depending on its position in the sky.

Russell's theory of descriptions

British philosopher Bertrand Russell built on the work of Gottlob Frege (see pp.86–87), and used formal logic to reveal the underlying structure of common linguistic expressions.

Underlying logic

Russell (1872–1970) argued that the grammar of ordinary language, such as its nouns and adjectives, can hide the underlying logic of expressions. He believed that many philosophical problems can be solved by translating what is said in ordinary language into terms that express this underlying logic.

For example, Russell argued that a proper name, such as "John," takes its meaning from the person it refers to. And so, when we say "John is bald," we ascribe a property (baldness) to John. Russell contrasts these with the phrases "The King of France" and "The King of France is bald," which have similar grammatical structures but a different underlying logic. For Russell, "The King of France" is not a name, but what he called a "definite description"—that is,

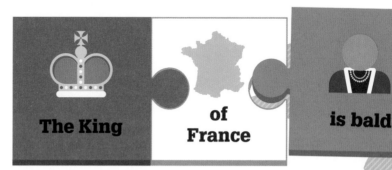

The King | of France | is bald

a phrase that describes a property of something that has yet to be identified. Russell noted that the statement "The King of France is bald" (like its negation, "The King of France is not bald") is neither true nor false because there is no King of France. Moreover, he argued that, being neither true nor false, it is logically meaningless.

Russell proposed that the way to make sense of the statement is to break it down into its constituent logical propositions. He identified three of these: there is a thing that is the King of France; no more than one thing is the King of France; and if anything is the King of France, then it is bald. Together, these propositions are the logical elements of the statement "The King of France is bald."

Russell concluded that it is only once we know the logic of such statements that their meaning and truth value can be assessed.

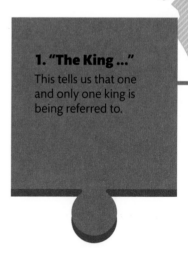

1. "The King …"
This tells us that one and only one king is being referred to.

Logical analysis

Russell considered whether the statement "The King of France is bald" involves an existential claim: that states that a certain thing exists and that it has a certain characteristic.

> "A logical theory may be tested by its capacity for dealing with puzzles."
>
> Bertrand Russell, *On Denoting* (1905)

2. "... of France ..."
This identifies the king
as the King of France.

3. "... is bald."
This tells us that if there
is a King of France, then
he is bald.

EXISTENCE IS NOT A PROPERTY

Russell argued that many philosophical problems arise
from assuming that "existence" is a property of things.
What he means is that when we say, for example, that
a unicorn is horselike and has a horn on its head, we
are describing properties that collectively *are* the unicorn.
However, when we say that it "exists," we are not adding
to the unicorn's properties—we are simply saying that
something in the world has the properties of a unicorn.
Likewise, if "existence" were a property, then the claim that
unicorns do not exist would mean that something exists
that has the property of nonexistence. Russell's claim
could be seen to undermine many traditional arguments,
such as Anselm's proof of God's existence (see pp.46–47).

Picturing the world

Ludwig Wittgenstein was one of the most influential philosophers of the 20th century. In his first major work, the _Tractatus Logico-Philosophicus_, he presented what came to be called his picture theory of meaning.

Mirroring reality

In the _Tractatus_, Wittgenstein (1889–1951) examined the nature of language with a view to tracing the limits of what we can know and talk about. He was apparently inspired by the way that traffic accidents were reconstructed in Paris courtrooms at the time he was writing—using toys to represent the cars and people involved. Wittgenstein believed that language works in a similar way—that it enables us to "picture" the world, which is made up of facts, which are an existing combination of objects. For example, the words "grass" and "green" are the building blocks, or "atoms," of the meaningful statement "The grass is green," which is a picture of a fact in the world. According to Wittgenstein, statements that cannot be reduced to such building blocks are effectively nonsense, because they fail to describe reality. The propositions of science, therefore, have sense, whereas those of ethics and aesthetics—statements of value—do not.

Atoms of meaning

Wittgenstein's picture theory of meaning is often described as "logical atomism," for it states that a meaningful proposition is one that is based on "atomic" statements that relate to the observable world. If a sentence cannot be analysed into these atomic statements, it is meaningless. For Wittgenstein, language enables us to form pictures of the world that we share with one another. Therefore, when we understand each other, it is because we share the same pictures of the world.

1 I'M ON A BEACH
If someone is alone on a beach, they can share that fact via language. Language is like a camera that takes pictures of the world.

2 "I'M ON A BEACH"
If someone says "I'm on a beach," their words are representations of themselves and the beach, and picture them and the world around them.

MEANINGFUL

However, for Wittgenstein, "nonsense" did not mean "worthless." Rather, he said that ethical statements try to say "things that cannot be put into words … They are what is mystical." They are, as he put it, attempts to say what can only be shown (see box).

Wittgenstein believed that the philosopher's role was to distinguish sense from nonsense and to help to construct a clear and logical language. He said that language and the world mirror each other, and that logic enables us to correct any apparent mismatch between the two. He argued further that philosophers had generated a great deal of confusion by failing to understand the pictorial nature of language, and that the whole of metaphysics—which dwells on things that transcend the physical world—was misguided.

SAYING AND SHOWING

Wittgenstein claimed that a meaningful statement is one that contains "atomic" statements, or pictures of facts in the world. However, he also distinguished between "saying" and "showing", arguing that while his theory of meaning defined the boundaries of what can be said, there are other kinds of insights that can only be "shown." This means that not everything that lies outside the strict bounds of "sense" is worthless. For example, things can be shown in literature, art, and music that can never be said directly. Our moral and aesthetic judgements are attuned to what is shown in what Wittgenstein described as a "mystical" way.

"It is not how things are in the world that is mystical, but that it exists."

Ludwig Wittgenstein, *Tractatus Logico-Philosophicus* (1921)

3 "SHE'S ON A BEACH"
When two people understand each other, they share the same pictures of the world.

4 "THE BEACH IS ROMANTIC"
According to Wittgenstein, words depict things in the world. However, they do not depict values, such as "romantic."

MEANINGLESS

Meaning and observation

In the mid-20th century, a group of thinkers known as the Vienna Circle proposed that only logical truths and statements about the physical world have meaning. Their position became known as logical positivism.

The verification principle

Logical positivism was heavily influenced by Wittgenstein's picture theory of meaning (see pp.90–91). Its central rule was the "verification principle," according to which a statement only has meaning if it is logically true or can be verified by observation. The goal of logical positivism was to rid philosophy of speculation and to bring it in line with modern science.

In 1936, British philosopher A. J. Ayer (1910–1989) published a famous defense of logical positivism. In *Language, Truth, and Logic*, he argued that only empirical, tautological, or mathematical statements are meaningful—that is, those that can be verified by observation, logic, or mathematics. He was influenced by Hume's distinction between matters of fact and relations of ideas (see pp.64–65) and argued that statements that are neither of these are not merely wrong, but meaningless. Ethical statements, for example, such as "Killing is wrong," do not express meaningful ideas (which, according to Ayer, must relate to the physical world), but emotions. Such expressions are meaningless, although they may serve to stir people's sympathies or to change their behavior.

MEANINGLESS STATEMENT

THAT'S A LOVELY COAT

> "...all utterances about the nature of God are nonsensical."
>
> A.J. Ayer, *Language, Truth, and Logic* (1936)

Meaningful statements

According to logical positivism, there are two types of meaningful sentences: logical statements (such as "Purple is a color") and factual statements (such as "It's raining outside"). In the following example, four statements are made, but only two of them pass the positivists' test of meaning—namely, that they are either logical truths or relate to the observable world. The other two statements are meaningless.

MEANINGLESS STATEMENT

LYING IS WRONG

LOGICAL STATEMENT

YELLOW IS A COLOR

FACTUAL STATEMENT

IT'S RAINING

MEANINGFUL OR MEANINGLESS?

According to logical positivism, the two statements on the right are meaningful because one ("Yellow is a color") is logically true and the other ("It's raining") is about the world. However, the other two statements ("That's a lovely coat" and "Lying is wrong") are neither true nor false, but meaningless.

Dispensing with metaphysics

Rudolf Carnap (1891–1970) believed that philosophers had spent too much time speculating about the nature of reality. Instead, he proposed that philosophers should restrict themselves to analyzing language only.

Logic and language

A member of the Vienna Circle (see pp.92–93) and an admirer of Wittgenstein's picture theory of meaning (see pp.90–91), Rudolf Carnap believed that philosophy should be a rigorous, empirical discipline. He studied both Frege (see pp.86–87) and Russell (see pp.88–89) and came to the conclusion that statements made in ordinary language can be ambiguous and therefore lead to philosophical confusion.

However, like Russell, Carnap believed that such confusion can be avoided by using logical analysis, which reveals the underlying logic of ordinary language. In fact, he thought that philosophers had caused a great deal of confusion by using language ambiguously instead of restricting themselves to analyzing language itself. For Carnap, philosophers should clarify language in the same way that physicists explain the world—by revealing its fundamental laws, only in the philosopher's case, the laws revealed are those of logic.

Philosophy and science

Carnap's main aim was to bring an end to metaphysics—that is, the discussion of ideas that do not relate to the physical world. He used the verification principle (see pp.92–93) to argue that since metaphysical statements cannot be verified by experience, they are meaningless. For example, the concepts "God" and "soul" transcend experience, so the statements "God is good" and "The soul survives death" are strictly meaningless. They are examples of what Carnap calls "pseudosentences," or sentences that appear to have sense, but in fact have no content whatsoever.

For Carnap, it was impossible to conceive of any sort of experience or observation that would support a metaphysical claim, so the metaphysical theories of the past should be abandoned. These included Plato's theory of the Forms (see pp.34–37), Descartes' notion of the *cogito* (see pp.52–55), and Hegel's concept of *Geist* (see pp.70–73). According to Carnap, all of these violate the rule that an idea must relate to the physical world for it to have meaning.

In *The Logical Structure of the World* (1928), Carnap argued that a genuine philosophical statement is neither true nor false, but simply a clarification of a scientific concept. In other words, philosophers should not construct theories about the world. Such theories are the business of science, and they should stand or fall on the basis of physical evidence alone.

VALUE JUDGMENTS

According to Carnap, ethical and aesthetic statements, like metaphysical claims, are meaningless because they fail to describe the world. If someone says "It is raining outside," they are saying that a certain state of affairs exists, and we can check to see if they are right. However, if someone says "Rain is beautiful" or "Stealing is wrong," there is no equivalent thing in the world that the words "beautiful" and "wrong" relate to. For Carnap, this renders the words neither true nor false, but meaningless.

Truth, sense, and nonsense

According to the verification principle, a statement is meaningful if it is true by definition (for example, "Triangles have three sides") or if it can be backed up by experience (for example, "This triangle is blue"). Carnap argued that by these criteria, metaphysics is meaningless and should therefore be eliminated. His theory of meaning was influenced by Wittgenstein's picture theory of language, according to which sentences only have meaning if they can be reduced to statements about things in the world.

METAPHYSICS IS NONSENSE

SCIENTIFIC STATEMENTS CAN BE TRANSLATED INTO LOGICAL LANGUAGE ...

... AND SO CAN OBSERVATIONAL STATEMENTS.

HOWEVER, METAPHYSICAL STATEMENTS CANNOT BE TRANSLATED

AND SO THEY ARE NEITHER TRUE NOR FALSE, BUT MEANINGLESS.

A private language is impossible

In his book *Philosophical Investigations*, Ludwig Wittgenstein overturned his own picture theory of meaning (see pp.90–91), arguing instead that the meaning of a word is its use.

The private language argument

In *Philosophical Investigations*, Wittgenstein argued that the traditional idea of the meaning of a word being an object it refers to cannot be true. If it were true, he claimed, then a private language would be possible, for "meaning" would simply be a matter of an individual associating a word with an object. But, he argues, a private language is impossible.

Wittgenstein asks us to imagine someone growing up alone on a desert island. They might use the sounds "red" and "green" to distinguish between certain colors, but if they misused the sounds, they would not be aware of their mistake. Even if they set up a rule book to help them, they would never know whether or not they were interpreting the rules correctly—they would need a rule book for the rule book, and so on. What they lack, Wittgenstein argued, is a community of language-users—words require rules, and rules are necessarily public, shared conventions. Wittgenstein compared language to a game of chess: if we don't know how to play, then we cannot even start the game (see pp.98–99).

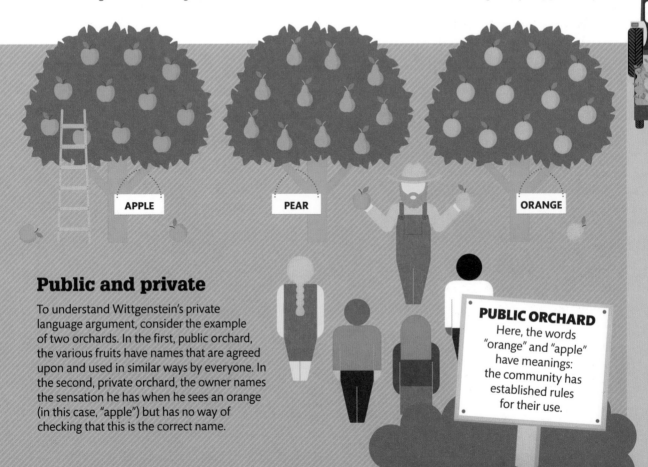

APPLE

PEAR

ORANGE

Public and private

To understand Wittgenstein's private language argument, consider the example of two orchards. In the first, public orchard, the various fruits have names that are agreed upon and used in similar ways by everyone. In the second, private orchard, the owner names the sensation he has when he sees an orange (in this case, "apple") but has no way of checking that this is the correct name.

PUBLIC ORCHARD
Here, the words "orange" and "apple" have meanings: the community has established rules for their use.

Wittgenstein's argument undermined centuries of philosophical assumptions. René Descartes, who is widely regarded as one of the founders of modern philosophy (see pp.52–55), argued that he could doubt everything except that he was conscious—even the existence of other people. The private language argument claims that such a thought is impossible, for thoughts require words, and words depend on the existence of other people. It was an observation that had huge implications, particularly in the field of the philosophy of mind (see pp.144–163).

"The meaning of a word is its use in the language."

Ludwig Wittgenstein, *Philosophical Investigations* (1953)

PHILOSOPHY AS THERAPY

Wittgenstein compared his philosophy with certain aspects of psychotherapy, stating in *Philosophical Investigations* that "the philosopher's treatment of a question is like the treatment of an illness." The illness, in this case, affects traditional philosophy, which was largely concerned with metaphysical questions, and the cure is the new (Wittgensteinian) way of thinking. For Wittgenstein, philosophical problems arise when we lose our way in language or are tricked by "grammar" into thinking, for example, that the word "I" refers to a mental entity, or that "believing" is an internal process (see pp.148–149). Wittgenstein argued that philosophers should not construct theories to solve philosophical problems, but should dissolve philosophical problems by showing that they arise from the misuse of language.

APPLE

PRIVATE ORCHARD
Here, in a world of one person, the sound "apple" lacks the community needed to establish rules for its use, so it has no meaning.

Wittgenstein's language-games

In *Philosophical Investigations*, Ludwig Wittgenstein argued that the meaning of a word is its use in particular contexts. To explain this idea, he used the notion of "language-games."

Language-games

Wittgenstein argued that a word only has meaning in the context of human activity. For example, to understand the word "bishop" in a game of chess is to know that a certain piece should be used in certain ways but not others. Wittgenstein argued that the same is true of all words: that to grasp their meanings is to know the rules for their use. This idea goes against the intuitive thought that the meaning of a word is an object that it refers to (see pp.86–87).

The word "art," for example, seems to represent a single thing; in fact, it not only describes a wide range of activities, but also activities that do not have a single, essential thing in common. Instead, they have overlapping similarities that Wittgenstein called "family resemblances." For example, when we say "That film was a work of art," we play a particular language-game in which "art" means something like "genius." On the other hand, when we talk of "The art of painting,"

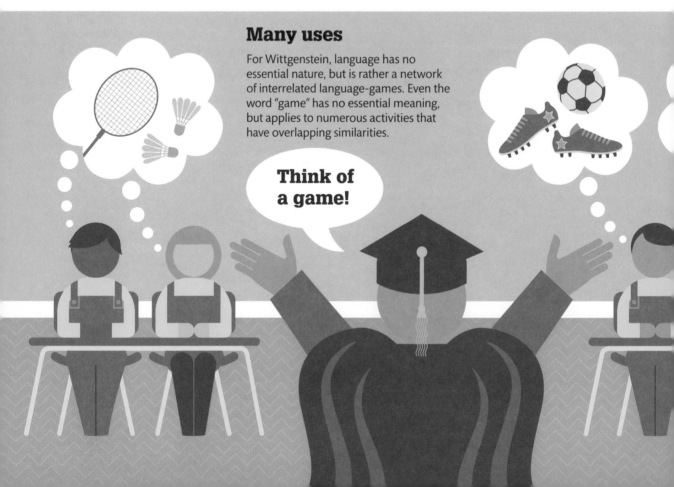

Many uses

For Wittgenstein, language has no essential nature, but is rather a network of interrelated language-games. Even the word "game" has no essential meaning, but applies to numerous activities that have overlapping similarities.

Think of a game!

we play a different game in which "art" means something like "discipline" or "profession."

Indeed, we also use words to flatter, scold, or influence people, using phrases that have little or no literal meaning. Wittgenstein's point was that any attempt to analyze language to reveal its essential structure is misguided because language has no essential structure. As Wittgenstein admitted, this reversed the view that he expressed in his earlier work, the *Tractatus Logico-Philosophicus* (see pp.90–91).

"... think of the whole process of using words ... as one of those games by means of which children learn their native language."

Ludwig Wittgenstein, *Philosophical Investigations* (1953)

MEANING IS USE

According to Wittgenstein, the ability to understand words is not a matter of knowing exact rules and definitions, but rather of being able to use them in relevant contexts. There is no ultimate foundation for this activity: the meanings of words are defined by the ways in which we use them, and not the other way around. As Wittgenstein said: "If I have exhausted the justifications, I have reached bedrock, and my spade is turned. Then I am inclined to say, 'This is simply what I do.'"

Science and falsification

The philosopher of science Karl Popper challenged one of our oldest ideas—namely, that scientists should construct theories and then show that they are true.

Science and pseudoscience

According to Popper (1902–94), a theory should only be called "scientific" if it is falsifiable—that is, if there are conditions under which it can be shown to be false. This undermines the idea that scientists should make theories and then demonstrate that they are true—a process that, Popper argued, gives credibility to all kinds of "pseudoscience."

For Popper, an example of pseudoscience was Alfred Adler's theory of "individual psychology."

Popper noted that if one man drowns a child and a second man dies to save a child, both, according to Adler, may be motivated by inferiority complexes—the first empowering himself by committing a crime, the second doing so by being selfless. Popper claimed that he could think of no human behavior that could not be interpreted in terms of Adler's theory, and that, far from proving the truth of the theory, this showed that it was not a theory at all—or at least,

not a scientific hypothesis. Popper contrasted this with Einstein's theory of general relativity, which was scientific precisely because it was open to being falsified by observation. So far, however, the theory has yet to be refuted.

By claiming that science is a process of conjecture, Popper avoided the "problem of induction" (see p.65), which states that scientific theories are unjustified because they cannot be proven to be true.

FALSIFICATION AND VERIFICATION

Popper considered the statement "All swans are white." "All swans" describes an infinite set of objects, so no matter how many white swans we observe, we can never prove the claim that all swans are white. However, we need only see a single nonwhite swan in order to falsify it. Falsification, then, has the merit of being achievable, whereas verification (proving a theory to be true) does not. Moreover, falsification reminds us of what science should be about—namely, disproving our provisional theories, rather than encouraging belief in things that cannot be proved. For Popper, the Marxist theory of history (see pp.74–75) and Freud's theory of the unconscious are in this sense unscientific.

A BLACK SWAN falsifies the theory that all swans are white.

The problem-solving pursuit

Popper argued that science attempts to solve the practical problems of the world and does so by formulating theories and then performing experiments to test and falsify those theories. He believed that the growth of scientific knowledge is thus the constant reformulation of theories that have been disproven by falsification. The best theories survive attempts at falsification, but this does not guarantee that they, too, will not be falsified in the future.

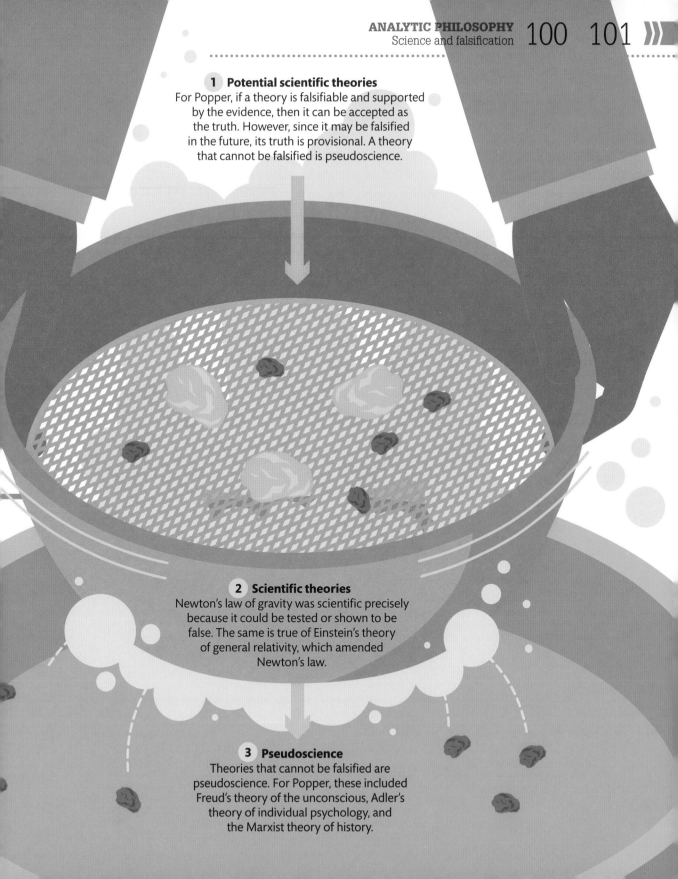

1 Potential scientific theories
For Popper, if a theory is falsifiable and supported
by the evidence, then it can be accepted as
the truth. However, since it may be falsified
in the future, its truth is provisional. A theory
that cannot be falsified is pseudoscience.

2 Scientific theories
Newton's law of gravity was scientific precisely
because it could be tested or shown to be
false. The same is true of Einstein's theory
of general relativity, which amended
Newton's law.

3 Pseudoscience
Theories that cannot be falsified are
pseudoscience. For Popper, these included
Freud's theory of the unconscious, Adler's
theory of individual psychology, and
the Marxist theory of history.

The nature of scientific truth

US philosopher Willard Van Orman Quine was critical of the idea that philosophers should limit themselves to analyzing language. Instead, he proposed that philosophy is a branch of science.

Philosophy as science

Willard Quine (1908–2000) was a fierce critic of logical positivism (see pp.92–93), particularly its claim that philosophers should limit themselves to analyzing language. However, he was also against the idea that philosophers should speculate about the nature of the world, or that philosophical knowledge is in any way different from scientific knowledge.

ANALYTIC TRUTHS

In *Two Dogmas of Empiricism* (1951), Quine attacked the positivists' reliance on the distinction between analytic and synthetic statements (see pp.68–69). According to this distinction, analytic statements are true by definition, while synthetic statements are true or false depending on the facts.

Quine argued that even the statement "All bachelors are unmarried men" (an apparently analytic statement) is only true because humans have had experience of what it is to be married. In other words, the word "bachelor" only has meaning in connection to a wider body of knowledge. Quine argued that positivists ignore this connection when they claim that analytic statements are true independently of facts, and so can serve as the fundamental units of thought.

For Quine, philosophy is effectively a branch of science, rather than a separate discipline that gives science its theoretical foundation. As he wrote, "it is within science itself, and not in some prior philosophy, that reality is to be identified and described."

Quine's definition of "science" was broad and included history, psychology, and sociology, which he saw as extensions of "common sense." However, he considered physics to be the model for all knowledge: ultimately, everything can be understood in terms of physical processes.

Interconnected beliefs

According to Quine, human knowledge is an interconnected "web of belief." Simple statements of observation, such as "it is snowing outside," lie at the edge of this web, where they are formulated according to experience. The truth or falsehood of such statements is easily checked. However, Quine argued that the same is not true of scientific statements, which are related to numerous other statements that make up an entire body of knowledge. In other words, scientific claims cannot be checked against experience in isolation of the theories that they belong to. Quine noted that this means that scientific statements cannot be accepted or rejected on the basis of evidence alone. Rather, they are judged according to their contribution to the strengths of a theory as a whole. Pragmatic considerations therefore play a pivotal role in how we assess scientific claims—such as how simple they are and how well they can be used to make predictions.

Among other things, Quine's argument showed that the positivists' claim that sentences can be meaningful on their own, independently of theory, is incoherent.

The web of belief

For Quine, knowledge is a web of interconnected beliefs. Logic and mathematics lie at the center of the web, while observational statements lie on the periphery. Between these lie the theories that we construct to account for our experience. According to Quine, each statement depends on the entire web for its coherence.

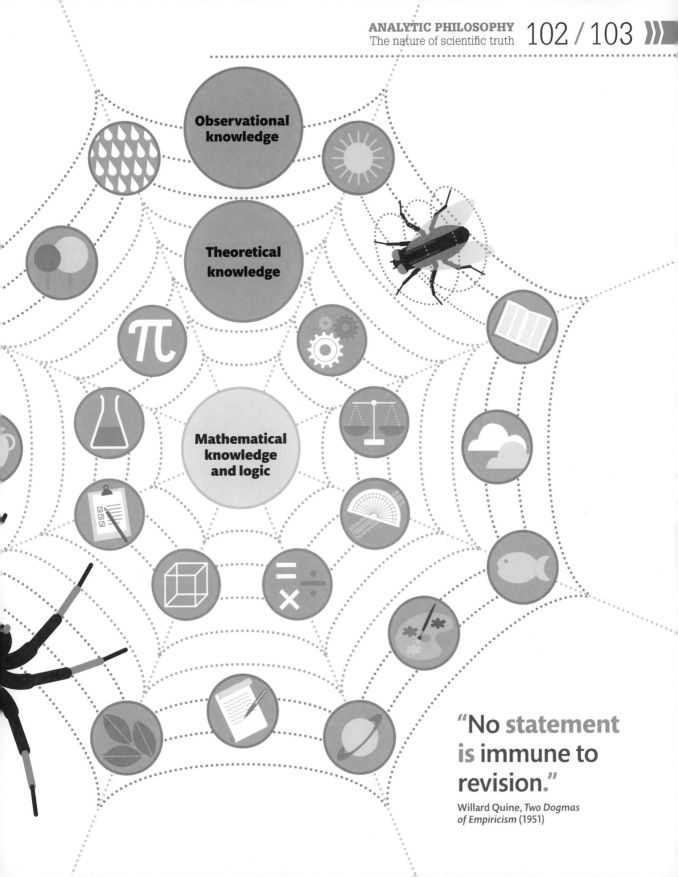

Observational knowledge

Theoretical knowledge

Mathematical knowledge and logic

"No **statement** is immune to revision."

Willard Quine, *Two Dogmas of Empiricism* (1951)

Words as actions

The philosopher J. L. Austin (1911–1960) argued that the meaning of a word is not an object or state of affairs in the world, but the effect it has on the person or people being spoken to.

Describing and influencing

In *How to Do Things with Words* (1955), J. L. Austin challenged the traditional view that the primary function of language is to describe. At the time, this view was held by many positivists (see pp.90–93), who advocated Wittgenstein's picture theory of meaning, according to which words are effectively pictures of the world (see pp.90–91). By then, Wittgenstein had disowned his earlier theory and had argued instead that language has countless functions (see pp.96–99), such as to persuade, to entertain, and to encourage. Austin agreed with the later Wittgenstein, but unlike Wittgenstein, he thought that the functions of language are finite and could be classified.

Austin made a preliminary distinction between what he called "constative" and "performative" sentences. He defined constative sentences as descriptions of states of affairs and performative sentences as words that are uttered to achieve a certain goal. The former, being descriptions, are either true or false, while the latter are either effective or ineffective in achieving their aims. However, Austin went on to claim that this distinction was inadequate, arguing that all constative sentences are performative in some sense. In other words, whenever we say anything, we are trying to influence the world in some way. For this reason, he redefined sentences as "speech acts."

Doing things with words

To develop his theory further, Austin distinguished what he called the locutionary, illocutionary, and perlocutionary acts of speech. The locutionary act is

Acts of speech

According to Austin, speech is an active, performative exercise: when we speak, we want to elicit responses from others and perhaps even influence their beliefs. The true meaning of a sentence is thus its intended social function, or what Austin called its "illocutionary force." He contrasted this with the locutionary and perlocutionary aspects of sentences—that is, the physical act of speaking and the actual effects that sentences have on others.

"Sentences are not as such either true or false."

J. L. Austin, *Sense and Sensibilia* (1962)

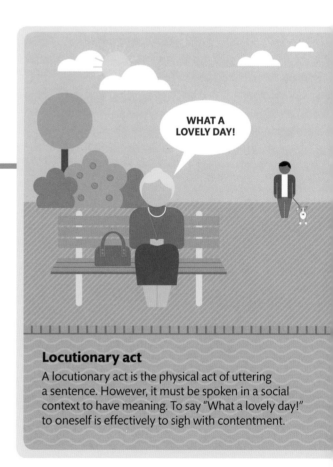

Locutionary act

A locutionary act is the physical act of uttering a sentence. However, it must be spoken in a social context to have meaning. To say "What a lovely day!" to oneself is effectively to sigh with contentment.

the simple, physical act of uttering a sentence. However, the locutionary act is also an illocutionary act, which is the intended effect of speaking a sentence—such as to warn, to apologize, or to instruct. A locutionary act is therefore an act *of* saying something, whereas an illocutionary act is an act performed *by* saying something. Austin's third category, the perlocutionary act, is the intended or unintended consequence of the illocutionary act on the person or people being spoken to. A warning, for example, can have the perlocutionary effect of being a hostile gesture, when no such effect was intended.

In Austin's view, to understand a sentence is to understand all three performative aspects about it. He argued that words are effectively tools whose meanings are the effects they have on the world, rather than pictures designed to represent it.

ORDINARY LANGUAGE PHILOSOPHY

Austin belonged to a school of thought known as "ordinary language philosophy." Ordinary language philosophers argue that the meaning of a word is the meaning it has in everyday language and that philosophical problems arise when words are taken out of their natural contexts. For example, in ordinary language, we say that we "understand" something when it is clear to us what something means. However, it is less obvious what philosophers mean when they talk about understanding. The philosophical use of the word is abstract and suggests that there is a "process" or "faculty" of understanding, which raises the question of what sort of process or faculty it is—for example, is it "mental" or "physical"? Neither of these questions arises from our ordinary use of the word.

Illocutionary force

If someone says "What a lovely day!" in a social context, they may be doing so to foster a friendship. Their words have meaning because of their intended consequences.

Perlocutionary effect

For Austin, the meaning of a sentence is also the effect it has on other people. If someone is greeted by someone else, they may respond romantically, whether the effect was expected or not.

Scientific revolutions

US philosopher and historian Thomas Kuhn challenged the dominant views of how the physical sciences work and transformed our understanding of the philosophical framework of scientific practice.

Paradigm shifts

Kuhn (1922–1996) believed that science does not always progress in a linear and gradual way. In fact, in *The Structure of Scientific Revolutions* (1962), he argued that the most significant advances in science take the form of revolutions, which he called "paradigm shifts."

For Kuhn, a "paradigm" is a view of the world that a scientific theory presupposes. A paradigm shift is therefore a change in our view of the world, as opposed to an extension of our existing ideas.

According to Kuhn, "normal science" is what goes on between revolutions, when scientists have

an agreed-upon view of the world. Newtonian physics, for example, was a paradigm that existed from the 17th century until the early 20th century, and because of it, scientists had a framework of shared assumptions. One of those assumptions was that time is absolute, or that it passes at

Avenues of knowledge

For Kuhn, while science has progressed along one particular route, there are many other routes it could have taken. A "true" route is one that solves the most important problems of the day.

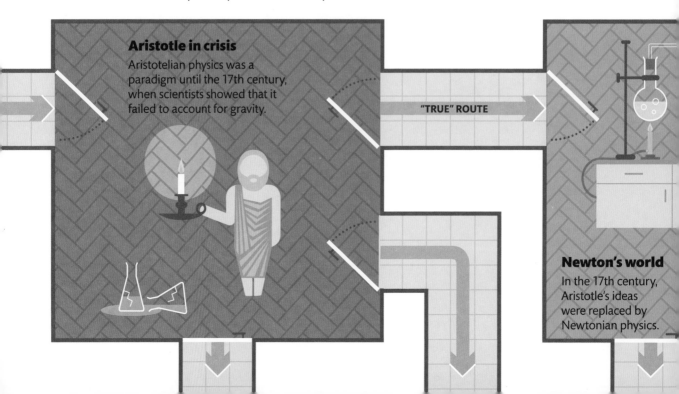

Aristotle in crisis
Aristotelian physics was a paradigm until the 17th century, when scientists showed that it failed to account for gravity.

"TRUE" ROUTE

Newton's world
In the 17th century, Aristotle's ideas were replaced by Newtonian physics.

the same rate wherever one is in the universe. In 1905, however, Albert Einstein showed that time is in fact relative, or passes at different rates depending on one's perspective. This idea completely undermined Newtonian physics and forced scientists to adopt a new, Einsteinian, paradigm.

Truth and progress

However, Kuhn argued that although Newton may have been wrong about the nature of time, the difference between Newton and Einstein is not that Einstein's theory is "truer" than Newton's.

In all likelihood, one day Einstein's ideas may be replaced. Instead, Kuhn claimed that science, in any age, enables us to do certain things, and that it is the things that we can do today (build computers, make vaccines, and so on) that make our science seem "true."

For Kuhn, paradigm shifts are not stages in our progress toward the truth—they are more like milestones in our evolution or in our ability to adapt to the world. Scientific truth is thus a matter of consensus, so it is always subject to change, both between different cultures and at different times.

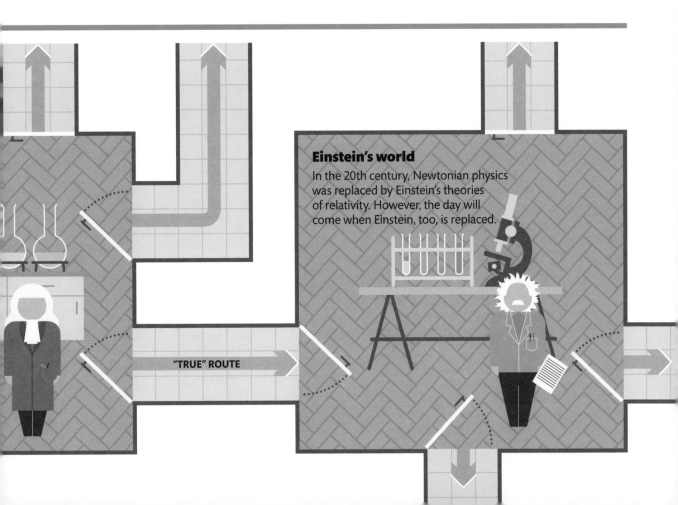

Einstein's world

In the 20th century, Newtonian physics was replaced by Einstein's theories of relativity. However, the day will come when Einstein, too, is replaced.

"TRUE" ROUTE

Points of view

A number philosophers have argued that it is impossible to think objectively or without being influenced by one's viewpoint. However, Thomas Nagel (1937–) claims that objectivity is possible within limits.

Points of view and objectivity

The idea of objective thinking suggests that there is a way of looking at the world that is not influenced by our particular, subjective viewpoints, which are shaped by our cultural and biological conditioning. To look at ourselves objectively is to see ourselves "from the outside" and to understand which of our beliefs are subjective and which are true regardless of who we are. Over a series of books and articles, Thomas Nagel discusses the extent to which this is possible.

For Nagel, the physical sciences are models of objectivity: they provide us with knowledge about the world and give us ways of testing that knowledge. In describing human beings, science tells us that we are creatures that have particular kinds of bodies and that these give us our human point of view.

However, Nagel argues that there is only so much that science can reveal. For example, science can tell us all sorts of things about bats, such as what they eat and how they communicate, but not what it is like to *be* a bat. In other words, it can tell us what bats are like from *our* perspective (from the outside), but not what they are like from *their* perspective (from the inside). Nagel's point is that science shows that there are numerous creatures in the world whose experiences, or points of view, are wholly unlike our own. All we can do is speculate about the nature of their experience, in the same way that someone who is blind can only speculate about the experience of sight.

For Nagel, knowledge is "a set of concentric spheres, progressively revealed as we detach gradually from the contingencies of the self." By thinking objectively, we leave our particular perspectives behind, but our objectivity is limited: it gives us an outside view of a world that is filled with other perspectives, each of which has its own unique sense of its own existence.

The view from nowhere

According to Nagel, thinking objectively means thinking outside the boundaries of our subjective perspectives. The further we leave these perspectives behind, the more objective our thinking becomes. The end goal of this process is to reach a vantage point that least depends on our biological and cultural perspectives—a view that Nagel calls "the view from nowhere." The physical sciences, for example, operate in this "nowhere": they describe things that are true for everyone, and not just for the scientists themselves. In *Points of View* (1997), the philosopher A. W. Moore calls the representations that are produced from no point of view "absolute representations," for they describe the world with "complete detachment."

THE NATURE OF CONSCIOUSNESS

In 1974, Nagel published a paper titled *What is it like to be a bat?* In it, he argued that if something is conscious, then there is something that it is like to be that thing: in other words, that to be conscious is to have a perspective. His argument relies on the idea that to be conscious is always to be conscious *of* something, and that the character of what we perceive depends on our senses. For these reasons, creatures with different senses perceive the world in different ways, so being a bat is very different from being a shark or a dog. Nagel's argument is a criticism of the materialists' claim that consciousness can be fully explained by describing a creature's brain (see pp.152–153).

> "What is wanted is some way of making the most objective standpoint the basis of action."
>
> Thomas Nagel, *The View From Nowhere* (1986)

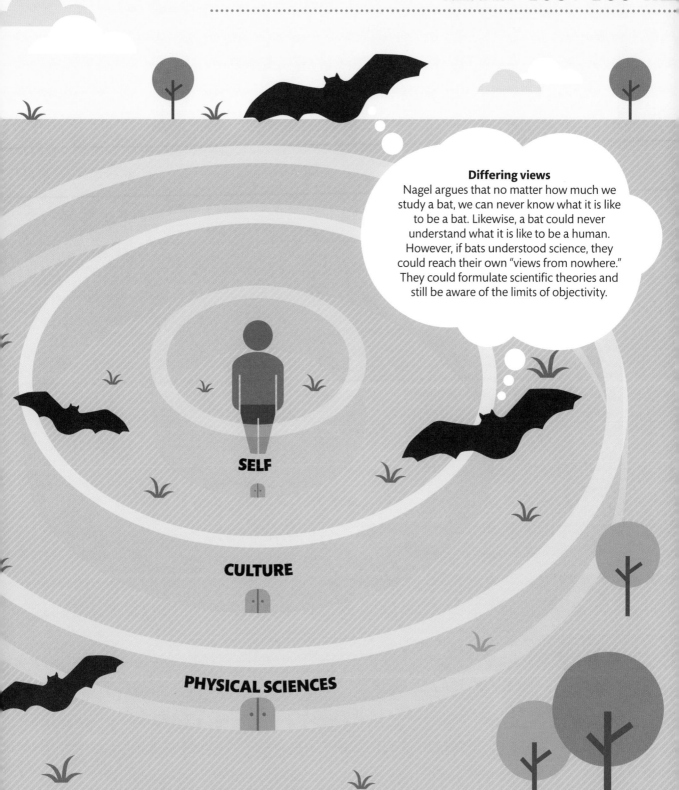

Differing views
Nagel argues that no matter how much we study a bat, we can never know what it is like to be a bat. Likewise, a bat could never understand what it is like to be a human. However, if bats understood science, they could reach their own "views from nowhere." They could formulate scientific theories and still be aware of the limits of objectivity.

SELF

CULTURE

PHYSICAL SCIENCES

Feminist epistemology

In studying the theory of knowledge (epistemology) from a feminist perspective, feminist epistemologists seek to identify and challenge harmful gender biases that prevail in many areas of knowledge.

A feminist view of knowledge

Feminist philosophers of epistemology and science have identified gender biases at the core of theoretical knowledge in disciplines such as physics, medicine, and law. They argue that women continue to be marginalized in most areas of knowledge as a result of the fact that dominant models of knowledge and the methods used to acquire knowledge both conceal and reinforce sexist biases. Stereotypically "feminine" modes of knowing (for example, practical forms of knowledge, such as how to look after children or the elderly) are underestimated and devalued.

As a consequence, women often lack self-confidence and authority in their chosen discipline and may be assumed to be less capable scientists, researchers, or academics than their male counterparts. Feminist philosophers argue that cognitive and scientific practices need to be assessed and reformed in order to ensure that women are fairly treated in these traditionally "masculine" fields.

Different perspectives

Feminists argue that women face greater adversity than men in our male-dominated society (see Standpoint theory, right), which gives them a different understanding of a situation. A man may think he can assess a situation objectively, but his perspective is skewed by patriarchal practices and harmful assumptions.

View from above

What a wonderful, clear view I have from the top of the mountain! Here I am, master of the objective view! I see everything clearly.

Men only

Many areas of theoretical knowledge have been created by men for men's purposes. As a result, they may contain many unquestioned biases.

Questioning gender biases

This feminist view of epistemology does not necessarily imply that all knowledge is determined by gender. Feminists claim, however, that types of knowledge that are important to women's interests are gendered. In doing so, they are not claiming that objectivity is not possible or desirable, but are raising questions about objectivity, such as whether it is possible or necessary to overcome specific gendered perspectives to achieve objectivity. They also question whether an unbiased view is always desirable and ask what makes a certain perspective or situation a privileged one, and in what sense. They also consider whether or not men can put themselves in women's shoes, and women in men's, in order to gain a new and valuable perspective.

STANDPOINT THEORY

Along with feminist empiricism and postmodern approaches (see pp.140–141), standpoint theory is one of several distinctive feminist approaches to knowledge. Standpoint theorists, including Sandra Harding (1935–), argue that the social position of women represents a standpoint (point of view) of a disadvantaged or oppressed group. This standpoint allows women to see the shortcomings of the male-dominated practices and institutions that oppress them.

Women's standpoint is privileged because they have direct knowledge of what it means to be oppressed, so they are capable of a more insightful critical reflection. The oppressors—groups of powerful men—tend to ignore harmful assumptions and the consequences of their actions.

The aim of standpoint theory is to achieve a collective understanding among women as a social group and to reveal these shortcomings and harmful assumptions. On this basis, feminists can act politically to fight against the representation of women as objects of men's desires and subordination and to promote women as capable of holding all forms of knowledge, as well as people whose needs and interests should be properly taken into account in every area of knowledge.

Feminist epistemology

The adversity faced by women reveals that the tools and workings of traditional knowledge are in need of critical examination because they often produce limited and gender-biased knowledge.

Oppressed standpoint

I must find new ways to get to the top of the mountain, but I'll keep going in order to achieve objectivity and gain knowledge that is free of gender bias.

CONTINENTAL PHILOSOPHY

In the 20th century, European philosophers pursued
a different approach to that of the analytic school.
They focused more on the nature of life itself—
on what it means to be human.

CONTINENTAL PHILOSOPHY

The phrase "continental philosophy" was first used in the 19th century by British philosophers who wished to distinguish what they saw to be their own tradition of empiricism from the more speculative form of philosophy practiced in mainland Europe. The label stuck, however, and provides a useful distinction between two broad approaches to philosophy, especially in the 20th century.

The rift between the two schools widened with the establishment of analytic philosophy, which was inspired by the work of Bertrand Russell. At the same time, philosophers in mainland Europe were coming to terms with the legacy of a century of German idealism. The continental tradition did not have the empirical roots that British philosophy had, and since the 17th century had been steeped in rationalism and idealism. Where British philosophers developed the pragmatic ideas of utilitarianism and liberalism, a more speculative undercurrent flowed on the continent, rising from the revolutionary ideas of Voltaire, Rousseau, and Marx; through the German idealists Kant, Hegel, and Schopenhauer; and culminating in the iconoclastic Nietzsche.

In the 20th century, continental philosophers placed even more emphasis on subjective experience. This produced a human-centered approach to philosophy that first appeared in the work of Edmund Husserl, whose "phenomenology" was the basis of a lot of future continental philosophy. Husserl argued that philosophers should not speculate about things that are beyond our comprehension, but instead focus on the things that we can and that we do experience. Husserl's ideas were taken up by Martin Heidegger, who proposed that philosophers should study the nature of experience itself. This idea of analyzing subjective experience appealed particularly to French philosophers, including Jean-Paul Sartre, the leading figure of the "existentialist" school of thought. Philosophy was very much a part of the French literary as well as academic tradition, and as such had anticipated the subjective perspective of modern continental philosophy. Sartre and his partner Simone de Beauvoir also developed Heidegger's idea that we should all aim to live "authentically." They argued that we have no essential nature and that we should each live according to our own principles.

Other strands of philosophy also emerged from the continental tradition. A combination of the critical approach advocated by Kant and a reinterpretation of Marx's ideas gave rise to a school of critical theory that tried to counter the rising tide of totalitarianism before World War II. This process of analysis of social and political issues flourished after the war. Michel Foucault, for example, identified ways in which society at large exercises power over individuals. His ideas greatly influenced subsequent structuralist and poststructuralist thinkers, who revealed the extent to which ideas and power are interconnected.

Objects in the mind

The German philosopher Franz Brentano argued that all mental acts—such as thoughts, emotions, and perceptions—are about something, namely an object towards which the mind is directed.

Intentionality

The term "intentionality" was originally used by scholastic philosophers (see pp.46–47), who argued that God exists in reality, as well as in our minds. Brentano (1838–1917) reintroduced the term as part of his theory of consciousness from a first-person perspective and attempted to lay the foundations of a scientific psychology.

In his book, *Psychology from an Empirical Standpoint* (1874), Brentano argued that every thought or mental state we have is about something. When we sense,

remember, imagine, or desire something, we direct our minds toward that thing. For example, we might picture that thing in our mind, we might have an opinion on it, or it might provoke an emotion in us. Brentano named this directing of the mind toward something "intentionality" and called the things toward which we direct our minds "intentional objects." For Brentano, mental states are about intentional objects, and intentional objects exist inside our minds whether or not they exist outside our minds (as real objects in the physical world).

Mental (intentional) objects

Intentional objects include objects of perception, recollection, or imagination and objects of desire or those toward which we have feelings. These intentional objects exist within our mind whether or not these things exist outside our mind. We can be directed toward one and the same intentional object in various ways: for example, by directly sensing it, remembering it, or having a feeling toward or an opinion about it.

Mental objects
Objects that are inside the mind (or "immanent") can be representations of real objects or nonexistent objects. Brentano called these representations in the mind "presentations."

The real
Physical objects exist outside the mind, independently of us. When we sense real objects, they become objects in our minds.

Brentano argued that there can be no unconscious mental acts. This is because we are always aware of the objects toward which our mental acts are directed, and so are always aware of the mental acts themselves. He called the most basic kind of mental phenomena "presentations," which we have when we picture an object in our minds. Other kinds of mental acts, such as judgments (which involve an affirmation or denial of the existence of objects), desires, and emotions, are based on and require presentations.

DIFFICULTIES WITH BRENTANO'S INTENTIONALITY

A major problem with Brentano's ideas is that he never clearly defined the terms he used to describe consciousness. This means that there has been confusion about the concepts he used to describe mental objects, such as "presentation" and "immanent object." It is also unclear whether his use of the term "intentional object" refers to the real object or its mental representation.

THE REAL BOOK AS WE PERCEIVE IT

ITS MENTAL REPRESENTATION

Experienced objects
Objects that have been sensed or remembered become objects inside our minds: they become mental representations of the real.

Emotions
Emotions and desires are also about things, since they are directed toward an object.

Nonexistent things
Not all mental acts are about real objects. We can have a "presentation" of something that has no counterpart in the real world.

Phenomenology

Founded by Edmund Husserl, phenomenology is concerned with phenomena, or things that appear to us. It involves laying aside our assumptions about whether or not external, physical objects exist.

The phenomena of consciousness

Edmund Husserl (1859–1938) believed that a scientific approach to the study of consciousness and experience from a first-person point of view would give us definite answers to questions about subjective experience that philosophers had been debating for centuries. He called this approach phenomenology.

Husserl defined phenomenology as the science of the phenomena of consciousness. The standard definition of a phenomenon is something that appears to us—that is, what we experience, mean, or intend. Husserl makes a distinction between phenomena and objects, however. He argues that objects exist outside our consciousness and beyond the limits of our perception, whereas phenomena are how these objects appear within our consciousness.

Changing attitude

In what Husserl calls our "natural attitude" toward things, we assume that objects and a world beyond our own consciousness exist. We perceive, remember, imagine, and desire what we assume are the objects themselves, but we do not investigate these mental acts of perception, remembering, imagining, and desiring. That is to say that because we assume that the objects themselves exist, we do not examine how these objects appear as phenomena within our consciousness. Husserl argues that we can

Epoché

Science aims to give us certain answers to questions about the world, but scientific findings depend on experience, and experience is subject to assumptions and biases. Phenomenology "brackets out" our assumptions and puts them to one side in an "*epoché*." Epoché involves a change of attitude from the "natural attitude" to the "phenomenological attitude."

In the natural attitude, we assume the existence of external objects. In the phenomenological attitude, we suspend our judgment about the existence of external objects and instead focus on, and describe, our inner experience of these objects. This enables us to grasp the essence of our experience of objects and what makes it possible for us to make sense of them.

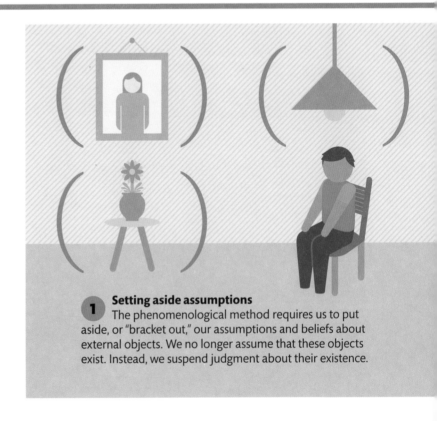

1 **Setting aside assumptions**
The phenomenological method requires us to put aside, or "bracket out," our assumptions and beliefs about external objects. We no longer assume that these objects exist. Instead, we suspend judgment about their existence.

change our attitude and pass from the natural attitude to what he calls the phenomenological attitude. This change in attitude is called phenomenological "reduction" or "epoché."

If we carry out the *epoché*, we lay aside (or "bracket out," as Husserl calls it) our assumption that objects beyond our consciousness exist. Instead, we focus on our consciousness and how these objects appear as phenomena in our consciousness. For Husserl, this enables us to make a pure description of the contents of our consciousness, free from any assumptions. Our consciousness is not at all empty, but full of the intentional objects (see pp.116–117) toward which we direct our minds.

"Experience by itself is not science."

Edmund Husserl

PHENOMENOLOGY VS. LOGICAL POSITIVISM

According to logical positivism (see pp.92–93), the only meaningful statements are logical propositions and statements about the physical world that can be verified by observation. Statements that express a subjective opinion or judgment are meaningless. This means that a logical positivist would argue that subjective answers to philosophical questions are meaningless.

For Husserl, logical positivism is flawed because it assumes that fundamental questions and issues about human existence are meaningless, and so unanswerable. Husserl argues that phenomenology can help us answer philosophical problems with the same degree of certainty with which we can answer scientific and mathematical questions. By laying aside all of our assumptions, we can build a secure foundation for knowledge of subjective experience that will enable us to make meaningful philosophical statements about our experience of life.

2 **Objects and phenomena**
This enables us to distinguish between an object (the chair) and a phenomenon (the chair as we perceive it). We might destroy the chair, but we can still remember or imagine it. The phenomenon can survive the object.

3 **Focusing on consciousness**
If we reflect on our own perception or memory of a chair, this means we can focus on our inner experience of objects and examine how they appear to us within our consciousness.

Time consciousness

Edmund Husserl (1859–1938) argued that time consciousness, or our awareness of time, is the most basic form of human consciousness.

Present, past, and future

To explore how humans experience time, Husserl analyzed an actual moment of consciousness. He used the example of hearing a melody. For Husserl, when we hear a note of a melody at a precise moment, the sound of this note creates a "primal impression," or a new "now-moment." This new sound pushes away the most recent moment. As that most recent moment moves into the past, our consciousness holds onto it, so that what is retained takes on the character of being just past and no longer immediately present. Husserl calls this process of holding onto the recent past "retention."

Husserl argued that the past of something is made up of a continuity of retentions. This continuity of retentions makes it possible for us to perceive an object as one particular thing rather than as a multiplicity of things or just a messy chaos. Every retention brings with it a further retention. When a present moment of time slips into the past, it becomes connected to a retention of

The flow of time

Husserl argues that the experience of hearing a melody brings together the primal impression of the immediate now; the retention of the immediate past; and protention, or the anticipation of, the future.

"All consciousness is consciousness of something."

Edmund Husserl

the past moment that immediately preceded it. A chain of retentions, connected with the present moment reaches into the past like a comet's tail. When we hear a melody, we are not only retaining past sounds but also expecting or even anticipating—by drawing on past retentions—the new sounds that are about to come. Husserl calls this forward-looking aspect of time consciousness "protention."

For Husserl, the three basic elements of time consciousness— primal impression (present), retention (past), and protention (future)—allow the immediate present to be connected to the past and the future as humans experience, and are aware of, the passing of time.

Immediate moment
At any given immediate moment, a new note is sounding.

1 Primal impression
The new note that is just sounding creates a primal impression, or a new now-moment.

2 Retention
The sound from the immediate past is no longer present, but it is retained in our consciousness.

3 Protention
We expect to hear new sounds that will occur in the immediate future.

What is it like to be human?

In his form of existentialist philosophy, Martin Heidegger explored what it means to be human, and most importantly, what it is like to exist as a human being living in the world.

Existentialist phenomenology

Heidegger (1889–1976) was influenced by Edmund Husserl's phenomenology (see pp.118–119), but he transformed the phenomenological method to address what he believed were more fundamental questions about meaning and being. While Husserl argued that we find meaning by understanding the structure of consciousness, Heidegger argued that we can only find meaning by analyzing what it is like to be human in our day-to-day existence.

Heidegger maintained that various attempts to define the human being as consciousness, subject, or self, are inadequate because they look at human life from the outside. He argued that in order to understand what it means to be human, we should not ask abstract questions about human existence, but should think about it through lived experience. Instead of asking "What is a human being?", we should ask "What does it mean to exist as a human being in this world?"

What to ask

For Heidegger, we can only understand our existence in this world by asking questions about our own experience, such as "What is it like to be human?" Scientific questions, such as "What is a human?", will not help us to reach this understanding.

What is the human?

A Scientific Treatise on Human Nature

Human existence

In Heidegger's view, if we are to understand what it means to say that something is, we need to understand what it means to exist as a human being. This is because humans are the only beings for whom the meaning of existence and being is a question. Animals, plants, and inanimate objects, for example, do not ask questions about their being and reality, but humans do ask such questions. Heidegger argued that "*Dasein*," or the state of "being there" in the world is what defines us as humans. We are not isolated subjects cut off from the world that we want to know about, but rather are beings who are "always already" in the world. For Heidegger, to be in the world means to dwell in a familiar environment, and being-in-the-world is both simpler and broader than mere knowledge or perception. It refers to how things we engage with affect our existence and how they make us feel.

BEING-IN-THE-WORLD

In his book *Being and Time* (1927), Heidegger describes the nature of being-in-the-world (*Dasein*) by exploring the attitudes of humans who exist in this world toward the various things that they encounter in this world. If humans encounter an object and their attitude toward that object is that it is potentially available for them to use in order to achieve something, then that object is what Heidegger calls "ready-at-hand". If humans merely look at or observe an object without engaging with and using it, then that object is "present-at-hand". In this way, Heidegger takes *human* being as a starting point for asking philosophical questions about being in general.

"Dasein is in each case mine and in the world."

Martin Heidegger

What is it like to be human?

What does it mean to exist as a human being in this world?

Life before death

Martin Heidegger argued that it is only possible for us to understand and engage with the things that matter most to us when we live an "authentic" existence and acknowledge our own mortality.

Being-toward-death

In *Being and Time* (see p.123), Heidegger argued that a fundamental human anxiety is our awareness that we are not the source of ourselves, so we do not have absolute power over our destinies. He claimed that this sense of "groundlessness," or lack of foundation, lies at the heart of our being and that it is connected to our awareness of our mortality. Heidegger called this attitude of living in the face of death "being-toward-death."

Being-toward-death is not an attitude that occurs occasionally, but is from the outset part of who we are, whether we acknowledge it or choose to ignore it. Heidegger argued that we must genuinely understand our own mortality if we are to live as our authentic selves. By acknowledging death, we acknowledge the outermost limits of our own experience. If we ignore our own mortality, we miss this fundamental dimension of our existence and become preoccupied with banal aspects of our day-to-day lives that are ultimately meaningless, so our existence becomes inauthentic. If we become aware of death, we reach a deeper understanding of ourselves and what it means to exist and have meaningful and authentic existence.

The call of conscience

For Heidegger, having a genuine understanding of our own mortality brings us back from our lostness in the world to our own true selves. Achieving it seems to occur spontaneously, but Heidegger claimed that it is prompted by the "call of conscience," which is being's most profound communication with itself: conscience cuts through the surface "chatter" of our lives and summons us into the presence of ourselves. It is a call away from the distractions that shield us from the truth—that we are temporary creatures, whose fear of death is relieved by facing it directly.

THE NATURE OF ANXIETY

Heidegger argued that one of the ways in which the authentic self manifests itself is through anxiety, or angst. He contrasted anxiety with fear, which he claimed was always fear of something in particular, such as a snake or a spider: when the snake or spider is removed, the fear disappears. Anxiety, on the other hand, is not a fear of anything in particular; it is a feeling of alienation from the world. This feeling of "groundlessness" is, for Heidegger, the birth of the authentic self—or, as he puts it, of *Dasein* (see pp.122–123), becoming individualized and self-aware. It is the moment in which, distanced from the world and other people, we are free to become ourselves.

Authentic existence

For Heidegger, existence is finite, ending with our deaths, and belongs not just in the present, but also in the past and future, which are interconnected. To understand what it means to exist authentically is to constantly project our lives on to the horizon of our death: to exist as "being-toward-death." To be is to be in time, and our being is, ultimately, a being-toward-death. But this is not a pessimistic view; instead, it enables us to make sense of the things that matter to us and to prioritize them things over less important things.

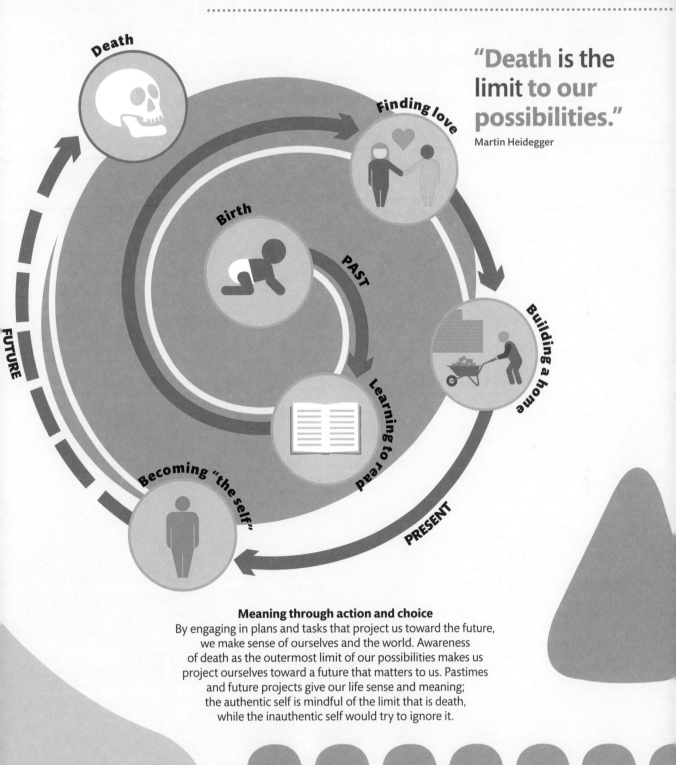

Death

Finding love

Birth

PAST

FUTURE

Building a home

Learning to read

Becoming "the self"

PRESENT

"**Death** is the limit **to our possibilities.**"
Martin Heidegger

Meaning through action and choice
By engaging in plans and tasks that project us toward the future, we make sense of ourselves and the world. Awareness of death as the outermost limit of our possibilities makes us project ourselves toward a future that matters to us. Pastimes and future projects give our life sense and meaning; the authentic self is mindful of the limit that is death, while the inauthentic self would try to ignore it.

Freedom and identity

Jean-Paul Sartre argued that freedom is one of the fundamental things that makes us human, but that we attempt to deny the existence of this freedom by deceiving ourselves and assuming fixed identities.

Being-in-itself and being-for-itself

One of the most important contributors to existentialism (the analysis of human existence in the world), Jean-Paul Sartre (1905–1980) was influenced by and critically engaged with the works of leading phenomenologists such as Edmund Husserl (see pp.118–121) and Martin Heidegger (see pp.122–125).

In his seminal work *Being and Nothingness: An Essay on Phenomenological Ontology* (1943), Sartre distinguished between different ways of existing. "Being-in-itself" characterizes the being of inanimate objects or animals, which are as they are made to be and lack consciousness and freedom to make choices. By contrast, "being-for-itself" is a mode of existence that has consciousness and freedom to choose

and act. Sartre claimed that humans are distinctive for having both kinds of nature. We have freedom, but, at the same time, our existence is defined by situations and identities that we simply accept, like personal history, age, gender, race, class, or professional status. Sartre believed that freedom is, however, inescapable. We may seek to flee the choices and decisions that come with freedom because we do not want to take responsibility for our actions, but we are "condemned to be free": to be constantly faced with these choices and decisions.

Playing a role

Sartre illustrates the distinction between existence and essence with the example of a café waiter, who excels in his professional role. Being a waiter seems to be part of his essence—the purpose and identity that are imposed on him—and he seeks to perform the ideal role of a café waiter. Sartre says that the waiter is trying to imprison himself in this role, but this is in principle impossible. This is because humans cannot escape their freedom. The waiter is not just a waiter. His existence—a state of being in which he is free to act as he chooses—is characterized by possibility. For Sartre, a person's identity cannot be reduced to the roles that that person plays in everyday life. Our existence as conscious, free beings is more important than the roles that we perform, or our essence.

I am the perfec
waiter, but I am f
to leave my job

Ah, Jacques! He really is the perfect waiter—so polite and efficient.

Bad faith

Sartre identified a fundamental kind of self-denial of consciousness and freedom, which he called bad faith. Bad faith is a kind of self-deceit about our freedom to transcend the identities we impose on ourselves.

Bad faith is not, however, lying. In the case of lying, the deceiver and the deceived are two parties. The liar is aware of his intention to lie and does not seek to hide it from himself. In contrast, with bad faith, the deceiver and the deceived are the same person. The deceiver knows the truth, which he conceals from himself, choosing instead to imprison himself in his role. Sartre thought that bad faith is a deep paradox of consciousness: we deny our freedom, but if we were not free, we would not be able to carry out this denial.

EXISTENCE AND ESSENCE

For Sartre, existence is the fact of being, while essence is its purpose, function, and definition. For everything in the world created by human beings, essence precedes existence, but for humanity itself, the reverse is true.

Sartre illustrates the distinction between existence and essence with a paper knife. The knife would not have been created if no need for it existed. Therefore, the knife's *essence* must have preceded the knife itself.

As an atheist, Sartre did not believe that a creator god had given humanity an essence. He argued instead that there is no human nature beyond that which we actively define for ourselves.

"Existence precedes essence."

Jean-Paul Sartre

No more bad faith!

Freedom
The waiter is free to reject his identity.

The "other"

According to Jean-Paul Sartre (see pp.126–127), we cannot view ourselves as separate from other people, or other minds, because we can only become self-aware when we are aware that someone else is watching us.

The problem of other minds

Many philosophers have viewed our relation to other people in terms of the "problem of other minds": how can we know that other people have minds and think and feel like we do? These philosophers seek to prove that other minds exist, and thus solve the problem of solipsism (the view that I am the only mind that I can know to exist). From Sartre's perspective, arguments that attempt to prove or disprove the existence of other minds fail for a number of reasons, the main reason being that they share a view of the "self" as separate from others and a view of other people as objects of knowledge for us.

Sartre challenges these assumptions, arguing that the self is inseparable from others and that our main relation to other people is a *lived* (immediate, first-personal) experience of them as *subjects* in concrete life situations rather than as *objects* of knowledge. He says that once we realize that other people view us as an object—and label us in any way they choose (see box)—we become aware of ourselves and see ourselves as objects of the other's gaze.

In Sartre's view, the existence of others cannot be proven, but we

The other's look

In Sartre's view, when we are aware that another person ("the other") might see us, we do not just notice two eyes directed at us. An open window or the movement of a curtain or door can be manifestations of the other's look. When we are looked at, we become aware of ourselves as vulnerable. This awareness is not some sort of knowledge; it is a *lived* experience of another person—the experience of feeling vulnerable or ashamed that arises from being seen by that person. We become aware of our own self, as an object, only in relation to the other person. The self therefore has its foundation in the other's look. Being seen by another is "an irreducible fact" of our being. Sartre concludes that our relation to other people (and their "mind") is an internal relation rather than a relation between two separated entities: it is a direct, lived relationship rather than a mediated form of objective knowledge.

Objectifying others

For Sartre, we become aware of conscious states such as shame when we are confronted with the gaze of another. To illustrate this, he imagined himself peeping through a keyhole. In this similar example, a man is spying on his partner, who is having an affair with another man. As he watches, he is totally absorbed in what he is doing—he is not explicitly aware of himself. But his look objectifies his partner and the other man.

CHEATER

LIAR

TRAITOR

can and do resist solipsism because we rely on our lived experience of others (how we experience them) to make us aware of ourselves and of how other people view and label us. As we become aware of the labels that other people attach to us, we might apply these labels to ourselves and lose awareness of our freedom (see box). But if we reassert ourselves and our freedom, we gain greater self-awareness.

"Through the revelation of my being-as-object for the Other ... I apprehend his being-as-subject."

Jean-Paul Sartre, *Being and Nothingness* (1943)

OUR UNEASY RELATION TO OTHERS

According to Sartre, we cannot control the way in which we are seen by someone else. How other people categorize us—as, for example, "nice" or "funny"—is unpredictable, as they can see us as they want to. The other person's freedom is, as Sartre says, "the limit of [our] freedom." Other people can attach, in their mind, certain labels to us and our "outside" objective appearance.

By objectifying us in this way, other people rob us of our inherent freedom (our existence as a being-for-itself) and instead turn us into a being-in-itself (see pp.126–127). We see ourselves as vulnerable. This alienates us from ourselves and our possibilities in the world because we lose awareness of our freedom and become restricted by the labels that other people attach to us. We regain our freedom by opposing objectification by others.

Being objectified

Suddenly, the man realizes that another person is watching him. He becomes aware of himself as an object for someone else and of their objectifying gaze. As he has negatively labeled his partner and the other man, so, in turn, the person who has caught him spying labels him.

Finding freedom

Under the gaze of the other person, the man's self eventually reasserts itself and opposes the other person's objectification; it seeks to regain and affirm freedom. As the self becomes aware of its freedom, the other becomes an object for the self. The self no longer feels ashamed.

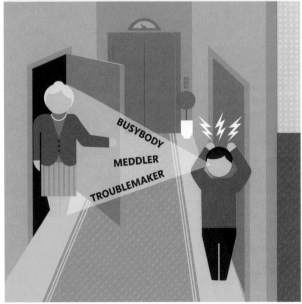

Gender identity

The activist and intellectual Simone de Beauvoir (1908–1986) had a huge influence on contemporary philosophy and feminist theory. Her ideas on the framing of woman as man's "Other" were groundbreaking.

The "Other"

In *The Second Sex* (1949), Simone de Beauvoir examined human consciousness from a first-person, phenomenological perspective, using existential ideas about freedom (see pp.126–127) to address the question of the difference between women and men. She draws a distinction between sex, which is biologically determined, and gender, which is a social construct. Gender has been used by men to make women their "Other" and to justify traditional views of women as inferior. Men and masculine features are seen as the absolute ideal of the human, whereas women have been characterized as deviant, imperfect, and the inessential "Other." At worst, the female body has been regarded as weaker than, or inferior to, a man's—Freud, for example, described a woman as a "mutilated man." At best, women have been regarded as a "mystery" in order to justify their secondary, alienated status as a "second sex."

The lived body

De Beauvoir argued that historically men have used sexual difference as a way of oppressing women—in particular, by requiring them to be passive, caring, and concerned with their appearance. Her argument was

Becoming a woman

De Beauvoir rejected the traditional view that biology determines what we are and that it is a woman's destiny, for example, to become a mother. She argued that such ideas were invented by men, chiefly for the purpose of subjugating women. Instead, she restated the existential claim that "existence precedes essence," arguing that we are not born with any particular gender identities and that women are not born women, but only become women through social conditioning.

In other words, women's nature is not fixed, but is constantly changing and developing. Furthermore, since women have freedom, they have the ability to liberate themselves from the demands that men have traditionally made of them. Her point was not that there are no gender differences, but rather that whatever differences there are should not be used as excuses for treating women as inferior.

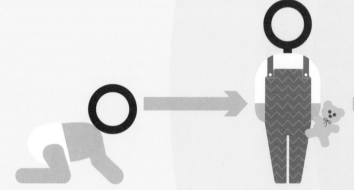

"One is not born but becomes woman."

Simone de Beauvoir, *The Second Sex* (1949)

Infancy
De Beauvoir observed that baby girls do not behave differently from baby boys and that they are not expected to do so.

Early socialization
However, as female infants get older, they are socialized in ways that make them behave like "girls," doing the things that "girls" stereotypically do.

not that women should be like men, or that sexual differences should be eliminated, but that differences, whatever they are, should not be used to subordinate women.

De Beauvoir saw sex and gender as essential aspects of human life. She argued that our existence is characterized by "being-in-the-world" (see pp.122–123) and shaped by our physical forms: women and men exist as embodied individuals engaged with the world. Her major idea was that embodied existence—and, in particular, the "lived body" (see pp.132–133)—is essentially gendered and sexed.

WHO IS TO BLAME?

Although women cannot be said to be to blame for their domination by men, de Beauvoir claimed that women are sometimes complicit in compromising their freedom. She identified three kinds of women who show what Sartre called "bad faith"—that is, who turn their back on their own essential freedom (see pp.126–127). The Narcissist denies her freedom by seeing herself as an object of beauty; the Woman in Love does so by submerging herself in the love of a man; and the Mystic does so by devoting herself to an absolute idea, such as God.

A WOMAN must assert her own identity to avoid compromising her freedom.

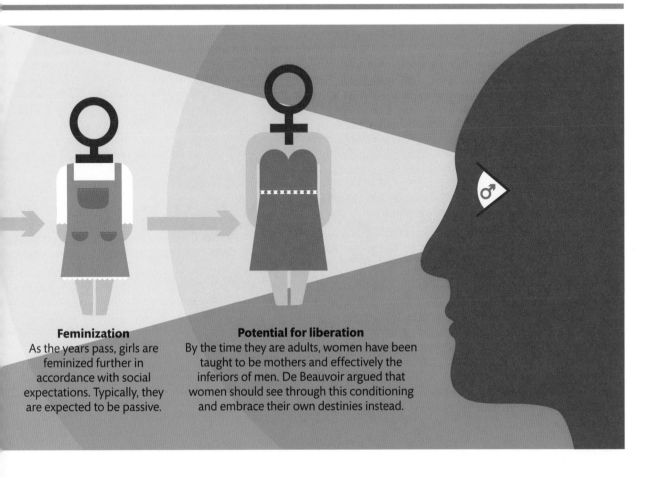

Feminization
As the years pass, girls are feminized further in accordance with social expectations. Typically, they are expected to be passive.

Potential for liberation
By the time they are adults, women have been taught to be mothers and effectively the inferiors of men. De Beauvoir argued that women should see through this conditioning and embrace their own destinies instead.

The lived body

Maurice Merleau-Ponty, influenced by Martin Heidegger's account of being-in-the-world (see pp.122–123), argued that the way we perceive the world is not purely intellectual but is also shaped by our bodies.

Phenomenology of the lived body

Merleau-Ponty criticized traditional understandings of the human body, namely the "intellectualist" approach and the "empiricist" approach. Intellectualism views the body in terms of our mental representations of it and neglects its material existence, ignoring the fact that the body is made up of matter. This fact becomes obvious when, for example, people encounter physical obstacles or become ill, or are injured. Empiricism, meanwhile, sees the body as a thing of the natural world but neglects its distinctive intentionality—that is, its conscious engagement with the world.

Merleau-Ponty argued that a person's body is not just an object that responds to external stimuli. Instead, he said, it should be thought about in terms of that person's engagement with the world and their ability

Perception as background

Merleau-Ponty took Heidegger's concept of being-in-the-world—the idea that to understand existence, we must first consider our own existence within the world we live in (see pp.122–123)—and added to it a new idea about the human body and perception.

In *Phenomenology of Perception* (1945), Merleau-Ponty challenges traditional beliefs about perception, arguing that it cannot be properly explained in terms of how sensory data is received and processed (as empiricists claim), nor in terms of thinking about objects and their sensory properties (as intellectualists propose). In his view, perception is a fundamental openness, a background that enables us to discern specific sensory features and that is "prereflective." For example, we can identify the ringing sound of a phone and reach for it only because we already have a (background) perception of the thing that is a phone; we do not need to reflect on it in order to reach for it, but instead act automatically.

In everyday life, we are neither mere spectators to the world's "show" nor armchair thinkers; we are actively engaged in specific environments. Perception is connected to action and movement. It is not simply produced—by either the physical body or the mind—but instead stems from an entanglement of the lived body and consciousness. For example, a swimmer perceives the water and interacts with it without thinking about it; her body has a consciousness that enables her to swim without reflecting on her movements and how they interact with the water.

Perceiving without thinking
Our perception of things involves an awareness of objects as a whole, including parts we cannot see, such as the interior of a house. This precedes our focusing on particular details.

to act with purpose. The "lived body" (a term first used by Husserl to describe the body as we experience it from a first-personal point of view) is not accessible to us like an object that we can see and touch from all sides, but is always present for us and enables us to access the world. The lived body is not a mere object, but is involved in all aspects of our existence.

The phantom limb

To illustrate this view, Merleau-Ponty used the phenomenon of the phantom limb (where someone who has lost a limb still feels the limb as part of their body). Merleau-Ponty argued that this phenomenon is neither merely the result of neural connections nor of purely mental processes. The empiricist explanation of the body is insufficient here, for given that the limb is no longer present, it cannot receive stimuli. Also, different patients tend to have different experiences of the condition. The intellectualist explanation also fails because the limb is vividly felt as present—far too vividly for it to have been generated by a mental representation such as a memory. Rather, Merleau-Ponty argued, the phantom limb has its source in the person's habitual ways of being and acting in the world. For this reason, the intention is still present, even though the limb is not.

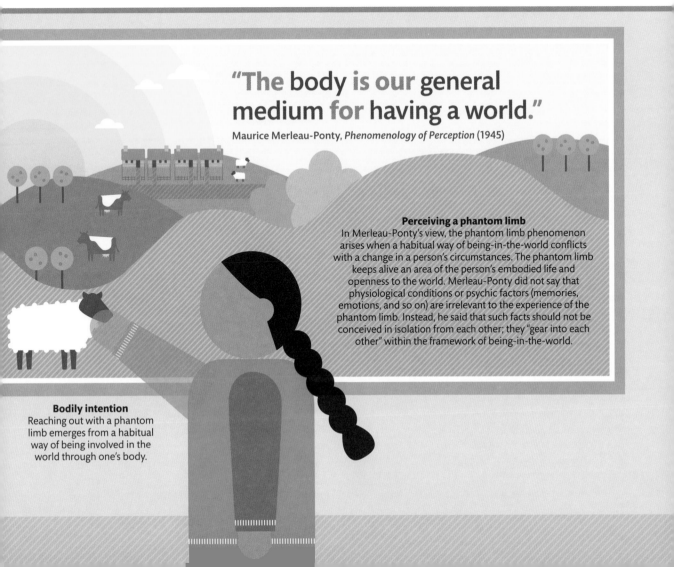

> "The body is our general medium for having a world."
>
> Maurice Merleau-Ponty, *Phenomenology of Perception* (1945)

Perceiving a phantom limb
In Merleau-Ponty's view, the phantom limb phenomenon arises when a habitual way of being-in-the-world conflicts with a change in a person's circumstances. The phantom limb keeps alive an area of the person's embodied life and openness to the world. Merleau-Ponty did not say that physiological conditions or psychic factors (memories, emotions, and so on) are irrelevant to the experience of the phantom limb. Instead, he said that such facts should not be conceived in isolation from each other; they "gear into each other" within the framework of being-in-the-world.

Bodily intention
Reaching out with a phantom limb emerges from a habitual way of being involved in the world through one's body.

Critical theory

Developed as a response to the rise of 20th-century capitalist society, critical theory aimed to free individuals from ideological, cultural, and political forms of domination.

Emancipation

Led by a group of scholars based in Frankfurt, Germany, in the 1930s, critical theorists examined modern capitalist society, seeking to identify and expose its limitations—in particular, the norms and institutions that define society and that can exert power over individuals. Critical theory attempted to uncover not only sources of domination, but also possibilities for social change, with the eventual practical aim of human emancipation. A "real democracy," according to Max Horkheimer (1895–1973), leader of the Frankfurt School, is one in which "all conditions of social life that are controllable by human beings depend on real consensus."

Instrumental rationality

Horkheimer and Theodor Adorno (1903–1969) were critical of liberalism and the "instrumental rationality" that seeks to identify efficient means for specific ends, and thus control and manipulate relevant factors in order to reach set goals. They argued that the liberal, capitalist ideologies that are used to promote social, economic, or political progress—resulting, for example, in mass production and rampant consumerism—have led to the decline of the individual. The rationality of liberalism, therefore, needs to be reconsidered for the genuine pursuit of social freedom.

Discursive rationality

More recently, Jürgen Habermas (1929–) argued for a more discursive, collaborative approach to rationality, framing it as a social enterprise to be carried out within the public sphere. He believed that assessing ethical and political norms cannot be the result of detached "armchair" thinking, but can only occur through public discussion, which should be open to all those affected by an issue. This approach emphasizes social diversity and complexity and enables people to be seen as individuals existing independently in their own socio-historical circumstances.

> "The limited freedom of the bourgeois individual puts on the illusory form of perfect freedom."
>
> Max Horkheimer, *Critical Theory* (1972)

Liberation from liberalism

Critical theorists argued that liberal rationality no longer sets us free, but has instead turned into a new form of enslavement. They seek to overturn various forms of social, economic, and political control over individuals.

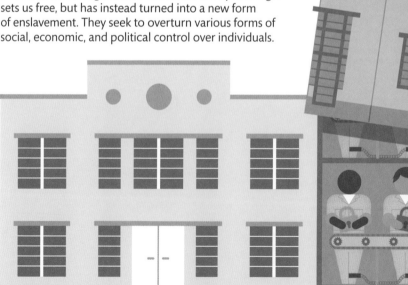

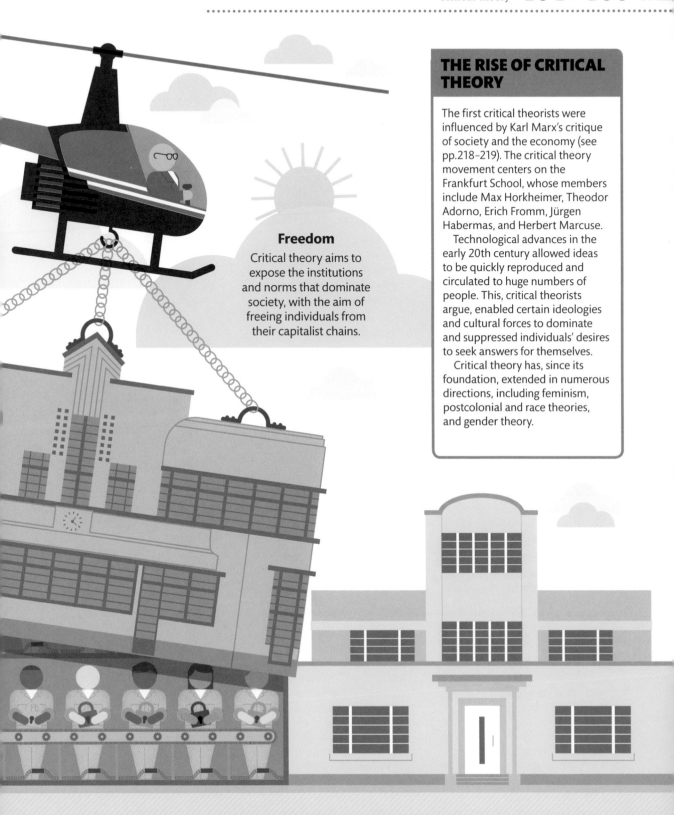

THE RISE OF CRITICAL THEORY

The first critical theorists were influenced by Karl Marx's critique of society and the economy (see pp.218–219). The critical theory movement centers on the Frankfurt School, whose members include Max Horkheimer, Theodor Adorno, Erich Fromm, Jürgen Habermas, and Herbert Marcuse.

Technological advances in the early 20th century allowed ideas to be quickly reproduced and circulated to huge numbers of people. This, critical theorists argue, enabled certain ideologies and cultural forces to dominate and suppressed individuals' desires to seek answers for themselves.

Critical theory has, since its foundation, extended in numerous directions, including feminism, postcolonial and race theories, and gender theory.

Freedom

Critical theory aims to expose the institutions and norms that dominate society, with the aim of freeing individuals from their capitalist chains.

Power plays

Michel Foucault (1926–1984) was a prominent social theorist, historian of ideas, and philosopher associated with postmodernism (see pp.138–139). His work challenged traditional ideas about power.

Disciplinary power

Foucault's philosophy challenged both traditional philosophers and important thinkers of his own time, such as Jean-Paul Sartre (see pp. 126–127). He was influenced to some extent by existentialism and phenomenology, as well as the work of Friedrich Nietzsche (see pp.78–79).

Foucault regarded power and knowledge as being intimately interconnected and being used to control and dominate individuals. In *Discipline and Punish* (1975), he considered new forms of control and punishment at work in the modern prison. He identified what he calls "disciplinary power," which is exerted not only in prison, but also in other institutions such as schools, hospitals, and industry. This is a mode of control that pervades all levels of society.

The tactics and techniques of modern disciplinary power are designed to sustain power structures throughout society by imposing self-regulation on the populace. Foucault thought that this modern "disciplinary power" replaces the "sovereign power" (of, for example, kings or judges) found in feudal social structures.

Conforming individuals

Disciplinary power achieves control over individuals by making them conform voluntarily to the norms and standards of society. It brings about the "normalization" of individuals (especially "deviant" persons) by requiring them to fit into existing systems such as education. The process is also intended to produce efficient workers.

At the same time, the infrastructure for the monitoring and observation of individuals— such as the surveillance camera— effectively controls individuals by identifying deviant behavior for punishment. Foucault also applies his theories on the relationship between power and identity to sexuality, a theme developed by Judith Butler in her work on gender, sex, and sexuality (see pp.140–141).

Punishment
Close surveillance is a more efficient and less severe form of control than previous systems based on physical punishment.

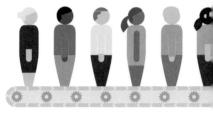

Diverse workforce
The capitalist economy requires vast numbers of individuals from a variety of backgrounds to work in industry.

Entering education
Education appears to open up new opportunities for students with a wide range of potential skills and abilities.

Normalization

Foucault calls the crucial technique for exerting disciplinary power over individuals "normalization." Individuals who are observed, examined, and judged as having failed to comply with required norms and regulations (such as those in industry) or to meet certain standards (of good, "normal" behavior, for example) are considered "deviant" or "abnormal." The behavior of such individuals is deemed to require correction—potentially through coercive tactics and procedures. Techniques of disciplinary control thereby turn individuals into the objects of scientific (or pseudoscientific) knowledge and domination.

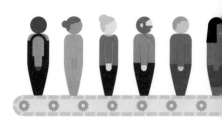

"Disciplinary power [...] is exercised through its invisibility."

Michel Foucault,
Discipline and Punish (1975)

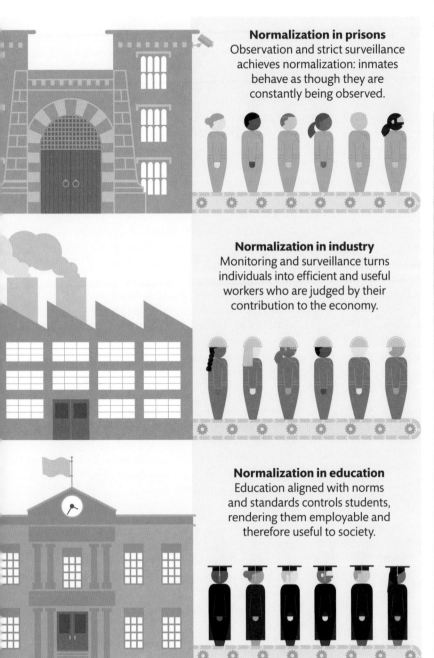

Normalization in prisons
Observation and strict surveillance achieves normalization: inmates behave as though they are constantly being observed.

Normalization in industry
Monitoring and surveillance turns individuals into efficient and useful workers who are judged by their contribution to the economy.

Normalization in education
Education aligned with norms and standards controls students, rendering them employable and therefore useful to society.

THE PANOPTICON

Foucault used the example of Jeremy Bentham's Panopticon prison, which Bentham designed in the late 18th century, to illustrate his idea of modern disciplinary power. The architectural model of the prison includes individual cells encircling a central observation tower, from which each of the inmates could be watched. The idea was that because the inmates could be observed at any time, they would behave as though they were constantly under inspection. Foucault considered this technique to be a prototypical example of using disciplinary power to exert control over the individual.

The Panopticon was never built, but this 1928 prison in Crest Hill, Illinois, followed Bentham's original design.

Deconstruction

Jacques Derrida was an influential postmodern thinker whose thesis of "deconstruction" laid down a detailed linguistic challenge to both the prevailing views of the day and accepted philosophical tradition.

Dismantling philosophies

The idea of "Deconstruction" proposed by Derrida (1930–2004) owed much to Martin Heidegger's earlier notion of "*Destruktion*," which itself challenged the Western metaphysical tradition—the branch of philosophy concerned with the nature of reality and our perception of it. Derrida continued Heidegger's critique of metaphysics and, in particular, its "logocentrism"—the idea that truth exists as a separate entity to the language ("*logos*") used to describe it. Derrida famously declared "There is no outside-text," meaning we cannot grasp what is beyond the language used to discuss philosophical concepts.

Derrida argued that the meaning of a word is not a representation of some "truth" that exists "out there." Instead, words draw their meaning from their links and oppositions to other terms. In traditional metaphysical thinking, binary oppositions such as essence/appearance, speech/writing, mind/body, being/nothingness, and male/female have gained acceptance. Derrida points out that these oppositions involve a biased prioritization of one term over the other in a hierarchical relationship decided arbitrarily.

Not only is this theoretically inadequate, but it can be ethically or politically dangerous, potentially resulting in violence or injustice against the things represented by the "inferior" item in each pair.

As a philosophical approach, deconstruction investigates these binary oppositions and exposes the biases that underlie them. It does not seek to reconcile the terms of opposition, but aims to destabilize and rethink the differences between traditional opposites.

Différance

Derrida further explored the meaning of words with his idea of "*différance*," a play on words that implies both difference and a deferral of meaning. He argued that meaning comes from differences between words, but that arriving at meaning is deferred because of the way we use language—terms are qualified, explained, and contextualized by the other words surrounding them. For Derrida, *différance* means that when we examine "truths," theories, and ideas, we must deconstruct the words used to refer to them, remaining alert to the fact that meaning is never as straightforward or explicit as it may seem.

POSTMODERNISM

Postmodernists argue that the world as we know it is "discursively constructed"—that there is no fixed or stable relationship between individuals and the world, and that difference is at the heart of all things. Postmodernists endorse multiple viewpoints and emphasize the "contingency"—reliance on other factors—of scientific and other rational attempts to make sense of things. They challenge the authority of reason and objectivity and argue that choosing one theory over another is a result of individual decisions rather than of rational, objective justification.

Questioning meaning

Meaning is created by the "play" of differences between words, which can be limitless and indefinite. Rather than perceiving concepts as existing in paired opposites, Derrida encourages us to question the basis of our understanding, actively deconstructing the meaning of a text by challenging implicit hierarchies, breaking traditional binary pairings, and looking for gaps—which Derrida termed "*aporias*" (Ancient Greek for "puzzles" or "contradictions")—in meaning.

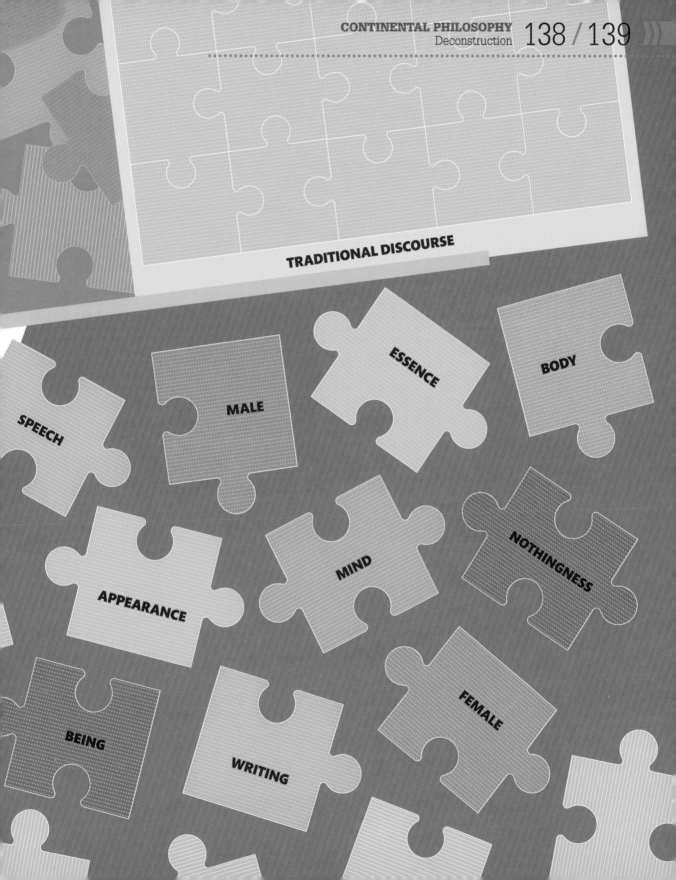

TRADITIONAL DISCOURSE

ESSENCE

BODY

MALE

SPEECH

MIND

NOTHINGNESS

APPEARANCE

BEING

FEMALE

WRITING

Feminist postmodernism

Third-wave feminists, influenced by postmodernism (see pp.138–139), question the idea that sex and gender are biologically determined. They aim to overturn dominant "feminine" and "masculine" ideals.

Gender as a performance

In *Gender Trouble* (1990), Judith Butler argues that gender is a sort of performance. Acted out repeatedly, gendered performances have solidified in time and created the illusion that gender has an essential nature, which is either male or female.

Such performances, Butler claims, reinforce dominant norms and ideals relating to the traditional gender binary (feminine and masculine) and (hetero)sexuality, and marginalize and oppress those who do not conform, such as gay or transgender people.

Butler argues that these norms are socially constructed and rooted in language as "regulative discourses." Such discourses shape which forms of sex, gender, and sexuality are "socially acceptable,"

and enable dominant groups to exercise power over others. Butler argues that we must contest these norms in order to destabilize the view of a gender binary and compulsory heterosexuality.

Against essentialism

Essentialism, simply defined, is the view that all women across cultures and time share essential features or experiences. An essentialist might, for example, say that sex is defined

Redefining gender

Many contemporary feminists believe that universal claims about women, gender, and sex are wrong. Such claims, they say, obscure the diversity of women's situations and strengthen male-female power hierarchies. Butler argues that not only gender but also sex is socially constructed and reinforced.

Sex and gender are both socially constructed
Third-wave feminists, including Butler, argue not only that gender is socially constructed, but that sex (having a "male" or "female" body) is, too, through language. They question the biological foundations of gender.

by essential biological attributes we are born with (a view called "biological foundationalism").

Butler argues that essentialism is a political fiction that serves existing oppressive patriarchal regimes. In her critique of the category "woman," she rejects the view that the word refers to a unified gender identity and proposes a new understanding of the complexities of gender identity that intersects with other aspects of a woman's identity, such as race.

THE THREE WAVES OF FEMINISM

The traditional (pre-1960) view of gender and sex was that they are both the product of biology—that is, that sex determined gendered behavior and roles. Second-wave feminists (1960s–early 1980s) believed that sex is biological, but that gender is a social and cultural creation. Third-wave feminists (1990s–) argue that "sex" and "the body" are not simply biological categories: differences between male and female bodies are, in part at least, socially constructed.

THIRD-WAVE FEMINISTS question the idea of essential female characteristics.

"**Gender is a kind of imitation** for which there is no original."
Judith Butler, *Gender Trouble* (1990)

Gender roles
Butler seems to liken us to actors in a puppet show, performing gendered scripts, and asks how we can disrupt these norms to promote justice for both women and men.

...e size does not fit all
...tler argues that an idealized
...w of women is a dangerous
...sion that has an oppressive
...wer and damaging effects.

PHILOSOPHY OF MIND

Throughout history, people have puzzled over the nature of conscious experience. In the modern age, the questions became more pointed: What is the mind? How does it relate to the body?

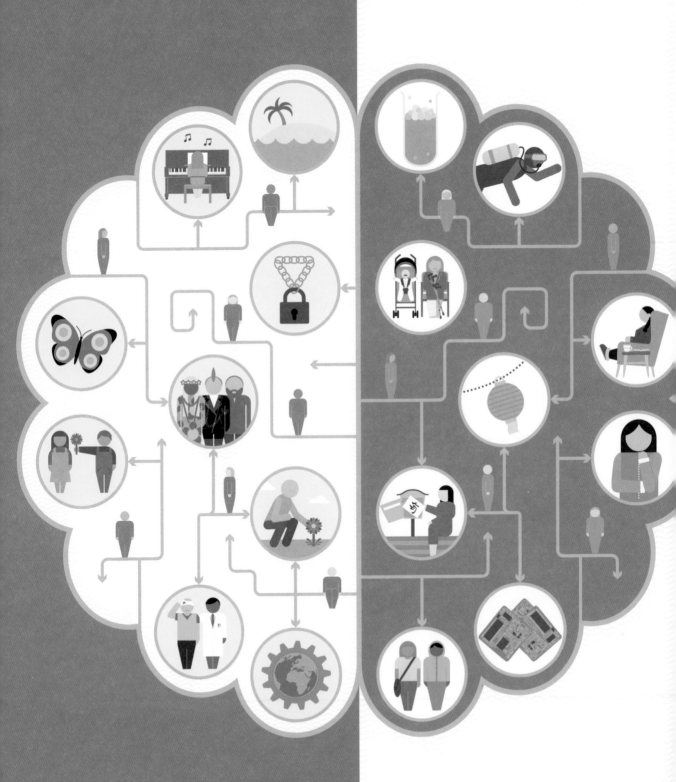

PHILOSOPHY OF MIND

Unlike ethics and political philosophy, which deal with numerous subjects, the philosophy of mind focuses on a single problem—namely, the nature of what we understand as "mind." Its central questions are: What is consciousness? What is a mind? How do minds relate to physical bodies?

Questions about mind are metaphysical questions, because they concern the nature of things in the world and their answers fall into two broad categories. The first is called "dualism," which claims that there are two kinds of things in the universe, one of which is matter and one of which is mind. The second is called "monism," which claims that there is only one kind of thing in the universe—either matter, mind, or something else of which matter and mind are attributes.

The question of how the mind relates to the body is a relatively recent one. It dates from the 17th century, when René Descartes divided the world into two: into the material world, which he argued is predetermined and runs like clockwork, and the immaterial world, in which the human mind is located. He made the distinction, because all around him, "science" was taking root: Galileo and Kepler had laid Aristotle's cosmology to rest, meaning that a new view of the universe was required. However, Descartes saw that if the universe runs like clockwork, as scientists were claiming, then human freedom is impossible.

So he argued that there is an immaterial world in which the immaterial mind holds sway. This is the classic dualist position: that the mind and the body are distinct things, and that they remain so even if their interaction is a mystery. Although it fell out of favor for many years, dualism is having a resurgence today, largely due to the shortcomings of monist accounts of the mind.

Today, most monists are "materialists," or "physicalists," who claim that consciousness is simply a neurochemical function of the brain. From this view, pains, joys, hopes, and intentions are all ultimately physical in nature. Some argue that ideas such as "mind" and "consciousness" are little more than "folk psychology"—that is, part of a family of concepts that we use in everyday life but are not rooted in scientific fact. Another form of monism is "behaviorism," which has its roots in the philosophy of language. Behaviorists claim that words such as "clever" and "kind" describe outward, bodily behavior, which we then mistake for internal, "mental" processes. Ludwig Wittgenstein made a similar point, arguing that questions about the mind tend to arise when "language goes on holiday." Wittgenstein was neither a monist nor a dualist, but argued instead that metaphysical questions—particularly those that involve distinctions between the "mind" and the "body" and the "inner" and "outer" realms—are the result of linguistic confusion.

Dualism

The idea that reality is dual in nature—that it is made up of both physical and mental elements—was championed by the 17th-century French philosopher René Descartes.

Mind and body

According to Descartes, physical objects exist in space and are governed by physical laws: a tree, for example, has a certain height, width, mass, and location. However, he argued, the same is not true of the human mind or its attributes: beliefs, pains, hopes, decisions, and plans have no such characteristics, so they cannot be regarded as physical. For Descartes, the mind has no material substance—it is a pure subject of experience that goes beyond the otherwise clockwork machinery of the world. Only humans, he believed, enjoy such freedom; all other creatures are determined by the laws of nature (see pp.54–55).

Having split the world into mind and matter, Descartes questioned how the two interact. He suggested that they "commingle" in the pineal gland of the brain, but was unable to say how they do so. Indeed, explaining the interaction between mind and matter is difficult for a dualist, for the mind (being immaterial) can never be found to see how it works: it is always the *subject* of experience, but never its *object*. And so, if ever a physical object, such as a brain or a computer, is presented as *being* a mind, a dualist knows in advance

Qualia

Philosophers use the word "qualia" to describe the immediate contents of experience—what it feels like to hear a particular sound, for instance. Frank Jackson used this example: Mary lives in a black-and-white world, in which she learns everything there is to know about color from books and television documentaries. She is then taken out into the real world and experiences color for the first time. What she is introduced to are qualia—qualities that, according to dualists, cannot be explained by materialist accounts of the mind (see pp.152–153).

A materialist may say that Mary knows everything there is to know about color, even in her black-and-white world, simply by studying it.

that it is not. Likewise, if a materialist (see pp.154–155) states that pain is simply electrical activity in the brain, this only deepens the mystery, for we know that that conscious awareness—the feeling of being stung by a bee—is bound up with bodily processes. The mystery is the nature of that bond, and how a physical brain can do anything as strange as *feel*.

The hard problem

Today, what is called the "hard problem of consciousness" reformulates Descartes' thought:

that no amount of science gets us any closer to understanding what it is to *be* conscious—to have direct experience of colors, scents, and sounds. According to this view, science describes the world as it is "out there," and does so from the vantage point of experience. But the vantage point itself—the place where experience occurs—can never itself be seen: the subject of experience can never become its object. As David Chalmers, a defender of "naturalistic dualism," puts it: "Studying consciousness tells us more about how the world is fundamentally strange."

EPIPHENOMENALISM

One problem faced by dualists is the possibility that the universe is "causally complete" (see pp.152–153). According to this view, human behavior is completely explained by bodily processes, which leaves nothing for the mind to do other than to experience the body's workings. The biologist T.H. Huxley held this view, calling the mind an "epiphenomenon," or by-product, of the brain. He likened the mind to a clock's bell, which plays no role in keeping the time.

Mary's entry into the world highlights the dualists' case – that color is not a theory, but an experience.

"Except our own thoughts, there is nothing absolutely in our power."

René Descartes, *Discourse on the Method* (1637)

The limits of language

In the 1940s, the philosopher Ludwig Wittgenstein raised questions about the nature of language that cast doubt on the very idea of a "philosophy of mind."

Shadows of grammar

In his *Philosophical Investigations*, Ludwig Wittgenstein (1889–1951) argued that the meaning of a word is not an object it refers to, but a rule that governs its use. Such rules, he said, must be public, shared conventions, which can change according to context (see pp.96–97). With this claim, he undermined Descartes' assumption that knowledge starts with the individual, and that certainty can be gained through direct, private experience (see pp.52–53). According to Descartes, we learn the word "pain" by associating it with a feeling and then applying our experience to other people. Wittgenstein, however, argues that the opposite is true: we learn the word "pain" while interacting with others, whose behavior we describe. We say that someone is "in pain" when they act in certain ways, just as we might say that someone is "angry" or "clever" according to their behavior.

The crucial point is that our relationship with our private feelings and sensations, far from being a bedrock of certainty, is not one of "knowing" at all. A person could never say, for example, "I think I am in pain, but I may not be." According to Wittgenstein, to say "I am in pain" is not a description; it is pain-behavior itself—a cry for help.

Indescribable pain

For Wittgenstein, language is intersubjective—a phenomenon established between subjects, or people, rather than between a subject and itself. The criteria for saying that another person is in pain, for example, are behavioral. However, this is not the case when we say that *we ourselves* are in pain, because there are no criteria for describing private sensations (see box, right). To say "I am in pain" is effectively a cry for help.

Whereof one cannot speak

Even more problematic for Wittgenstein was Descartes' use of the word "I" in the phrase "I think, therefore I am." In everyday usage, the word "I" is used to distinguish one individual from another: if a teacher asks, "Who wrote on the board?" and a pupil says, "I did," the pupil does so to distinguish themselves from the rest of the class. But Descartes uses "I" to distinguish his mind from his body, creating a void in which he locates his "thought." For Wittgenstein, using the word "I" in this way is meaningless, as it lacks its logical neighbor of "others." He said it is an example of what happens when "language goes on vacation."

Wittgenstein's point is not that there is no such thing as the mind or consciousness, but that we lack the words with which to frame such metaphysical questions—or rather, that when language is kept on the "rough ground" of ordinary usage, such questions disappear. As he said in his earlier work, the *Tractatus Logico-Philosophicus*: "Whereof one cannot speak, thereof one must be silent."

"Help!"
To say one is in pain is to call for help rather than to describe one's "inner" feelings.

> ## "An inner process stands in need of outward criteria."
> Ludwig Wittgenstein, *Philosophical Investigations* (1953)

BEETLE IN A BOX

Descartes claimed that we can doubt that other people are conscious, but not that *we* are conscious. Wittgenstein, on the other hand, argued that there is nothing in consciousness that *only we* can know. He imagined a community in which everyone keeps a "beetle" in a box: "No one can look into anyone else's box, and everyone says he knows what a beetle is only by looking at his beetle." In such a world, the word "beetle" could refer to any number of things (even empty space), and so would have no meaning. The same would be true if the word "pain" described a purely private phenomenon: whatever it referred to could not be shared. However, if it cannot be shared, it cannot have meaning, for, according to Wittgenstein, meaning is a public, shared convention (see pp.96–97).

Doctor

Behaviorism

Behaviorist philosophers claim that the "mind/body problem" (see pp.146–147) is an illusion created by a certain misuse of language—one that mistakes descriptions of behavior for mental attributes.

Ghost in the machine

In claiming that there is only one kind of substance in the universe, namely matter, behaviorism is both a "monist" and a "materialist" doctrine. The philosopher Gilbert Ryle popularized the idea in 1949, in his book *The Concept of Mind*. He argued that dualists make a "category mistake" when they describe the mind as a nonphysical thing, which they then endow with supernatural powers such as "seeing" and "thinking." For Ryle, this "ghost in the machine," as he calls it, creates an infinite regress (a never-ending sequence of reasoning): if it is not the physical eye that sees, but some ghostly mind-eye behind it, then the ghostly eye needs another eye behind it to do its seeing, and so on. Ryle's answer is that there are no mental processes: there is only physical behavior, which we wrongly objectify as the "mind." This goes far beyond Wittgenstein's claim that subjective phenomena lie outside the realm of sensible discourse (see pp.148–149).

For behaviorists, to be in a given mental state (such as happiness) is to behave in a certain way (such as to laugh and smile). Attributes such as intelligence are best understood as adjectives describing the body rather than nouns denoting nonphysical entities or properties. Logical behaviorism, as advanced by Rudolf Carnap, takes this further, claiming that to say "I am happy" *means* "I am smiling, laughing, and so on," which few would defend today. However, Carnap's view highlights a problem with behaviorism—that it omits the phenomenon of experience. Few would say that their pain, for example, is a way in which they behave—an objection that strengthens the dualists' case.

INTERNALIZED SPEAKING

A common objection to behaviorism is the fact that we spend so much of our time *thinking*, which has nothing to do with behavior, but is instead an entirely internal, mental process. However, behaviorists argue that thinking is simply internalized speaking, and that speaking is by definition behavioral. Just as we learn to speak in a family group, so we learn arithmetic by being shown the rules by a teacher. At first, we write our calculations down, then we learn to make them in our heads. However, we are "thinking" as much with a pen as without one. This argument is loosely based on Wittgenstein's "private language argument," which claims that language is a public activity that can never begin with the individual (see pp.96–97).

Thinking aloud
Whether we think publicly, on paper, or privately, in our heads, is irrelevant, according to Ryle.

Thinking quietly
Ryle argues that thinking "in one's head" is simply internalized speaking.

> "Minds **are not** bits of clockwork; they are just bits of not-clockwork."

Gilbert Ryle, *The Concept of Mind* (1949)

Social skills are the ability to understand and adopt social norms.

Organizational ability is a way of interacting with the environment.

Intelligent make-up

According to behaviorism, mental attributes are simply functions of behavior. To be intelligent, for example, is to possess a certain set of abilities, such as to do math, or to speak articulately. These attributes are evident in a person's behavior; they are not private properties of the "mind."

Math ability involves following established rules.

$x + y =$

Artistic sensitivity includes the ability to play music.

Articulateness is the ability to make oneself clearly understood.

Problem-solving is a way of changing the world for the better.

✓ NEED TO KNOW

❯ **Ludwig Wittgenstein** did not consider himself a behaviorist, but he is often categorized as such (see pp.148–149). His ideas greatly influenced Gilbert Ryle.

❯ **Logical behaviorism** has its roots in the positivist doctrine of verificationism (see pp.92–93).

❯ **Behaviorist psychology** was pioneered by John B. Watson and B. F. Skinner in the 1920s.

The mind-brain identity theory

In the late 1950s, the philosophers U. T. Place, J. J. C. Smart, and Herbert Feigl reformulated an old idea: that mental states are simply physical states of the brain.

The mind machine

In *Is Consciousness a Brain Process?*, U. T. Place claimed that the behaviorist argument—that mental states are defined by behavior—is insufficient, and that mental states are a way of describing neurological events (see pp.154–155). He argued that the distinction between the concepts "sensation" and "brain state" is similar to that between "lightning" and "electrical discharge." In both cases, the former phrase is like an informal, personal report and should not be taken literally, whereas the latter is a scientific claim and means exactly what it says. Place also argued that the first kind of statement can be reduced to the second, and so, just as lightning is in fact an electrical discharge, pain is in fact a particular state of the brain.

J. J. C. Smart and Herbert Feigl came to the same conclusion, but claimed that "sensation" and "brain state" are related in the way that Frege links "morning star" and "evening star" (see pp.86–87). In each case, both terms have their own meaning but refer to the same thing: in Frege's case, the planet Venus; in Smart and Feigl's, the brain. Hilary Putnam noted that an alien species might experience pain, but have no brain, suggesting that mental states need not be of the same physical "type". Instead, he proposed that we identfy mental-state "tokens," such as a specific individual's pain, with specific physical tokens, such as the relevant parts of an individual's body.

Identity crisis

A major limitation of the identity theory is that it cannot account for subjective experience (see pp.54–55). This has been a problem since the idea was formulated by the Greek Atomists, who claimed that the soul was made of physical atoms (see pp.30–31). Indeed, when Thomas Hobbes popularized the theory in the 17th century, it only strengthened Descartes' dualist alternative, for all its mysteries.

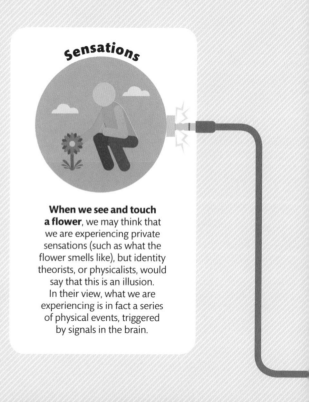

Sensations

When we see and touch a flower, we may think that we are experiencing private sensations (such as what the flower smells like), but identity theorists, or physicalists, would say that this is an illusion. In their view, what we are experiencing is in fact a series of physical events, triggered by signals in the brain.

Causal completeness

One argument for the identity theory lies in what is known as the "causal completeness" of the universe. Sight, for example, begins with photons passing through the lens of the eye and ends with a physical reaction, such as flinching from a flame. The entire process is marshaled by the brain, which sends signals to the body to trigger the relevant reaction, leaving no role for the mind to play. From this perspective, the mind is irrelevant, or a "ghost in the machine," in the words of Gilbert Ryle (see pp.150–151).

PREESTABLISHED HARMONY

Gottfried Leibniz addressed the fact that in a causally complete universe, the mind is causally ineffective. For Leibniz, the mind and the brain are separate entities, but do not interact with each other. They *seem* to interact, but that is only because God arranged the world to keep the two in step. They exist in what Leibniz called a state of preestablished harmony. His idea is similar to Baruch Spinoza's concept of parallelism (see pp.58–59).

Emotions

According to physicalists, emotions, like intentions, are behavioral states that are observable, and as such, unmysterious. To be angry or depressed is to be disposed to behave in certain ways, and these depend on the chemical make-up of an individual's brain.

Intentions

How can one person's intention to give another person flowers, for example, be a physical event in the brain? For physicalists, to "intend" something is no different from "doing" something: it is a shorthand description of a particular set of behaviors, all of which are describable by science (see pp.150–151).

Identity

Our personal identity, from our ethnicity and language to our particular way of dressing, is either biologically or culturally conditioned—and cultural conditioning, physicalists argue, is nothing other than behaving in certain ways.

> "Philosophy **is the** disease **of which it should be the** cure!"
>
> Herbert Feigl, *Inquiries and Provocation: Selected Writings, 1929–1974*

Eliminative materialism

In recent years, various materialist philosophers have abandoned the mind-brain identity theory in favor of an even more radical position – namely, eliminative materialism.

The science of mind

Unlike defenders of the identity theory (see pp.152–153), who argue that statements about the mind can be reduced to statements about the brain, eliminative materialists claim that since mental states do not exist, there is nothing to identify them with.

An example of this view, held by the philosophers Paul and Patricia Churchland, is that a person may think she is sad because her dog has died, but in fact she is sad because her serotonin levels have dropped. Indeed, her sadness is nothing other than her lowered serotonin levels, and their lowering is linked to the physiology of her "love" for her dog. Saying that she is sad may elicit sympathy and help from others—which are also physical processes—but the truth is that a certain physical process (X) has caused another physical process (Y), which in turn has caused other physical processes (Z). Explaining behavior in terms of "beliefs," "desires," and "reasons" is, according to eliminativists, similar to explaining diseases in terms of miasma, or ascribing mental illnesses to demonic possession. Such ideas, they say, belong to a time before empirical science, when folk tales and superstition were all that people had to rely on.

Daniel Dennett argues that we ascribe intelligence to a system when we are ignorant of its design: for example, we might say that a computer "knows" how to play chess because we fail to grasp its workings. For Dennett, complex systems appear intentional (capable of thought) when viewed "from the top down," but mechanical when viewed "from the bottom up." Eliminativists claim that we ascribe joys, pains, and sensations to ourselves in a similar way: because we fail to know our workings.

Phlogiston theory
In the 17th century, Johann Joachim Becher attempted to explain the processes of combustion and rusting. He suggested that fire is caused by the release of an element called "phlogiston" into the air.

Oxidation
The phlogistion theory was superceded by the theory of oxidation in the 18th century. Antoine Lavoisier discovered that both combustion and rusting are caused by a chemical reaction between certain substances and an element in the air. He called the new element "oxygène."

The fate of folk psychology

The everyday language we use to explain human behavior, including such concepts as "belief," "desire," and "intention," are what philosophers call "folk psychology." According to eliminative materialists, folk psychology is effectively a failed scientific hypothesis and, as such, it should join the list of other failed hypotheses.

Miasma theory

For centuries, throughout the world, many diseases were thought to be caused by "miasma," or "bad air," released by rotting organic matter. Swamps and bogs were considered particularly miasmatic, and so were avoided when possible.

Folk psychology

Today, as in the past, many people believe that their lives are influenced by their "beliefs," "desires," and "intentions." Likewise, they believe that their moods, thoughts, and sensations are nonphysical phenomena that exist in the special, private domain of the "mind."

Germ theory

In the 19th century, the chemists Louis Pasteur and Robert Koch demonstrated that many diseases are caused by microorganisms invading the body. Bacteria, viruses, and fungi are among the many "germs" now known to cause disease.

Neuroscience

Eliminativists believe that, one day, neuroscience will replace folk psychology. They argue that nothing about human beings is private or takes place in a separate domain called the "mind." All of our moods, thoughts, and sensations are simply bodily processes.

The crucible of science

Eliminativists claim that science has shown that the "mind" is a fictional entity.

Functionalism

In the 1960s, several philosophers put forward a functionalist theory of mind, taking ideas from Aristotle and modern computer science. Functionalism focuses on what the mind does, rather than what it is.

Can a machine think?

According to Aristotle, to know a thing is to know its purpose. Likewise, for functionalists, the important thing about the mind is not what it is, but what it does. The function of pain, for example, is to alert us to the fact that we are injured, just as the function of the heart is to pump blood around the body. Intelligence is also a function—an ability to do math, for instance.

When asked "Can a machine think?", the computer scientist Alan Turing famously replied, "Can a submarine swim?" His point was that how we use the word "swim" is a matter of convention and that the same is true of the word "think." He then devised a thought experiment to show that a machine could be said to "think" under certain specific circumstances (see below).

The Turing test

Developed by Alan Turing in 1950, the Turing test provided criteria for assessing artificial intelligence. A human, a machine, and a human adjudicator are isolated in separate rooms. The adjudicator has no idea which room contains the machine and which contains the human. He communicates with the machine and the other human via printouts, on which he also receives their replies. If, after a certain number of questions, he is unable to distinguish between the two, then the machine has passed the test. It can be said to be intelligent, and upgrades of its system can be said to increase its intelligence (see box, above right).

Questions

The adjudicator sends questions into the rooms in which the machine and the human are isolated. He does not know which room the machine or the human is in. His goal in asking the questions is to distinguish which is which.

✓ NEED TO KNOW

> **In *De Anima*,** Aristotle defined the soul as "the first actuality of a natural body having in it the capacity of life." The soul, or mind, is thus an activity of a thing: its potential becoming actual.

> **Thomas Hobbes's** conception of the mind as a "calculating machine" was a precursor to modern functionalism (see pp.56–57).

> **Modern functionalism** was developed as an alternative to the mind-brain identity theory (see pp.152–153) and behaviorism (see pp.150–151).

In *The Nature of Mental States* and other articles, Hilary Putnam developed this idea, arguing that mental states are comparable to software: they are functional states of "computational machines," such as brains. Just as computers are able to process electronic inputs to make outputs, so the brain can turn perceptual inputs (the information we gather through our senses) into behavior. This powerful idea remains influential today. However, critics argue that calling the mind a computer puts the cart before the horse—that computers are built to simulate human activity and that "processing" is only a minor aspect of consciousness (see pp.146–147).

ARTIFICIAL HUMANS

The Turing test (see below) raises a number of interesting questions. Suppose, for example, that the machine in the room is far more sophisticated than the one used in the test. Suppose it is identical to a human being and is no longer kept in the room. Suppose it walks among us and is programmed to react with apparent emotion. If we are happy to call it "intelligent" because it passes the Turing test, are we happy to say that it "feels"? If not, is that merely because we built it? It can always be argued that *we* are equally "built"—by physics, biology, and evolution.

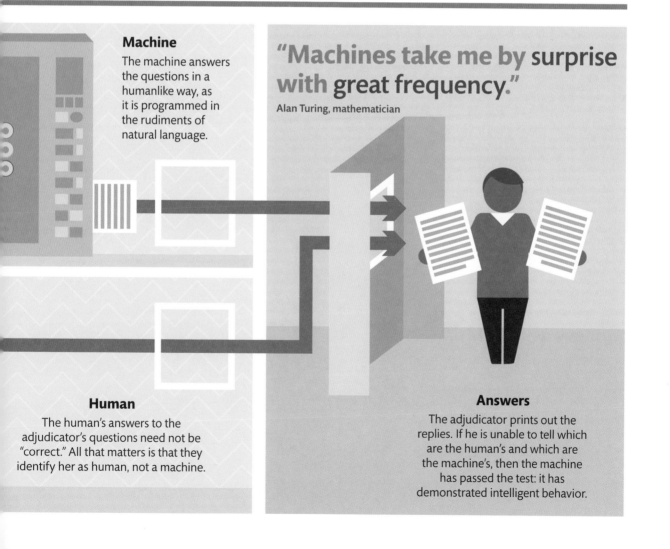

Machine
The machine answers the questions in a humanlike way, as it is programmed in the rudiments of natural language.

"Machines take me by surprise with great frequency."
Alan Turing, mathematician

Human
The human's answers to the adjudicator's questions need not be "correct." All that matters is that they identify her as human, not a machine.

Answers
The adjudicator prints out the replies. If he is unable to tell which are the human's and which are the machine's, then the machine has passed the test: it has demonstrated intelligent behavior.

Biological naturalism

The philosopher John Searle argues that functionalists are misled by the computer model of the mind (see pp.156–157), which is at best a useful metaphor. He sees the mind as a natural property of matter.

The Chinese room

According to Searle, the mistake that functionalists make in their model of the mind arises from confusing the syntax of a sentence with its semantics. The syntax of a sentence is its grammatical structure, which can be reduced to symbolic logic. Its semantics, however, are the meanings it conveys. The same semantics can thus be conveyed by an infinite number of languages, which have unique syntactical structures.

Searle makes the following analogy. A person sits in a room and has cards marked with Chinese characters passed to them under the door. The person has no understanding of Chinese, but has a rule book that instructs them on how to respond: "If character X appears under the door, then respond with character Y," and so on. The person can communicate using this system and could even be mistaken for someone who speaks Chinese. For Searle, this is how computers work: they have instructions but no understanding; syntax but no semantics. And so, when a functionalist claims that the mind and the brain

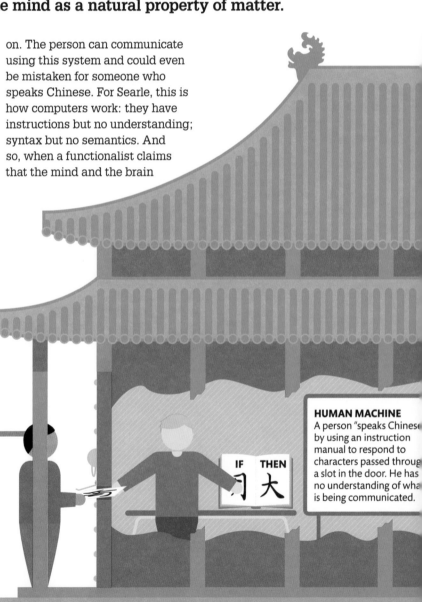

HUMAN MACHINE
A person "speaks Chinese" by using an instruction manual to respond to characters passed through a slot in the door. He has no understanding of what is being communicated.

Evidence of nothing

Searle's "Chinese room" argument demonstrates the limitations of functionalism. Searle argues that just as the person in the room does not understand Chinese, so a computer that passes the Turing test cannot be said to "think" (see pp.156-157).

are like a computer and its software, they omit what they try to explain: the phenomenon of understanding.

Searle's own position is known as "biological naturalism." He says that both dualism (see pp.146–147) and neurological reductionism (see pp.154–155) are mistaken. For him, consciousness is a biological phenomenon and may perhaps be caused by the brain. Indeed, mental properties are a type of physical property—ones that, science may show, provide us with subjectivity.

LEIBNIZ'S MILL

In the 17th century, Gottfried Leibniz (see pp.62–63) made an argument that is similar to the "Chinese room." He asks us to imagine a machine that simulates human behavior and supposedly has "perception." It could be the size of a mill, so we could enter it and watch its workings. We would not, he argues, conclude that it is conscious: "Thus it is in a simple substance, and not in a compound or in a machine, that perception must be sought for."

"My car and my adding machine understand nothing: they are not in that line of business."

John Seale, *Minds, Brains, and Programs* (1984)

The person in the room obviously speaks Chinese.

MAILBOX

MESSAGE RECEIVED
A native Chinese speaker reads the message communicated by the person in the locked room and comes to the wrong conclusion: that the person speaks Chinese.

Panpsychism

In recent years, many philosophers have taken a new interest in dualism (see pp.54–55)—and in the ancient idea of a "universal mind".

The hard problem

The philosopher David Chalmers claims that we have yet to solve the "hard problem" of consciousness—namely what it is to *be* conscious. In doing so, he revives the dualist claim that no amount of physics can explain what it is to *feel* (see pp.146–147). Chalmers observes that if materialism were true, experience would not be necessary. If I burn my hand on a stove, and the fact that I take my hand away is explained by neurological processes, why do I need to feel pain? Why are we not, effectively, "zombies"—creatures identical to humans, but lacking subjectivity?

Unlike thermostats, which also react to temperature changes, humans have an extra, "inner" dimension, which resists physical description. But in a world of physical objects, how has this come about? One answer is that the mind, while not a "substance" in Descartes' sense (see pp.52–53), is a fundamental

Russellian monism

In his 1927 book *The Analysis of Matter*, Bertrand Russell argued that science describes the extrinsic (external) properties of matter, such as the shape, quantity, and disposition of things, but says nothing about matter's intrinsic (internal) nature—about what it is in itself. Indeed, according to this view, the inability of science to describe intrinsic natures is what creates the mind-body problem, which is effectively a conceptual vacuum. "Russellian monists" argue that consciousness is a hidden property of matter: it cannot be examined by science, yet it is present in everything, from rocks to humans, in varying complexity.

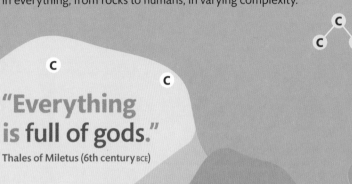

"Everything is full of gods."
Thales of Miletus (6th century BCE)

C = CONSCIOUSNESS

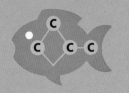

property of the universe. According to this view, known as "panpsychism", matter and mind are always bound together. Stones are not "aware" because they lack sensory organs, but mind exists within them. For panpsychists, the things that we would describe as "conscious" are merely those that are biologically similar to us. This idea was prevalent in the 19th century, and was only displaced by

positivist ideas, which have since fallen out of favor (see pp.91–93). It was originally formulated by Anaxagoras (see pp.28–29), and was recently defended by the physicist David Bohm.

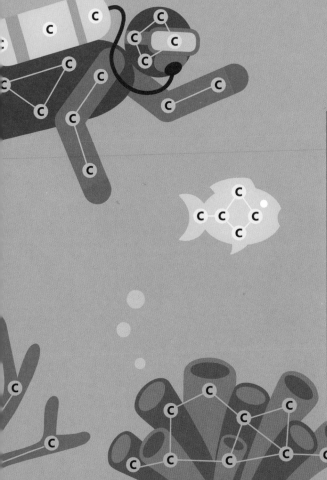

SCHOPENHAUER'S WILL

German philosopher Arthur Schopenhauer (1788–1860) was an important figure in the development of panpsychism. He was influenced by Kant's distinction between the phenomenal world of the senses and the world of the thing-in-itself (see pp.66–67). However, while Kant thought that the thing-in-itself is unknowable, Schopenhauer said that humans have special access to what they are in themselves. Through introspection, he argued, we encounter the "Will"—which, far from being a desire, is the driving force of the universe.

Schopenhauer, however, was a pessimist. He believed that the Will is inherent in everything in the world, but is impersonal, aimless, and without consciousness. It is the cause of our insatiable desires, which bring about suffering, and to find peace we must learn to overcome it through compassion.

The nature of the body

The linguist Noam Chomsky argues that the mind/body problem is one that could only be formulated for a brief time during the 17th and 18th centuries.

The mechanical philosophy

Throughout the medieval period, Aristotelian ideas prevailed in Europe, chiefly in the form of scholastic philosophy (see pp.46–49), which married Aristotle's ideas with Catholic beliefs. Aristotle argued, for example, that a rock rolls downhill because it belongs at the center of Earth, while fire rises in an attempt to reach the heavens. By the 16th century, magnets and iron filings were said to be "sympathetic" to each other, and so attract. The scientific revolution, which began in the 17th century, sought to replace such supernatural explanations with causal, mechanical ones (see pp.50–51). The assumption was that once the causes of a thing are known, there is nothing left to

Science and intelligibility

According to Chomsky, science underwent a revolution in the 17th century that remains largely forgotten today. The belief then was that science would explain the mysteries of the world, but Newton showed that this is not always possible. Often, the best science can do is generate models of the world that enable us to discuss it, which should not be confused with understanding the world as it is.

SYMPATHY

1 The world explained
In medieval Europe, everything was, in a sense, explained. Life, the world, and the heavens were described in scholastic terms, with no distinction between "body" and "mind." A magnet attracts iron because the two were said to be "sympathetic."

2 The world redefined
In the 17th century, Descartes split the world into two: body and mind (see pp.146–147). Crucially, he defined "body" in purely mechanical terms, describing physical systems as machines that have purposes and are driven by the equivalent of gears and pulleys.

explain. This was illustrated in 1739 by the French engineer Jacques de Vaucanson: he built a mechanical duck that ate, digested, and defecated kernels of grain. This "mechanical philosophy" was first adopted by Galileo Galilei ("the father of modern science") and pursued by his successor, Isaac Newton.

At the end of his life, Isaac Newton claimed to have failed at his task. What had foiled him was the force that he had discovered: gravity. For gravity does nothing if not "act at a distance"—drawing Earth around the Sun without pulleys, cogs, or chains. He called gravity "so great an absurdity" that no one could entertain it—and yet there it was, effectively a "supernatural force" governing the heavens. Matter, in short, became a mystery again, and scientists

redefined the nature of their task. They became less concerned with "understanding" the world as such than formulating theories that rendered it intelligible – a far humbler task than Galileo had envisaged.

For Noam Chomsky, this has implications for the philosophy of mind. His point is that matter, far from being a simple mechanism that the mind can be said either to *be* or to *interact* with, is itself something we have no clear definition of. Following C. S. Peirce, Chomsky distinguishes "problems," which fall within our cognitive abilities to solve, from "mysteries," which lie outside our cognitive scope. According to this view, mind, matter, and their possible interaction may perhaps be a mystery, but maybe in the way that a clockwork duck is a mystery to a real one.

3 **The world becomes a mystery**
Newton concluded that one of the two substances described by Descartes doesn't exist—namely, body. The phenomenon of "action at a distance," as displayed by gravity, shows that the world is not mechanical and is, therefore, a mystery.

What moves the Moon?

4 **Rendering the world intelligible**
Although body, or "matter," remains a mystery, scientists and philosophers can still construct models to describe it. Their aim is to create a model of matter that accounts for the mind without reducing it to something else.

RIGHT AND WRONG

The branch of philosophy that studies the nature of
moral values is called "ethics." Its central questions
are: Where do our morals come from? What are
our grounds for holding them to be true?

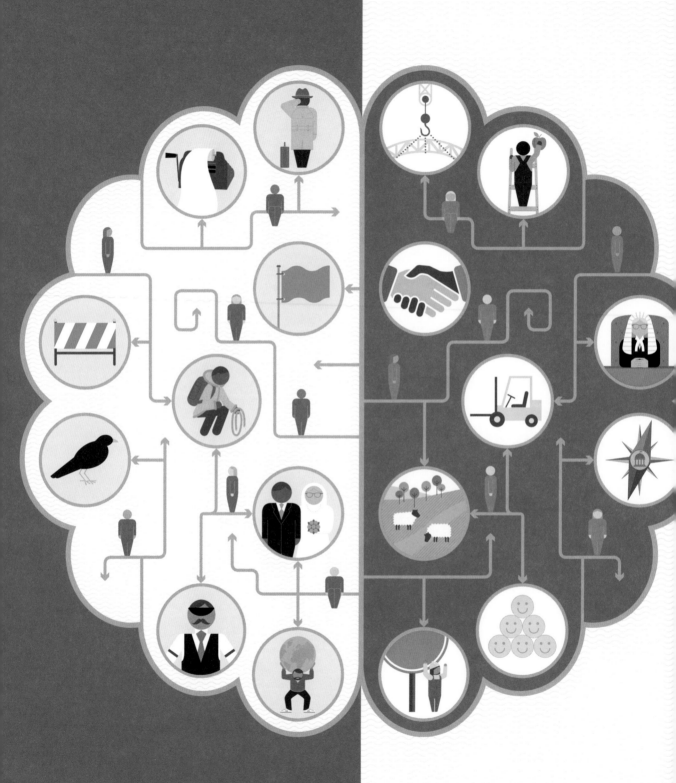

RIGHT AND WRONG

Many people think of morality as a set of rules that requires us to perform certain actions and refrain from others. However, what happens when two rules contradict each other? Knowing the right thing to do is not always as simple as following a rule—raising a question over the nature of moral authority. The nature of this authority is one of the central questions of ethics.

Aristotle believed that ethics only starts with rules. He argued that conflicts between rules force us to think for ourselves, and it is just this exercise of "right reason" that constitutes morality. However, by denying moral rules, he was not claiming that we cannot have "rules of thumb," or guidelines on how to behave. His point was simply that rules can never be absolute, or eternally binding.

However, many philosophers disagree with Aristotle. Some believe that morality is a collection of rules that is embedded in human nature. Immanuel Kant, for example, believed that morality is governed by categorical imperatives, or universally binding rules that are arrived at by rational thought. For Kant, the moral value of an action should thus be judged in terms of its motive, or whether or not it flows from the moral law. The utilitarian philosopher Jeremy Bentham also believed in rules, even arguing that only one is required: that we act in a way that maximizes the happiness of the greatest number of people. So, for utilitarians, the morality of an action is not a question of its motive, but rather its consequences in the world.

Others philosophers follow David Hume, who argued that reason is the "slave of the passions." By this, he meant that a moral act is simply one that brings about a desired state of affairs. According to this tradition, to say "lying is wrong" is another way of saying "I don't like lying," as morality is simply an expression of personal preference, which cannot therefore be rationally justified. Philosophers who hold this view regard emotion, rather than reason, as the basis for moral decisions and actions.

One thing that most philosophers agree on is that morals are a matter of choice. Unlike the laws of physics, moral rules can be broken, but they can only be broken freely. Someone who steals, for example, is only acting immorally if they freely choose to steal. If they feel compelled to steal, then we tend to judge them differently—perhaps as being in need of help. For this reason, determinism—the idea that our behavior is fixed by the laws of nature—renders morality void. As Jean-Paul Sartre argued, it is our ability to act freely that makes us moral agents.

Contemporary moral philosophy falls into two broad categories: first- and second-order ethics. First-order ethics involves thinking about specific moral problems. These include whether human cloning is morally acceptable, whether animals have rights, and whether the law should permit assisted suicide. Second-order ethics is more general and involves thinking about the nature of morality: whether it is a system of rules, whether or not we have free will, and whether we can justifiably claim to know right from wrong—or even that right and wrong really exist.

Rules and principles

Some philosophers believe that we need to follow rules to make moral decisions. Others argue that there are no moral rules, so we can only make moral decisions by assessing our particular situation.

To follow or not to follow rules?

Most people are brought up to see rules as central to deciding what is right and wrong. The moral rules that children are taught give them a framework for how they should always behave. Young children need this framework because they cannot yet reason for themselves. However, as children grow older, experience tells them that it is difficult to apply inflexible rules to specific situations. They will encounter situations in which one moral rule conflicts with another, or where following a moral rule could have dire consequences. There must, therefore, be more to morality than the rules we are taught as children.

Philosophers disagree about whether morality can consist of rules. Aristotle said that making a moral decision is not always a matter of applying a rule, and that often we instead have to exercise reason and judgment. Rules are only helpful up to a point because most moral judgments are affected by the situation in which they are made.

Moral particularism and moral generalism

One theory, moral particularism, goes further. It states that there are no moral principles because every moral judgment depends on the context in which it is made. No two contexts are the same, so every moral decision must be made on its own merits. The philosopher Jonathan Dancy (1946–) is the best-known advocate of moral particularism. Dancy argues that morality cannot be governed by rules because all reasons for performing an action or not performing an action depend on the context in which we might perform an action.

Philosophers who reject moral particularism are called moral generalists. They believe that morality is a matter of following rules, but not necessarily the inflexible rules that children were brought up on. They offer more general rules that can more easily be adapted to specific situations. The utilitarian view that we should do whatever produces the greatest happiness of the greatest number (see pp.186–187) is an example of a rule that a moral generalist would accept. Another example is the golden rule, or the idea that we should treat other people the way we would like to be treated. Moral generalists might apply rules such as these when they are faced with a moral dilemma.

THE GOLDEN RULE

The golden rule is the principle of treating other people the way we would like to be treated, or the idea that we should "do as we would be done by." This rule cannot give us specific instructions for making a moral decision. In order to follow it, we need to decide how we would like to be treated in a particular situation and what course of action would involve treating other people the way we would like to be treated. It is not a rule that can be taught to children because they are not yet able to reason for themselves. But it is a rule that can help moral generalists in the case of a moral dilemma.

Moral dilemmas

In everyday life, we often encounter moral dilemmas: specific situations that bring the general moral rules that we have been taught as children into conflict with each other. For example, we might have been taught that we should always be loyal and should always tell the truth, but there are many situations in which telling the truth would mean being disloyal to someone. When faced with a moral dilemma, a moral particularist would make a moral decision based only on the context of the situation. A moral generalist would still follow rules, but these rules are more flexible than the rules that children are taught.

MORAL PARTICULARISM

Moral particularists believe that we cannot use general rules to make a moral decision in a particular context. They would argue that our reasons for acting or not acting always depend on the situation we are in and that we can therefore only make moral decisions by assessing that situation.

MORAL GENERALISM

Moral generalists believe that moral rules can help us make moral decisions. But moral generalists follow rules, such as the golden rule (see box), which can be more easily adapted to particular situations than the rules that children are taught.

"Morality can get along perfectly well without principles."

Jonathan Dancy,
Ethics Without Principles (2004)

⟨ **LOYALTY**

TRUTH ⟩

Ethics and the law

The laws that apply in a particular country or region, the "laws of the land," are rules that everyone knows they must follow. Such rules govern our behavior and must not be broken.

Law of the land

Ignorance of the law of the land is not permitted as a defense against breaking these laws. This means that laws must be publicized in such a way that it is reasonable to expect everyone to know what they are. But what relation do the fundamental rules of morality, if they exist, have to the rules that make up the law of the land?

It is obvious that the rules of morality and the law of the land are different. We know this because laws are not always fair, and those that are unjust may be rejected. For example, many countries are currently questioning whether or not to allow assisted suicide. To do so would be to challenge existing laws that prohibit the taking of life. If some laws should not be passed and other laws should be passed, then morality somehow determines the law of the land. But if morality determines these laws, what determines morality?

Some philosophers believe that the moral rules we should follow are those we were taught in childhood; others believe in different moral rules; while others believe there are no moral rules at all. But who is right?

Moral knowledge

Working out which moral rules to follow, if any, and how to do so is a question of moral epistemology

Laws

It is the duty of a government to pass laws that uphold the moral law, thus ensuring harmony.

Wrong

NEED TO KNOW

> **Moral epistemology** is the study of our knowledge of moral rules or facts.

> **Moral particularism** is a theory that suggests there are no moral principles, because every moral judgment is affected by the context in which it is made, and no two contexts are the same.

> **Moral generalism** is the belief that morality is a matter of following rules, but not necessarily the rules learned in childhood.

Moral compass

The philosopher John Locke believed that the moral law has priority (in terms of time and importance) over the law of the land and argued that it is the duty of a government to introduce the laws that will uphold the "moral law," but never those that go further than the moral law (in introducing restrictions not justified by the moral law). He thought that if the laws passed by a government strayed too far from the moral law, this would justify rebellion against that government.

(the study of moral knowledge (see pp.174–75)). Whether we have to use reason every time we make a moral judgment, or if we have to apply a rule, how do we ensure that our judgment is correct? We cannot observe that an action is wrong, or conduct an experiment to tell us whether or not it is wrong, so science will not help. Some philosophers say we have a special intuition that allows us to "see" moral truth. Others argue that we acquire moral knowledge through our actions over time, building a moral sense from our experience.

> ## "The end of law is not to abolish or restrain, but to preserve and enlarge freedom."
>
> John Locke, *Second Treatise of Government* (1690)

HARMONY

Right

Laws

If a government passes laws that go beyond or against the moral law, people may rebel against them.

REBELLION

FIGHTING INJUSTICE

People have a tendency to rebel when faced with a law they believe to be unjust. In the UK in the 1980s, there were riots when the government tried to introduce a system of local taxation that many people felt was unfair. In the US in the 2000s, protests erupted when it became increasingly clear that black people were less protected by the law than white people. It seems many people believe rebellion is justified if the law of the land strays too far from the moral law.

BLACK LIVES MATTER is a movement that campaigns against the unequal treatment of black people.

Free will?

Most people believe that acting morally involves exercising free will: the ability to freely choose both our actions and the reasons for our actions. However, others argue that free will does not exist.

Rationality and morality

Free will is usually considered a necessary condition of being a moral agent—that is to say, being capable of acting rightly or wrongly. This is because free will involves freely choosing to carry out an action for a specific reason. An action can be considered morally justifiable if an agent has made a rational choice to act according to a moral principle. This suggests that rationality and free will are essential aspects of morality.

In spite of the fact that most normal adult human beings are rational, many human behaviors, such as emotional or instinctive reactions or compulsive behaviors, are nonrational—they are not performed for reasons, whether good or bad. And since moral agency requires rationality, nonrational actions are therefore not moral actions. This explains why young children are not full moral agents: even if they have free will, they have not yet developed the sort of

Does choice exist?

The traditional view of morality is that we can only act morally when we freely choose our actions. If we do not believe in free will, we could rethink this traditional view, arguing that morality depends on something other than the ability to freely choose our actions. Or we could accept this traditional view but argue that since free will does not exist, none of our actions are moral actions and therefore morality does not exist either.

HARD DETERMINISM
A person's sense of freedom is an illusion. People do not have free will. Instead, their actions are governed by the laws of nature and the conditions at the time.

SOFT DETERMINISM
The conditions that determine people's actions include people's beliefs and desires. This means that determinism is not incompatible with free will.

FREE WILL
There are many reasons why people might decide to perform or not to perform an action. They have the free will to choose which of these reasons to act on.

rationality (and understanding of right and wrong) that equips them to choose to behave in a certain way for moral reasons.

However, some philosophers question whether even normal adult human beings are moral agents. Psychologists believe that the human mind is made up of two "systems," only one of which involves rational thought (see pp.234—35). It has even been suggested that most apparently moral decisions made by adults could be said to be nonrational. An argument for this is that the reasons people give for their moral decisions are mostly "post hoc rationalizations." In other words, people often apply rational explanations for nonrational actions in retrospect.

THE FREE WILL DEBATE

Determinism

Determinists argue that the world is governed by laws of nature regardless of what people do or think. This means that people's actions and behaviors are also governed by laws of nature, and therefore that there is no such thing as free will.

Free will

Others believe the libertarian idea that people choose their actions for their own reasons, which have nothing to do with the laws of nature. Since people can freely choose to act in a certain way for a certain reason, free will must exist.

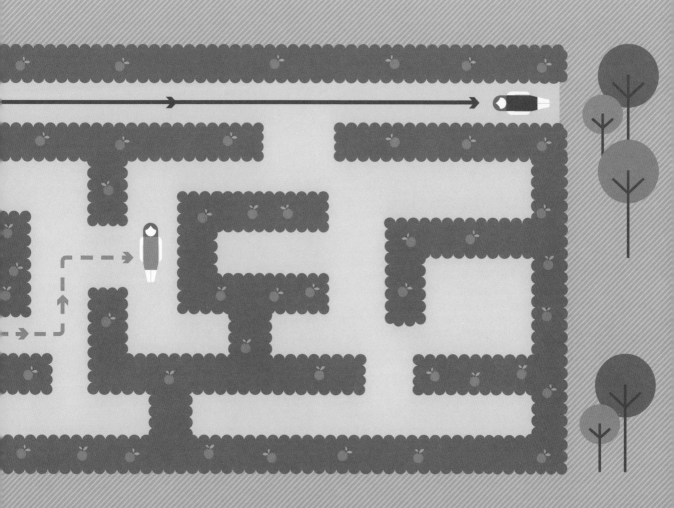

Do we have moral knowledge?

Most people assume that humans are capable of knowing what is right and wrong. However, some argue that when we think we are acting morally, this is not a matter of knowledge, but of emotion or biology.

Knowledge-how and knowledge-that

Moral knowledge is knowledge about what is right and what is wrong. To understand the nature of moral knowledge, it is essential to define what knowledge is. Knowledge generally falls into two categories: knowledge-how and knowledge-that.

Knowledge-how is knowledge of actions and skills that we have learned and that have become instinctive, such as riding a bike. We would find it difficult to explain this knowledge to other people. Knowledge-that is knowledge based on facts, feelings, or perceptions that we "know" are real. It can be put into words and explained to other people.

Does moral knowledge exist?

Moral knowledge is an example of knowledge-that. All kinds of knowledge-that are factive—that is to say, they express propositions that we cannot know unless those propositions are true. If moral knowledge exists, then our moral beliefs must be supported by moral facts, or at least by rational justification.

In everyday life, we assume we know what is right and wrong. However, some people argue that our moral beliefs are not grounded in facts or rationality, but in emotion, psychology, or evolution, and that moral knowledge is an illusion. Other people would say that we do have moral knowledge because we are capable of thinking rationally about morality.

"I believe the moral feelings are not innate but acquired ..."

John Stuart Mill, *Utilitarianism* (1863)

"BOO/HOORAY" THEORY

Noncognitivists (see pp.182–183) argue that moral beliefs are not a matter of knowledge and reason, but a matter of emotion. For noncognitivists, when we say that a course of action is morally right or morally wrong, we are not expressing a belief about truth or falsehood, but something more like an emotion. They argue that there are no objective moral facts, and therefore moral statements can only express the speaker's approval or disapproval of a course of action.

A popular version of noncognitivism is the "Boo/Hooray" theory of morality. This is the theory that to say, for example, "Murder is wrong" is, in effect, to say "'Boo murder!" To say "It is right to keep promises," on the other hand, is to say "Hooray to keeping promises." According to the "Boo/Hooray" theory, these statements do not express truth or falsehood, but emotional reactions.

Moral nihilism vs. moral knowledge

Moral nihilism is the view that nothing is right or wrong, and nihilists believe that there are no moral facts. If there are no moral facts, then there are no moral truths (see pp.176–177). And if there are no moral truths, then there can be no moral knowledge because there is nothing to know. Psychology, neuroscience, and evolutionary biology offer some arguments in support of this nihilistic view, claiming that science will one day show that moral beliefs are a product of human evolution and psychology.

The opposing argument points out that these scientific arguments are really just theories about what science might prove in the future, and that science is actually a very long way from showing that morality is merely biological. Until it does, we should consider the evidence we have for thinking that we do rationally justify our moral beliefs, that we do have free will, and that at least some of our behavior is not determined by our genetic inheritance or evolutionary impulses to adapt to our environment. This evidence suggests that we do have moral knowledge.

ARGUMENT	MORAL NIHILISM	MORAL KNOWLEDGE
JUSTIFICATION	**POST-HOC JUSTIFICATION** Some psychologists believe that what we see as explanations for our moral actions are nothing more than post-hoc rationalizations. In other words, when we have to decide between right and wrong, we often react emotionally rather than rationally, then attempt to explain our actions in retrospect.	**RATIONAL JUSTIFICATION OF MORAL BELIEFS** Science will never be able to successfully demonstrate that no one ever reasons about what is right and wrong. Many philosophers have spent much of their time thinking rationally about morality.
FREE WILL	**HARD DETERMINISM** Hard determinists (see pp.172–173) believe that there is no such thing as free will, and our actions are governed by the laws of nature and the conditions at the time. Some neuroscientific experiments support the view that free will is an illusion. If we cannot freely choose our actions, then we cannot offer rational explanations for them based on moral knowledge either.	**SOFT DETERMINISM** Soft determinists (see pp.172–173) believe that free will is compatible with determinism because the conditions that govern our actions include our beliefs and desires. If these beliefs include moral beliefs, then we are capable of choosing to act for moral reasons.
EVOLUTION	**EVOLUTIONARY ADAPTATION** Some evolutionary biologists believe that when humans think they are acting morally, they are merely adapting to their social environment. Humans are social animals, so it is advantageous for them to acquire a reputation for honesty, kindness, cooperation, and loyalty. Genes that are not conducive to acquiring this reputation are more likely to die out.	**ALTRUISM** Many human beings engage in altruistic behavior that is not easy to explain in evolutionary terms. Some altruistic acts are done in secret, so they will not help a person acquire a reputation for generosity. Sometimes people perform altruistic acts for the benefit of someone they will never meet. In this case, altruistic behavior will not help a person flourish in his or her social environment.

Does moral truth exist?

Conventional ways of discussing morality imply that moral beliefs (beliefs about what is right and wrong) are either true or false. But what exactly is moral truth? Might it not even exist?

Moral facts

If moral beliefs can be true or false, there is such a thing as moral truth. But if beliefs are made true by facts, then moral truth must depend on moral facts. Moral nihilists (see pp.174–175) argue that there are no moral facts, and therefore that there can be no such thing as moral truth. It would certainly be very difficult to establish the existence of moral facts by observation or experimentation. But over the years, philosophers have come up with theories that offer an account of the sort of facts that make moral beliefs true and help people make moral decisions.

Moral theories

Aristotle argued that an action is right if a virtuous person would perform it (see pp.180–181). For Aristotle, a virtuous person is someone who knows what is right, does what is right, and does what is right for the right reasons. Deontologists (see pp.184–185) believe that morality is based on unbreakable laws. Unbreakable moral laws, or the facts about what is right that are known by a virtuous person, could be the kind of moral facts on which moral truth can be based.

Noncognitivists (see pp.182–183) argue that moral beliefs are a matter of emotion rather than a matter of reason, and that moral statements therefore cannot be true or false. However, noncognitivists would also argue that we can arrive at the sort of moral facts that can help us make moral decisions by adopting a "stable and general perspective." This means finding out as much as possible about the things we approve or disapprove of and taking into account the opinions of people who disagree with us.

Nonmoral facts?

According to utilitarians (see pp.186–187), an action is right if it produces the greatest happiness of the greatest number (GHGN). Utilitarians would argue that this is a moral fact, and that we can understand the problematic concepts of right and wrong in terms of something we can already understand: human happiness. This means that no action is inherently right or wrong because the likelihood of it producing the GHGN depends on the context in which it is carried out. Utilitarians will not necessarily agree with each other about whether a particular action will

---

TRUTH WITHOUT OBSERVABLE FACTS?

Moral beliefs are not the only kind of belief that cannot be established to be true by observable facts:

> **New theories** cannot be established by observation or experiment, but only by argument from existing theories, rules, and axioms (accepted statements). These existing theories, rules, and axioms are not concrete facts, but abstract facts. That is to say that just like new theories, they cannot be established by observation either.

> **General claims** cannot be established by observation or experience because they are claims about states of affairs in the past, present, and future, and we cannot observe

the future. Such general claims and beliefs are made true by modal facts (facts about possibility and necessity), not concrete facts.

> **Analytic truths** (for example, "frozen water is ice") are truths that depend on the meaning of the terms that constitute the statement. They are true by definition and cannot be made true or false by observable facts in the outside world. In other words, they are not made true by concrete facts, but by conceptual facts.

produce the GHGN in a particular situation. And some people would say that seeing morality in terms of human happiness is an attempt to reduce moral facts to nonmoral facts.

The naturalistic fallacy

According to the philosopher G. E. Moore, utilitarians are guilty of the "naturalistic fallacy" of assuming that what makes us happy is the same as what is good. Moore argued that goodness cannot be reduced to notions of pleasure or happiness. For Moore, the fact that some actions are wrong is a "brute" fact that cannot be analyzed in terms of any other sort of fact. We can only determine the truth of a moral claim by looking to facts about inherent rightness and wrongness, and these facts can be detected by our special moral sense, or intuition. We may not observe the fact that a particular action is wrong. But we do "intuit" this fact through our special moral sense.

"Moral laws are merely statements that certain ... actions will have good effects."

G. E. Moore, *Principia Ethica* (1903)

Moral beliefs, truth, and facts

If beliefs are made true by facts, then the existence of moral truth depends on moral facts—facts about whether an action is right or wrong. It is difficult to argue that moral beliefs are straightforwardly true or false because moral facts—if they exist—cannot be established by observation. But many philosophical arguments rest on moral truth and moral facts.

Moral beliefs

Moral beliefs are beliefs about what is right and wrong. Most people would argue that beliefs can be true or false, and that if beliefs are true, they are made true by facts. Moral beliefs can therefore only be justified by moral truth, and moral truth can only be made true by moral facts. But can statements about what people believe to be right and wrong really be straightforwardly true or false? And what kind of moral facts might make these beliefs true?

Moral truth

Those who argue that beliefs are made true by facts understand truth as a relationship between a belief and a fact. Many statements are straightforwardly true or false. We can observe the factual evidence that makes them true or false or establish this evidence through experimentation. Statements about moral beliefs cannot be made straightforwardly true or false by empirically observable facts. But might there nevertheless be moral facts—facts that can make moral beliefs true or false?

Moral facts

If there are moral facts, they are not concrete facts. That is to say we cannot touch, look at, see, or hear moral facts, or conduct experiments to discover them. However, most philosophers believe that there are moral facts. For example, utilitarians believe that an action is right if it produces the GHGN, and deontologists (see pp.184–185) believe that an action is right if it falls under a rule that prescribes it. These are not facts that we can check by observation. But for utilitarians and deontologists respectively, they are facts that make moral beliefs true.

The fact-value distinction

David Hume (see pp.182–183) argued that we cannot arrive at a value (a statement about how things should be) from a fact (a statement about how things are) because values depend on what matters to us.

What are values?

Some philosophers believe that the key characteristic of value judgments is that we cannot construct arguments for or against them. Value judgments express deeply held convictions about what matters to us, or what we value. If we do not value something, it is very difficult to persuade us to value it. We could persuade someone to say that they value something, but if we do this by threatening them, their position will not be genuine. We might try to persuade someone to value something by saying it is a means to something they already value, but this might simply make them stop valuing the thing that they already value. Judgments about values seem to be pretty different from judgments about facts.

FACTS

"Is" statements

Descriptive statements ("is" statements) refer to facts. They simply say how things are. A descriptive statement straightforwardly expresses truth or falsehood.

Can we bridge the gap?

Hume made a distinction between "is" statements (statements that express "facts") and "ought" statements (statements that express "values," or what matters to us as individuals). He argued that people sometimes fall into the trap of using an "ought" argument in place of an "is" argument—that is, they confuse the roles of values and facts. According to Hume, any attempt to bridge the gap between facts and values will always involve assumptions about what matters. Judgments of values cannot be arrived at in the same way as judgments about facts.

> "The rules of morality are not conclusions of our reason."
>
> David Hume, *A Treatise of Human Nature* (1738)

VALUES

"Ought" statements

Prescriptive statements ("ought" statements) express values, or judgments about the potential "value" of a fact. These judgments are true or false only to the extent that things do or do not matter to us.

UTILITARIANISM

The GHGN

Utilitarians (see pp.186–187) would argue that a course of action does not create the greatest happiness of the greatest number (GHGN). This is a descriptive statement, which expresses a fact. They would then argue that we ought not to follow that course of action. This is a prescriptive statement, which expresses a value. But by arriving at a value from a fact, utilitarians have assumed that the GHGN matters to us.

RELATIVE OR ABSOLUTE MORAL TRUTH?

Statements that are absolutely true are true under any circumstances. Statements that are relatively true rely on facts that only exist relative to something. So are moral statements true absolutely or only relatively? If they are relatively true, what are they true relative to? Many believe that moral truth is not absolute because moral judgments and laws vary according to their context. This context might be a community, a culture, a situation, or even a person. Utilitarians could claim that the statement "we should do whatever produces the GHGN" is absolutely true, but argue that moral statements about whether a course of action is right or wrong are only true relative to whether that course of action would produce the GHGN in a given situation.

Aristotle's virtue ethics

Aristotle's theory of morality has more recently become known as "virtue ethics." Virtue ethics defines morally right actions as those that would be performed by a virtuous person.

Knowing what is right

According to Aristotle, a virtuous person is one who knows what is right, does what is right, and does what is right for the right reason. Reason is at the heart of virtue ethics—Aristotle believed that our capacity for reason separates us from other living things. Only humans can distinguish between where and what they are and where and what they ought to be. This means that only humans can, by being virtuous—by doing what they ought to do—get themselves from where and what they are to where and what they ought to be. Aristotle argued that the true function and purpose of humankind is to exercise reason in action. To exercise reason in action is to exercise the virtues (do what we know we ought to do) each time we act.

Acting virtuously

Only if we exercise the virtues in all of our actions will we achieve life's purpose—*eudaimonia*, which means "happiness" or "flourishing." To experience pleasure is not to experience *eudaimonia*. In Aristotle's view, the only way we can achieve *eudaimonia* is by acting, throughout our lives, in accordance with the virtues. We act virtuously only if we act for the right reason. Acting with the intention of achieving *eudaimonia* is not acting virtuously. We act virtuously only if we do what virtue requires of us because virtue requires it. If, by accident, we do what virtue requires of us but not because virtue requires it, our act may be virtuous, but we are not.

Gathering virtues

Becoming virtuous takes time. Each time we choose an action, we are choosing our future character. If we consistently make the right choices for the right reasons, we will acquire a good character. Aristotelian virtues fall into two categories: moral and intellectual.

THE GOLDEN MEAN

Aristotle said that to be virtuous, we must understand the nature of virtue. There is no instruction manual that tells us how to behave morally. The only way for us to determine what we should or shouldn't do is to identify, in each situation, the action that agrees with the "golden mean." This will be the action that avoids both an excess and a deficiency of certain characteristics. A courageous action, for example, avoids rashness (an excess of courage) and cowardice (a deficiency of courage). Not only might such an action be different in each situation, but it might also be different for each person. To be virtuous, we must therefore also understand ourselves.

Intellectual virtues

Theoretical and practical wisdom, the intellectual virtues, can be taught by parents and teachers.

"Virtue lies in our power, and so does vice; because where it is in our power to act, it is also in our power not to act."

Aristotle, *Nicomachean Ethics* (4th century BCE)

Asking for help

One problem with virtue ethics is that it gives us no clear rules for deciding how to act. Aristotle said we should look to the example of a virtuous person. When we ask a wise friend how we should act, we are following Aristotle's advice.

Moral virtues

The moral virtues cannot be taught; instead, they must be acquired. Even if we are born with a tendency to be honest, we are not born with the virtue of honesty. To have this virtue is to understand what it means to be honest, to be consistently honest, and always to be honest for the right reasons.

Virtuous act or agent?

Aristotle made a distinction between a virtuous act and a virtuous agent. He argued that when we face a moral dilemma, each of us must exercise moral reasoning in deciding how to act. When we do act, our act will be virtuous only if, in the context of that dilemma, it is the right thing to do. But we will be a virtuous agent only if we do the right thing for the right reason.

Humean ethics

According to the philosopher David Hume, the right action is the action that a "true judge" would approve of. The wrong action is the action that a true judge would disapprove of.

Acts of passion, not reason

At a glance, Hume's theory looks rather like Aristotle's virtue ethics (see pp.180–181). But Hume's "feeling approbation" (approving of) is different from Aristotle's "knowing what is right," and "true judges" are not the same as "virtuous persons." Hume was an advocate of "noncognitivism"—the view that morality is not a matter of reason and that, therefore, moral statements cannot be true or false.

Hume's ethics were built on his philosophy of mind—in particular, on his account of mental, or cognitive, states (see pp.178–179). He argues that cognitive states such as beliefs and knowledge cannot motivate actions. Actions can only be motivated by "passions," such as desires, values, and emotions. For example, knowing how to make a cup of coffee (a cognitive state) will not, in the absence of a desire for coffee (a passion), motivate a person to make one.

According to Hume, reason informs us of matters of fact and of relations between ideas. Only passion motivates us. Moral judgments, he says, are essentially linked to action; they cannot, therefore, express cognitive states such as beliefs and must instead express passions. This means that when we act on a moral judgment, it is passion that prompts us to act, not reason.

Moral judgments

Hume argues that if beliefs cannot motivate us, then moral judgments, which do motivate us, cannot express beliefs. Therefore, they must express passions. Unlike beliefs, passions cannot be true or false. It is undoubtedly true that moral judgments motivate us. To believe that lying *is* wrong is to believe that we *should not* lie. The move from "is" to "should" shows that the belief itself is motivating. Hume says that since this move takes us from beliefs (about what is the case) to values (what matters to us), moral judgments are not expressions of belief, but expressions of passion.

Hume's argument that moral judgments express passion rather than reason was revolutionary in its time. For example, the statement "lying is wrong" may seem to express a belief about a type of action ("lying," in this case) that is either true or false. But Hume would say this statement does not express a belief about the world, but rather a feeling—that the person speaking does not like lying. This is a highly subjectivist view—it suggests that there is no more to morality than our own likes and dislikes. Hume gives moral judgments a sort of objectivity by insisting that before an expression of approval or disapproval can be deemed moral, it must be made by one who adopts a "stable and general perspective."and thus becomes a "true judge."

The need for a true judge

Hume argues that in order to become true judges we must move from the "pre-moral deliverances of sympathy" of childhood to truly moral attitudes. These pre-moral deliverances of sympathy are those we experience when we empathize with others. If a child cries because her friend is crying, for example, she is experiencing such a state. To become a true judge we must therefore have a great deal more than the natural ability to empathize.

"**Reason is**, and ought only to be, **the slave of the passions.**"

David Hume, *A Treatise of Human Nature* (1738)

EXPERIENCE
Acquiring the knowledge required to become a true judge is a natural process. As we grow up, our parents and teachers and our experiences teach us that if, for example, we hurt our friends, we will lose them. Before our expressions of approval and disapproval can be counted as truly moral, we must, through our life experience, learn to consider every action from the perspective of those who will be affected by it, and then use this ability before deciding whether or not to act.

TRUE JUDGE

A stable and general perspective

To become a true judge, we must acquire a great deal of knowledge about the nature of the things we approve or disapprove of, and how facts about the world relate to one another. If we allow bias to skew our perspective, or fail to consider someone who will be affected by our actions, our attitudes of approval and disapproval will not qualify as "moral attitudes." If and when we do succeed in adopting a stable and general perspective, modern Humeans, such as Simon Blackburn, say that we "earn the right" to think of our moral judgments as true or false. Though these judgments are still expressions of passion, not reason, the passions they express are so informed by reason that they almost attain the status of beliefs.

Deontology

The theory of deontology (from the Greek word for "obligation") states that morality is based on unbreakable rules. The right action is the one that is performed according to the "moral law."

Inclination or obligation?

The most famous deontologist is Immanuel Kant. Kant believed that all of our actions are performed either to achieve a desired result or out of a sense of moral duty—our need to follow the moral law. Acts of the first kind are motivated by inclination (a form of passion). Kant thought that actions motivated by passion cannot be moral. They may be forbidden by the moral law, or they may conform to the moral law but be performed by an agent motivated by his or her own end rather than by the moral law. Kant believed, like Aristotle (see pp.180–181), that an act can be virtuous without the agent being virtuous. An act can only be a moral action, he argued, if the agent puts his or her inclinations aside and performs it out of duty (because it is required by the moral law). Our actions, therefore, are moral, as long as our intentions are good and we act "out of reverence for the law."

Deontologists like Kant think that acting morally depends on our acting because it is required by the moral law, not because it will achieve a desired result. But what is this "moral law"? Kant's version of it is the "categorical imperative."

Inclination
Hiker A offers the man his rope because he wants Hiker B to think he is courageous and kind. In doing so, he is acting out of inclination rather than moral duty.

HE

Moral high ground

Imagine a situation in which two hikers, Hiker A and Hiker B, come across a man who has fallen and is in desperate need of help. Each of them gives the man a rope. Their actions are identical, but their motives differ. Kant would say that Hiker B's motive ensures that she has acted morally. But Hiker A's motive means that he has not acted morally (even if his action was required by the moral law).

Imperatives

Imperatives tell us what to do—they are instructions. Kant made a distinction between two types of imperative. A hypothetical imperative tells us how to act in order to achieve a desired goal. It applies only to people who want to achieve that particular goal. In seeking approval for an action, a person is acting on a hypothetical imperative. The categorical imperative, on the other hand, applies to everyone, regardless of individual desires or circumstances. To recognize that an action is morally right is to believe it should be performed. In acting out of moral duty, a person is acting on a categorical imperative.

Formulas

Kant offered two main formulations of the categorical imperative. The Formula of Universal Law tells us that we should always act in such a way that we would be happy for everyone else to act in the same way in the same situation. In other words, moral rules must apply to everyone in all circumstances. According to the Formula of the End in Itself, no "end in itself" (Kant's term for a rational being) should be treated only as a means to the ends of others. In other words, we must not neglect the needs of others or dehumanize them in order to achieve our goals as individuals.

Moral duty
Hiker B throws the man her rope because she believes that it is the right thing to do. She is acting out of duty, and is therefore obeying the moral law.

The Formula of Universal Law
"Act only on that maxim through which you can at the same time will that it should be universal law."

The Formula of the End in Itself
"So act that you use humanity, whether in your own person or in the person of another, always at the same time as an end, never merely as a means."

> "Morality is not the doctrine of how we make ourselves happy. It is the doctrine of how we make ourselves worthy of happiness."
>
> **Immanuel Kant**

Utilitarianism

Utilitarian philosophy is based on the idea that the right action is the one that results in the greatest happiness of the greatest number (GHGN).

Consequences count

Utilitarianism focuses on the consequences of actions—the right action being the one with the most desirable consequences. According to John Stuart Mill, the only thing each of us desires is happiness, so our ultimate goal is for everyone to be happy. He defined happiness as "intended pleasure, and the absence of pain" and unhappiness as "pain, and the privation [absence] of pleasure."

The moral rules we learn as children, Mill argued, are unhelpful because we do not see them as rules that cannot be broken. Instead, we need a rule that can be applied in any situation—a rule to which there are no exceptions. The Greatest Happiness Principle (GHP) is such a rule. According to the GHP, an action is right only if it results in the greatest happiness of the greatest number (GHGN). Whether or not we intend to produce the GHGN when we act in a certain way is unimportant to utilitarians—they judge an action solely by its consequences.

The Greatest Happiness Principle (GHP)

The GHP tells us that the right action is the one that results in the greatest happiness of the greatest number (GHGN). To utilitarians, a truly moral agent is one whose actions, over time, successfully produce the GHGN.

Interpreting utilitarianism

The Greatest Happiness Principle, or GHP, can be interpreted in many different ways—for example, whether it is the quantity or quality of happiness that is most important, or whether the actions the GHP refers to are individual "token acts" (Act Utilitarianism) or general "action-types" (Rule Utilitarianism).

Quantity, quality, or both?

Jeremy Bentham, another famous utilitarian, believed that we need only look to the quantity of happiness produced, and that the enjoyment of "pushpin" (a board game) and poetry were of equal value in the "hedonic calculus." Mill, however, thought that both the quantity and quality of happiness were important, and said that the enjoyment of poetry (what he called a "higher pleasure") should count for more.

Act Utilitarianism

say "that lie is wrong" is to say that a
rticular lie is wrong. An act utilitarian
AU) checks every action against the
HP and chooses the action that will
sult in the GHGN. When lying would
romote the GHGN, an AU will break
he moral rule of thumb that lying is
rong. For an AU, therefore, there are
no absolute moral rules.

Observation and experience

Utilitarians (AUs, at least) will not accept that any of
our everyday moral rules are absolutely true or false.
They believe that the GHP is everywhere, always and
for everyone true. They also believe that we acquire
knowledge of morality by inductive means. We
observe or otherwise learn about the consequences
of various actions and, assuming the future will be
like the past, we think of those that are likely to
produce the GHGN as (likely to be) right and the
others as (likely to be) wrong. Moral knowledge is
not, therefore, as Kant would have it, discerned by
intuition, but by observation and experience.

Rule Utilitarianism

To say "lying is wrong" is to commit to the
belief that all lies are wrong. Rather than
looking at the consequences of every
action, a rule utilitarian (RU) refers to a set
of moral rules based on general "action-
types" that promote the GHGN, checking
individual actions against these rules. RUs
who won't break the rules even when an
action would violate the GHP are often
dismissed as "rule-worshippers."

"Actions are right in proportion as they tend to promote happiness."

John Stuart Mill, *Utilitarianism* (1863)

Existentialist ethics

Jean-Paul Sartre's existentialism denies the existence both of God and human nature (a set of shared characteristics that determines what we think and do). We alone can choose how we lead our lives.

Free to choose

Humans, Sartre argues, were not conceived in the mind of some deity to have a particular purpose, or "essence"—the characteristics that make us what we are. There is no divine purpose that determines how we should think and act, and no set of divine commandments that tell us how we should live. But nor is there any nondivine purpose or set of rules that do so. To think that human nature exists, Sartre says, is to fail to carry to its logical conclusion the belief that God doesn't exist. It is to leave intact the idea that something determines how we think and act—even if that something is not God.

According to existentialism, there is no set of objective rules that tells us how we should live our lives.

Recognition of this fact means that human beings are "radically free." That is to say, they are not defined by their natures, and their choices are not determined by their natures. Nor are they required to do, or value, anything dictated by a divine being. Instead, they must choose their values, beliefs, and actions for themselves. Every individual is the person they are only because of the choices they have made in the past. Individuals will become the people they become because—and only because—of the choices they will make in the future.

Bad faith

Sartre goes on to argue that we are in bad faith (see pp.126–127) if we attempt to persuade ourselves or others that we are not responsible for what we do with our freedom. For example, a person who says he was "carried away by passion" demonstrates bad faith, as does a person blaming her choices on her poverty.

Recognizing that we alone can choose how to live our lives underlines our subjectivity. Humans, Sartre argues, are the only beings that "propel themselves toward their future and are aware of doing so." Only we are able to "surpass" ourselves, to transcend what we are, and to become what we choose to become.

From abandonment to despair

The need to make responsible choices weighs heavily on us as human beings. This is partly because we feel "abandoned," bearing the responsibility for the choices we make alone. This causes us anguish as we recognize that the burden of decision-making falls on us alone and that nothing or no one can help us. Even if we seek guidance from someone we believe to be virtuous, we are making a choice—by choosing who to ask. If we are to live in good faith, therefore, there is nothing for it but to accept responsibility for our decisions. Even if it causes us despair, we must accept the freedom that we cannot escape and resolve to do our best with it. To refuse to act is to choose to refuse. By such acts, and failures to act, we create ourselves, so each of us is nothing more than the sum of our actions.

FREEDOM

We are free to choose for ourselves, so we must recognize that we are exercising free choice whatever decision we make, in whichever situation we find ourselves. Sartre admits that certain universal facts—for example, that we all die—place limitations on us. But each of us faces a unique combination of circumstances, as well as these universal ones. It is to each of these unique situations that we must individually respond. We cannot escape our freedom—we are "condemned to be free." Even to decide not to decide is to decide.

RESPONSIBILITY

With freedom comes the responsibility not only to choose for ourselves, but to choose for everyone. This is because to make a choice is to believe that choice is good—and that it is good for everyone. To choose is, in effect, to decide that this is how everyone else should live. Existentialists are thus able to claim that some choices are right (those that are responsible) and others are wrong (those that are not responsible or are taken in bad faith). The alternative would be to insist that our choices are arbitrary, and therefore that there is no such thing as right or wrong.

SEEKING GUIDANCE

Sartre offers an example of a young man who comes to him with a moral dilemma. Should the man, Sartre is asked, stay with the elderly mother who adores him and who has no one else to care for her? Or should he leave her and join the French Resistance against the Nazis? Sartre points out that conventional morality could justify either decision. But in asking the advice of an existentialist philosopher, the young man knew he would be told that he must make his own choice. He had, therefore, in a sense, already accepted his need to do so and was only postponing the decision.

"It is only in our decisions that we are important."

Jean-Paul Sartre, existentialist

Animal rights

In the past, humans rarely questioned the morality of using animals for all kinds of purposes. However, many people now argue that humans have duties toward animals, or even that animals have rights.

Rationality and sentience

The deontologist Immanuel Kant (see pp.184–185) claimed a being has rights if and only if it is an end in itself. Kant believed that to be an end in itself, a being must be both rational and autonomous. He argued that animals are neither rational nor autonomous and therefore have no rights. However, other deontologists argue that some animals choose how to act and therefore act for reasons, even if their "reasoning" differs from ours. According to these deontologists, animals are both rational and autonomous and therefore have rights, but not necessarily the same rights as humans.

Other philosophers believe that even if animals are not rational, they still have rights because they are sentient and so they, like humans, can feel both pleasure and pain. Utilitarians (see pp.186–187), who believe that actions are right insofar as they produce the greatest happiness of the greatest number (GHGN), would argue that a being with the capacity to feel pleasure and pain has rights, even if it cannot demonstrate rational thought. Descartes (see pp.52–53) did not believe that animals feel pleasure and pain. To him, animals are simply "automata."

Animal rights and the GHGN

Utilitarians who believe that animals are sentient also argue that animals should be taken into account when deciding which action will produce the GHGN. However, not all utilitarians believe that the happiness of animals is as important as human happiness. Even utilitarians who think that animals have as much right to be happy as humans face difficult questions about which actions will create the greatest happiness for animals and humans.

VEGETARIANISM AND VEGANISM

Some vegetarians and vegans believe that it is wrong to kill animals or cause animals to suffer. Others think that a vegetarian or vegan diet will minimize human suffering—for example, because they think such a diet is healthier or better for the environment than eating meat and dairy. Those who do eat meat and dairy products might justify it in terms of human happiness, arguing that it is better for their health, it gives humans a lot of pleasure, and it helps farmers to make a living.

KEEPING PETS

It could be argued that keeping animals as pets is cruel and that animals would be happier in the wild, where they would be free to fulfill their natural potential. But would animals really be happier in the wild? Many people would argue that pets enjoy human company and living in a safe, comfortable home. For some people, even if animals would be happier in the wild, the enormous pleasure that keeping pets generates for humans justifies any suffering caused to the animals.

Rights or duties?

The philosopher Roger Scruton believes that animals are rational but that they do not have rights because they are incapable of understanding duties. A human's right to life brings with it the duty not to kill others. A lion cannot understand the duty not to kill, so it cannot have the right to life.

However, Scruton argues that even if animals have no rights, we have duties toward them. For Scruton, our duties to animals matter because of the effect our actions have on them. Kant also believed that we have duties to animals, but only because humans who are cruel to animals are more likely to be cruel to other humans. According to Kant, our duties to animals are indirectly duties to other humans, whereas for Scruton, our duties to animals are direct.

The views of other people

Noncognitivists (see pp.182–183) believe that a stable and general perspective is necessary if we want our decisions about how animals are treated to be morally justifiable. To gain such a perspective, we must learn as much as possible about the subject and consult the views of other people, especially those whose views differ from our own. However, there is no consensus among philosophers about animal rights, despite efforts to achieve a stable and general perspective.

Virtue theorists (see pp.180–181) argue that something is right if a virtuous person believes that it is right. Although it is very difficult to know whether a virtuous person would say that animals have rights, a government might set up a committee of "the great and the good" to advise on issues such as medical research on animals.

"To be for animals is not to be against humanity."

Tom Regan, *The Case for Animal Rights* (1983)

SPECIESISM

Many people might argue that the suffering of animals matters less than human suffering because animals do not have hopes, fears, or life plans, for example. The utilitarian Peter Singer thinks that such an attitude is "speciesist." For Singer, speciesism is as morally unacceptable as racism or sexism, and we must always consider the impact our actions have on the pleasure or pain of animals.

LIKE ANIMALS, infants do not have life plans, but no one would argue that it is morally acceptable to kill infants.

ZOOS

Those who believe that it is morally wrong to keep animals in zoos might argue that human beings would not like to be kept in captivity. But it could be argued that some animal species would become extinct if there were no zoos. And some people think that the pleasure and educational benefits that humans get from zoos are enough to justify keeping animals in captivity.

RESEARCH ON ANIMALS

There are some animal rights activists who believe that any kind of animal testing, whether it is for cosmetic or medical reasons, is wrong, and that the suffering caused to animals can never be justified. Many people, however, would argue that carrying out research on animals is morally right because of the benefits that it brings to humans, particularly in the case of medical research that might lead to cures for diseases.

Euthanasia

Also known as "mercy killing," euthanasia is killing to end a person's suffering. Euthanasia is illegal in many countries and raises controversial questions about the sanctity of human life.

Forms of euthanasia

There are several different forms of euthanasia. Killing someone who chooses to die and is unable to take their own life is called "assisted dying" if the person is terminally ill and "voluntary" euthanasia (assisted suicide) if the person is not terminally ill. "Nonvoluntary" euthanasia involves the killing of a person who cannot consent to being killed, such as someone in a permanent vegetative state.

"Active" euthanasia involves an intervention to end someone's life, perhaps by injecting a large dose of sedative. "Passive" euthanasia involves withholding the treatment necessary to maintain life.

The moral justification of euthanasia

Some deontologists (see pp.184–185) might interpret the Sixth Commandment ("Thou shalt not murder") as an unbreakable moral law that states that it is wrong to kill another human being under any circumstances. A Kantian deontologist, however, might consider that if a person has rationally and freely chosen to die because of their suffering, it would be wrong not to help them.

Utilitarians (see pp.186–187) believe that euthanasia is right if and only if it would produce the greatest happiness of the greatest number (GHGN). If a person wants to die, his pain cannot be alleviated, and his family wants to end his suffering, a utilitarian would

Concerns about euthanasia

Numerous moral and religious laws forbid intentional killing, but do not forbid acts of which a foreseen consequence is that someone dies—not intervening to keep someone alive, for example. This means that even the most ardent deontologists who believe that laws that forbid intentional killing are unbreakable might still justify allowing someone to die to end their suffering. However, several questions concerning the justification and legalization of euthanasia must be considered. Can we ever be sure that the intention of someone who is preparing to use euthanasia is really to end suffering? Are we in danger of creating a climate in which people feel obliged to kill themselves?

WRONG

OVERESTIMATION
Research shows that healthy people often overestimate the pain and difficulties of people who are living with various conditions.

INTENTIONS
If someone is caring for an ill relative who says they want to die, the carer also wants the relative to die, and the carer kills the relative, it could be argued that this is murder if the carer acted on their own wishes.

SLIPPERY SLOPE
Legalizing euthanasia could lead to a slippery slope. Elderly or disabled people might feel that they ought to die rather than be a burden, and we might have less incentive to improve end-of-life care.

consider euthanasia morally acceptable in those circumstances. Not allowing the ill person to die would create more unhappiness than happiness for both him and his family.

Utilitarian Peter Singer argues that it is quality of life that counts, and not the sanctity of life itself. According to Singer, euthanasia should be permitted whenever consciousness (and the capacity for pleasure and pain) is irreversibly lost or when a person has categorically decided that their pain is such that life is not worth living. Singer supports a change in the current law and dismisses objections against assisted dying, assisted suicide, and even involuntary euthanasia based on the experiences and suffering of people living with long-term pain. If we prohibit voluntary euthanasia, Singer argues, these people must live with not only the pain itself but the fear of the pain continuing when they have no control over when it will end.

LEGALIZING VS. DECRIMINALIZING

Completely decriminalizing acts of euthanasia would make it permissible for anyone, at any time, to decide to end what they perceive as someone else's suffering. This would not produce the GHGN, nor would it necessarily result in everyone's being treated as an end in themselves (see p.185).

Legalizing euthanasia, however, would mean it could be regulated, stating the exact conditions under which it is permitted. Assisted suicide has been legalized in the Netherlands, Belgium, Luxembourg, Switzerland, Columbia, and Canada. The states of Oregon, Washington, Vermont, Montana, and California also permit assisted dying. In every country that has legalized euthanasia, the person to die must be an adult (except in Belgium and the Netherlands), mentally competent, and informed about their options, and they must volunteer to die (in writing or in front of witnesses). In such countries, the sanctity of life is less important than the quality of life from the perspective of the one who is living that life.

Even in countries where euthanasia is illegal, there are, under some circumstances, still ways of allowing patients to die if they want to end their suffering. One example of this is the act-omission doctrine: a doctor may deliberately walk slowly into the room in which someone is having a heart attack so the patient dies before the doctor gets there. This is passive euthanasia. It is the heart attack that kills the patient, not the doctor. Another example is the use of "double effect." Here, a doctor administers painkillers with the intention of ending suffering. A foreseeable consequence of the high dose needed might be the death of the patient. This is legal so long as the doctor did not intend to kill the patient, but to end their suffering. Legalizing euthanasia brings strict regulations that might make it more difficult for doctors to invoke double effect or the act-omission doctrine.

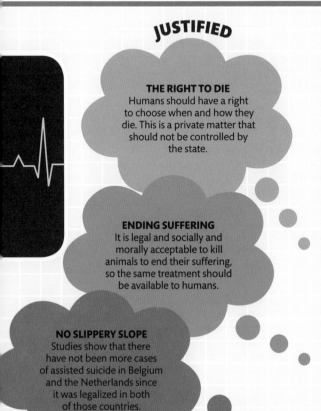

JUSTIFIED

THE RIGHT TO DIE
Humans should have a right to choose when and how they die. This is a private matter that should not be controlled by the state.

ENDING SUFFERING
It is legal and socially and morally acceptable to kill animals to end their suffering, so the same treatment should be available to humans.

NO SLIPPERY SLOPE
Studies show that there have not been more cases of assisted suicide in Belgium and the Netherlands since it was legalized in both of those countries.

"**There has been no slippery slope to disaster ... with medical assistance in dying in other countries.**"
Peter Singer, utilitarian

# Cloning

It is now possible in principle to clone human beings for both medical and reproductive purposes. However, human cloning is controversial and poses many ethical questions.

The purpose of cloning

Human cloning has two potential purposes: therapeutic cloning (cloning human embryos for medical research) and reproductive cloning (using cloning to produce new human babies). Both of these uses pose moral problems. Most countries have passed legislation banning reproductive human cloning, but therapeutic cloning is permitted in some countries under certain conditions.

The ethics of therapeutic cloning

Therapeutic cloning involves cloning a human being in order to conduct research on the resulting embryo. This might enable us to develop more effective diagnostic techniques and therapies for congenital conditions.

But is it morally acceptable to conduct research on a human embryo? A deontologist (see pp.184–185) who believes that

human life is sacred would think not. So, arguably, would any deontologist who believes that we should never use others as means to our own ends. The only way a deontologist could accept therapeutic cloning is if the embryo were deemed not (yet) to be a human being.

A utilitarian (see pp.186–187) would not oppose therapeutic cloning so long as it produced the greatest happiness of the greatest

Is cloning morally wrong?

Both therapeutic cloning and reproductive cloning are highly controversial. Since therapeutic cloning involves carrying out research on—and eventually killing—human embryos, the controversy around it is largely focused on the debate as to when human life begins. Reproductive cloning is even more controversial. It is banned in most countries, primarily for reasons of safety. Technology is improving all the time, and reproductive cloning has the potential to become a method of treating infertility, but there are many arguments against it.

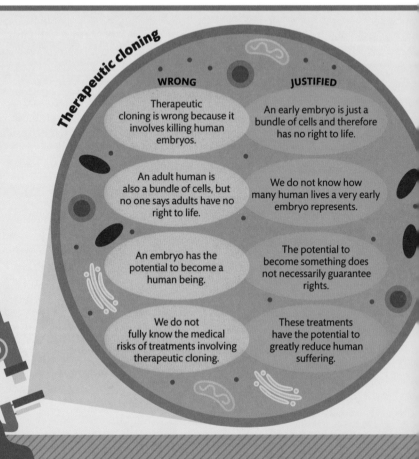

Therapeutic cloning

WRONG

Therapeutic cloning is wrong because it involves killing human embryos.

An adult human is also a bundle of cells, but no one says adults have no right to life.

An embryo has the potential to become a human being.

We do not fully know the medical risks of treatments involving therapeutic cloning.

JUSTIFIED

An early embryo is just a bundle of cells and therefore has no right to life.

We do not know how many human lives a very early embryo represents.

The potential to become something does not necessarily guarantee rights.

These treatments have the potential to greatly reduce human suffering.

number (GHGN), which it almost certainly would if it generated new diagnostic techniques and therapies.

Aristotle's virtue ethics (see pp.180–181) might suggest that we convene a committee of people who we think are virtuous, who can help us decide whether therapeutic cloning is morally acceptable. Hume, on the other hand (see pp.182–183), would recommend that we find out as much as we can about cloning and reflect on as many different views as we can (including views that we do not agree with) in order to arrive at a "stable and general perspective."

DOLLY THE SHEEP

Dolly the sheep was the world's first mammal to be cloned from an adult cell. She was born in July 1996, and her birth was announced in February 1997. She was produced by a technique known as SCNT: somatic cell nuclear transfer. The birth of Dolly proved that, in principle at least, human beings could be cloned. Within a few months of her birth, nearly every country in the world had banned reproductive cloning, because the technology was not yet advanced enough for reproductive cloning to be viable without posing great risks to human health. But this technology is improving all the time.

THE TAXIDERMIED REMAINS of Dolly the sheep are on display at the National Museum of Scotland in Edinburgh.

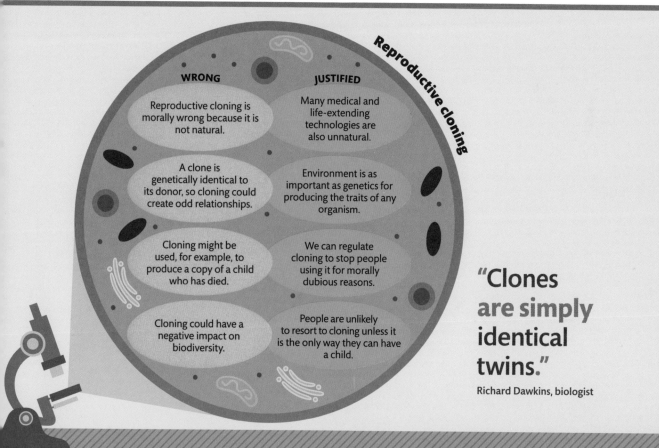

Reproductive cloning

WRONG

Reproductive cloning is morally wrong because it is not natural.

A clone is genetically identical to its donor, so cloning could create odd relationships.

Cloning might be used, for example, to produce a copy of a child who has died.

Cloning could have a negative impact on biodiversity.

JUSTIFIED

Many medical and life-extending technologies are also unnatural.

Environment is as important as genetics for producing the traits of any organism.

We can regulate cloning to stop people using it for morally dubious reasons.

People are unlikely to resort to cloning unless it is the only way they can have a child.

"Clones are simply identical twins."

Richard Dawkins, biologist

POLITICAL PHILOSOPHY

Political philosophy looks at the relationship between the individual and the state. Its chief concerns are the nature of political power and the ways in which it is justified.

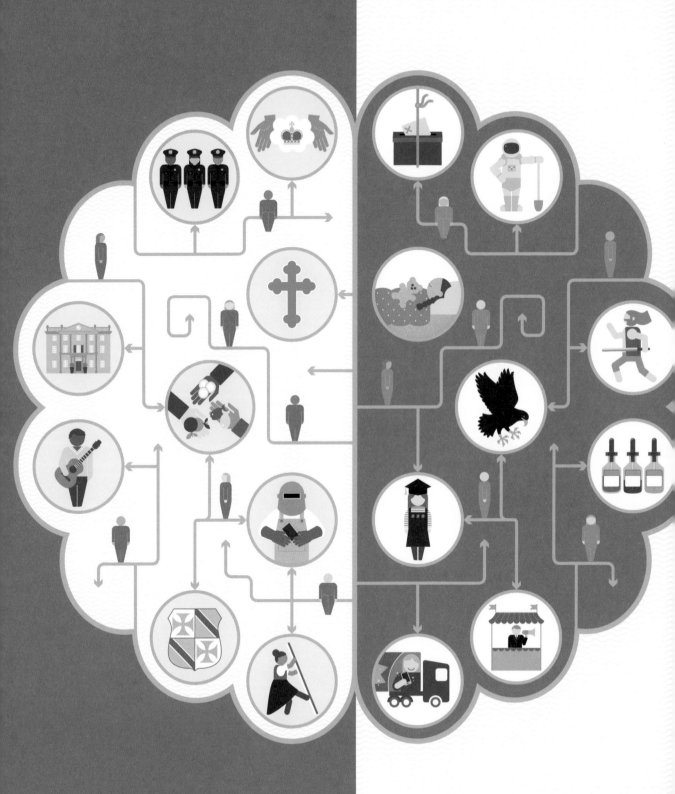

POLITICAL PHILOSOPHY

The field of political philosophy examines how society, the state, the government, the judiciary, and the individual relate to one another. It seeks to understand the nature of political power—particularly the arguments that are used by states to justify their authority.

Like all branches of philosophy, political philosophy analyzes arguments, particularly those that claim to be based on fact. For instance, it asks: What powers should the state have over its citizens, and what rights should its citizens retain? One answer might begin with a premise about human nature—that the powers of the state should be extensive, because without it, humans would descend into civil war. Likewise, if human nature is assumed to be more cooperative, a different, less pessimistic argument can be built. These were the differences between the ideas of Thomas Hobbes and John Locke.

The key questions of political philosophy include: Who should exercise political power—an individual (monarchy), an elite group (aristocracy), or the masses (democracy)? What is the basis of political obligation? What are property rights? Should existing political structures be conserved, allowing for gradual change, or should they be swept away in the name of justice? At the present time, democratic decisions have global repercussions, raising the question of whether democracy should be defended,

and if not, what the alternatives might be. Present-day concerns include the inequalities of power and wealth distribution both within and between societies, many of which are based on class, race, or gender. Philosophers ask whether we can ever be objective in answering these questions or whether our answers merely express our particular political leanings.

Some of these questions have a long history and were discussed even in Plato's time; others are much more recent. In fact, some questions once thought to have been settled have returned. For example, not so long ago, fascism was considered dead, permanently discredited by the horrors of the mid-20th century. However, depending on how we define the term, it may be back. How should we react? Other questions go even deeper. Today, some politicians claim that "objective truth" is a myth. They argue that there are no objective facts, only different ways of looking at the world, all of which are equally valid. They may argue, for example, that positions taken on the nature of climate change are all equally plausible. According to this idea, the truth is "tribal," or local to specific communities.

Perhaps all questions of political philosophy reflect a concern with the events of the age. However, they all have a common root: they oblige us to examine the nature of objective truth and to determine in what sense, if any, it differs from mere opinion.

Who should rule?

In the modern world, democracy—rule by the people—is widely considered to be the ideal form of government. However, in the past, philosophers have sometimes championed rule by a monarch or an elite aristocratic group.

Finding legitimacy

Various defenses have been made for rule by a minority group or a single individual. Ancient Greek and Roman rulers claimed to be descended from gods, or even named themselves deities. Plato made a more practical case for aristocracy (rule by the best) in the *Republic*. Disgusted by his mentor Socrates' forced suicide after being convicted of impiety by a citizen jury, Plato argued that in a democracy, an uneducated electorate could be swayed into making bad decisions by populists. Therefore, only a group of wise, impartial philosophers could be trusted to rule sensibly.

Medieval philosophers such as Thomas Aquinas, who asserted that government should reflect the heavenly order, put forward original theological justifications for monarchy (rule by an individual). This train of thought persisted into the 17th century, when Thomas Hobbes defended monarchy on the basis of "natural law" (see pp.202–203), by which a monarch protects society from falling into chaos.

Forms of rule

Although they may seem unpalatable today, vigorous cases have been made for both monarchy and aristocracy. These arguments tend to favor stability and security over the protection of individual freedoms.

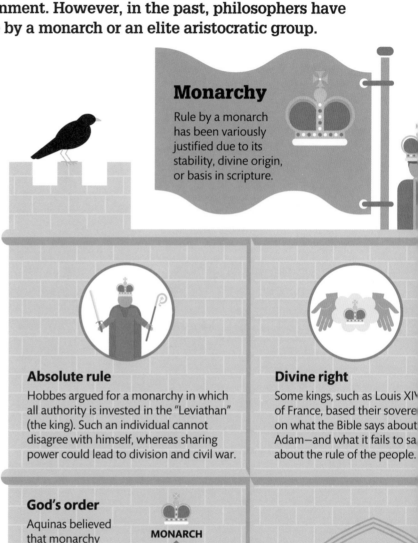

Monarchy

Rule by a monarch has been variously justified due to its stability, divine origin, or basis in scripture.

Absolute rule

Hobbes argued for a monarchy in which all authority is invested in the "Leviathan" (the king). Such an individual cannot disagree with himself, whereas sharing power could lead to division and civil war.

Divine right

Some kings, such as Louis XI◆ of France, based their sovere◆ on what the Bible says about Adam—and what it fails to sa◆ about the rule of the people.

God's order

Aquinas believed that monarchy reflects God's singular rule. It is checked by the aristocracy, which is drawn from the people, so it can still enjoy the representative benefits of a republic.

MONARCH

ARISTOCRACY

THE PEOPLE

PRINCIPLES FOR RULERS

Aristotle's *Politics* (c.335 BCE) gives advice to all rulers.

❯ **For the good of all** Rulers must govern for the good of everyone, not according to their own interests. If not, monarchy falls into tyranny, aristocracy into oligarchy, and democracy into mob rule.

❯ **By virtue** Those who are most virtuous have the strongest claim to authority.

❯ **Rule of law** Whether monarchy, aristocracy, or democracy, rulers must govern according to the law.

Aristocracy

In the *Republic* (c.380 BCE), Plato calls for rule by an elite caste of philosopher kings and queens.

IT'S FOR YOUR OWN GOOD!

Rule by the best

Plato believed that aristocratic rule by a select group of philosophers was the only way to prevent a descent through four stages of government, ending in tyranny.

1 Timocracy
Those with private property and military honor dominate society.

2 Oligarchy
The ruling class acts in its own interest, exploiting the poorest in society.

3 Democracy
Citizens abuse their freedom and pursue individual, conflicting wills.

4 Tyranny
An absolute ruler suppresses the populace with a despotic state.

? ? ? ?

Philosopher kings/queens

Plato argued that the only fit rulers are philosophers because they were:

❯ **Incorruptible** by power, wealth, or prestige.

❯ **Immune** to poor arguments and deceits that fool the uneducated.

❯ **Burdened by** no greater care than the philosophical desire for the truth.

❯ **Committed** to careful deliberation.

Justifying absolute rule

Some philosophers have argued that political authority protects humans from a "state of nature"—a hypothetical scenario that contrasts unfavorably with civil society and government.

Perpetual conflict

In *Leviathan* (1651), Thomas Hobbes (1588–1679) argued that, stripped of the veneer of civilization, men were rational but driven by their natural self-interest and "appetites and aversions" to compete and conflict. Writing during the bloodshed and upheaval of the English Civil War, this might be a forgivable conclusion, but the state of nature Hobbes describes is terrifying: life is "solitary, poor, nasty, brutish, and short."

Hobbes argues for the necessity of a sovereign (an absolute ruler ominously titled "Leviathan") who can bring order and peace, ending the state of perpetual war. Men—and women, named explicitly by Hobbes—agree to a social contract to establish this authority figure, who alone has the power to prevent a return to a state of nature. Hobbes goes on to identify key features of the agreement to set up the civil state, and the reason to obey the government—the terrifying state of nature is the only alternative. Citizens must surrender virtually all their rights—to resist is destructive of the essence of government. The contract is permanent and cannot be revoked—citizens are subjects in perpetuity.

At a time when others argued for a divine right of kings, Hobbes's justification for monarchy was unusual in that it was logical and reasoned, and controversial in assuming that there are rights in the state of nature.

Leviathan brings order

Hobbes argued that mankind's existence in the state of nature is so brutal that peace is only possible under an absolute sovereign, whose protection enables society to flourish.

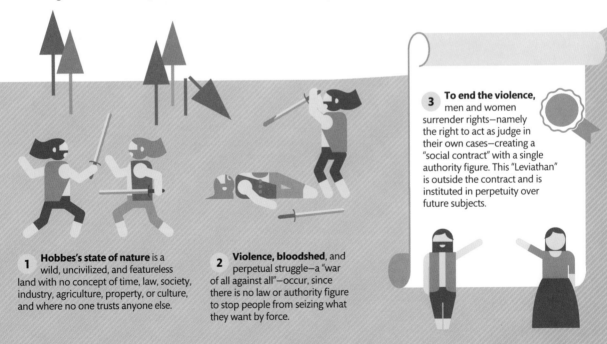

1 **Hobbes's state of nature** is a wild, uncivilized, and featureless land with no concept of time, law, society, industry, agriculture, property, or culture, and where no one trusts anyone else.

2 **Violence, bloodshed,** and perpetual struggle—a "war of all against all"—occur, since there is no law or authority figure to stop people from seizing what they want by force.

3 **To end the violence,** men and women surrender rights—namely the right to act as judge in their own cases—creating a "social contract" with a single authority figure. This "Leviathan" is outside the contract and is instituted in perpetuity over future subjects.

ARGUMENTS FOR ABSOLUTISM

》 **Parliamentary systems are inferior.** Due to their inherent instability, Hobbes settles on monarchy as the most stable form of state— a monarch cannot disagree with itself.

》 **Monarch needs absolute power to deter civil war.** The risk of a return to the state of nature is too great to allow citizens their rights.

》 **The social contract is irrevocable.** Citizens submit to absolute rule because peace under the Leviathan is preferable to anarchy and bloodshed in the state of nature.

ABSOLUTE RULE

WILL OF THE PEOPLE

RELIGIOUS POWER

MILITARY POWER

5 **To guarantee peace**, the Leviathan rules with absolute power—wielding the twin weapons of military and religious authority—and cannot be overthrown.

4 **Individuals surrender autonomy** to the Leviathan, who keeps the peace, enforces the social contract, and prevents society from returning to a state of nature.

Government by the people

Writing in the 17th century, John Locke developed a version of the "state of nature" and "social contract" to argue for a government that guarantees what he saw as God-given human rights.

Natural liberty

In contrast to Thomas Hobbes's "state of nature," that of John Locke (1632–1704) is one based on equality established by God, in which no one has more power than another, and men are free. But while "it is a state of liberty, it is not a state of license." Its populace is rational and disinclined to harm others or to steal their possessions. Unlike Hobbes's state of nature, Locke's is a peaceful place in which people respect each other, and where respect for property claims is a key principle. It is emphatically not a state of civil war.

People in the state of nature each retain the "executive power of the law of nature"—the right to act as judges in their own cases—so Locke argues that it is helpful to appoint a civil government to deal with some issues, such as competing property rights. Any such government must respect rights: "No one can be put out of his estate and subjected to the political power of another without his consent."

Built on consent

In Locke's theory, the government is founded with the consent of free, equal, propertied, rights-holding citizens and must behave in accordance with their wishes. Its primary function is to preserve property.

1 **Men and women exist in a "state of nature,"** and have God-given capacities for reason, cooperation, and property holding.

2 **Disputes about property** may arise, although people are disinclined to harm or steal from one another in the state of nature.

3 **Men and women agree to a social contract to form a government**, which can adjudicate on the competing property claims of its citizens, guaranteeing their God-given rights. In doing so, they leave the state of nature.

Limited government

Locke argues for a limited government, asserting that citizens are obliged to obey the government because it is formed with and acts upon, their consent. The only right people must surrender is the power to decide their own legal cases. Above all, the government's chief end is the preservation of property. Crucially, the social contract that forms the government is revocable. Locke is no revolutionary, but he states that: "When law ends, tyranny begins, and when that is the case, whosoever in authority may be opposed."

Locke's ideas underscored the Glorious Revolution of 1688 (against King James II of England) and were hugely influential to Thomas Jefferson when he wrote the Declaration of Independence 100 years later.

BOUNDARIES OF STATE POWER

❯ **All are subject to the rule of law.** In a civil society, "no man ... can be exempted from its laws"—even monarchs, law-makers, and political leaders.

❯ **No absolute power or divine right of kings.** Monarchs are not invested with their sovereignty by God, and their power is defined, not unlimited.

❯ **No coercion into "state" religion.** Individuals should have liberty with regard to religion, which should not be "propagated by force of arms."

❯ **Majority rule.** The state must have the consent of a majority of the people, who retain the right to rebellion.

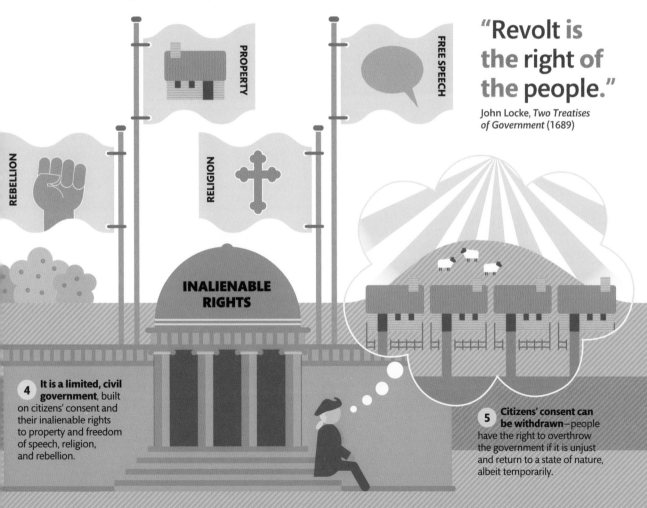

PROPERTY

FREE SPEECH

REBELLION

RELIGION

INALIENABLE RIGHTS

"Revolt is the right of the people."

John Locke, *Two Treatises of Government* (1689)

4 **It is a limited, civil government**, built on citizens' consent and their inalienable rights to property and freedom of speech, religion, and rebellion.

5 **Citizens' consent can be withdrawn**—people have the right to overthrow the government if it is unjust and return to a state of nature, albeit temporarily.

Popular sovereignty

In *The Social Contract*, Jean-Jacques Rousseau asked what kind of government could preserve the benefits of society—such as property and law—while still allowing everyone to remain as free as before.

Humanity in chains

Like Hobbes and Locke, Rousseau (1712–1778) based his theories on the idea of a "state of nature" and "social contract." His state of nature is a place in which people are primarily happy and cooperative and can enjoy freedom. But under government, society becomes more unequal, the rich dominate the poor, and violence and insecurity become endemic. As Rousseau wrote: "Man is born free, but is everywhere in chains."

Rousseau's solution was controversial and obscure. He proposed that "each of us must put himself under the supreme direction of the General Will, in which every member is an indivisible part of the whole." Rousseau gives no definition of this idea, but explains that it is not representative democracy, since law that has not been ratified by everyone is by definition void.

Forced to be free

Rousseau states that under the General Will, everyone "will be forced to be free" and that "the citizen consents to all the laws, even to those that are passed against his will. The constant will of all the members of state is the General Will." To avoid the danger of one particular group coming to dominate, Rousseau suggests that there should be no permanent political factions. This does not necessarily make Rousseau a totalitarian. On *The Social Contract*'s title page, he is described as a citizen of Geneva, a Swiss city-state that held all public votes in an open-air assembly, with no factions permitted. Resolutions emerged from public discussion, and all citizens were therefore attached to the ultimate decision. As Rousseau acknowledges, this can only occur in small republics, so his concept of the General Will may perhaps be more appropriate for local councils than nation states.

> ## "[In] the General Will ... members are an indivisible part of the whole."
>
> Jean-Jacques Rousseau, *The Social Contract*, 1762

From all and for all

Central to Rousseau's notion of the General Will is that citizens are part of something bigger than themselves—a collective decision-making process—and closely bound to the community of which they are a part.

GUIDING PRINCIPLES

Rational vs. affective

Rousseau opposed the Enlightenment drive toward rationalism that dominated his age, believing that reason can corrupt man's natural tendencies to freedom and happiness. Instead, he argued that feelings—the "affective"—should take priority. Pride in and love for community will lead to participation in the General Will.

RATIONAL   VS.   AFFECTIVE

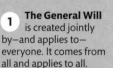

1 The **General Will** is created jointly by—and applies to—everyone. It comes from all and applies to all.

2 It is expressed in the form of laws that are not intrusive, but instead protect individual freedoms.

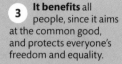

3 It benefits all people, since it aims at the common good, and protects everyone's freedom and equality.

Popular sovereignty

There is no need for a sovereign or representatives in government—the people enact direct democracy themselves.

DEMOCRATIC SYSTEMS

Direct democracy

In a direct democracy, every citizen votes on policy. It was first seen in ancient Athens in the c.5th century BCE, when citizens voted on policy issues in a public square. For Rousseau, freedom means obedience to a law that we have had a direct hand in making.

Representative democracy

The most common modern democratic system, representative democracy involves citizens electing politicians to act as their representatives. Rousseau condemned this as a betrayal of power that the citizen alone should exercise.

General Will

Voting as an assembly of citizens—free of political parties, social groupings, or factions—people exercise popular sovereignty.

Education

Citizens should be educated from an early age to nurture their natural good tendencies, further inclining them toward the General Will.

How are property rights justified?

In his *Second Treatise of Government*, John Locke examined how property is acquired in a "state of nature" and how rights to it are justified, protected, and passed on.

Property begins in a state of nature

Thomas Hobbes argued that property requires an agreement between people, which can only occur under the protection of a government (see pp.202–203). Locke disagreed, arguing that property is acquired in a "state of nature" (see pp.204–205). He believed the world was given by God to people in common, and that every person has property in themselves—literally possessing their own body—in their labor and in what they produce. When a person works the land and has "mixed his labor with it … he thereby makes it his property." There is no limit to how much property can be acquired, as long as each person "leaves enough and as good for others to follow him," not taking more land than is necessary to provide for their own needs, producing more than can be consumed, or wasting the common stock. To avoid waste, people may trade surplus perishables—such as plums—for goods that will keep—nuts, for instance—without violating the justice of the way property is first acquired.

Locke sees no injustice in trading produce for money. As the value of money is not based on labor or property, it allows for the accumulation of wealth and inequality. Also, Locke's view that property claims are made by laboring on the land implies that unclaimed land can be seized simply by working it, which could be seen as a justification for colonialism.

5 Property is passed on by inheritance, renewing the social contract and legitimizing the government.

4 Money and excess goods are exchanged, even if it leads to imbalances of wealth.

Inheritance brings consent

Locke argued that by inheriting property, people tacitly consent to a government that they had no part in creating because they need that government to protect their property rights. In doing this, they renew the "social contract" and confer legitimacy on the state. Locke's argument may have been an attempt to deter regular elections, which risked upsetting property allocation.

MINE!

1

People "mix" their labor with the land, thereby staking a property claim.

Social contract renewed

2

People agree a social contract, creating a government that protects their property claims.

Individuals take from the "common stock" what they need to survive, but may also trade surplus goods.

3

Flaws in Locke's theory

Locke's justification of property runs into problems on several counts. He is unclear on how much labor is required to claim a property and what constitutes labor itself. For instance, if an astronaut grows carrots on Mars, has labor been mixed with the whole planet, or just a part of it? Is it sufficient to fence off a property, or does this simply lay claim to the strip of land on which the fence stands? If someone owns tomato juice and pours it into the sea, do they then own the sea?

MARS

UM ...

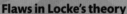

UTILITARIANS AND PROPERTY

Utilitarian philosophers (see pp.186–187) justify property and wealth not through how they are acquired and exchanged, but by whether their distribution produces the greatest happiness of the greatest number. For instance, a utilitarian might argue for a progressive income tax, since the financial pain to higher-rate taxpayers is outweighed by the benefits that the majority of people receive from public services that the government can fund with tax revenue.

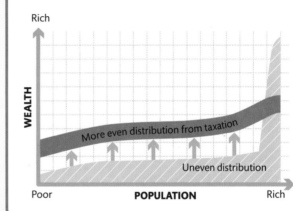

Rich

WEALTH

More even distribution from taxation

Uneven distribution

Poor **POPULATION** Rich

Consent and obligation

In a democracy, government rests on the consent of the governed, but the source of this consent and the obligations it confers upon the citizens of a state have implications for the nature of government.

Why should we obey?

Thomas Hobbes thought that our obligation to obey the government derives from our desire to prevent a return to a "state of nature," which was so unpleasant that no abuse of power by the state could be worse. John Locke offered the alternative view that we are bound to obey the state by consenting to its creation through a "social contract."

However, most people are born into a society with a preexisting contract, so they have no chance to object to it. Locke argued that consent can be given tacitly, as well as explicitly—using government services, inheriting property, or traveling freely on the highway may amount to giving tacit consent.

This is a much-debated idea. A passive act, such as inheriting property, does not appear to signal approval for the government or generate an obligation to obey it. However, Locke avoids the question of reopening the social contract for every new generation.

Explicit consent

The issue of consent was revisited in Nozick's 1974 work *Anarchy, State, and Utopia.* As part of an argument in favor of a libertarian society, he introduced a thought experiment in which local residents find a broadcast system and decide to start a public entertainment service. Each person runs the station for a day. Nozick questions whether, after enjoying listening to the music and stories for months, residents are obliged to participate.

Nozick's answer is unequivocal: "surely not." He argues that giving a benefit to someone who has had no say in its creation cannot create an obligation. Nozick thus rejects Locke's argument that inheriting property, traveling on a highway, or receiving any other unsolicited benefit can generate obligation. Tacit consent of a government does not create the obligation to obey it— only explicit consent can do so. For the libertarian Nozick, tacit consent therefore provides no justification for any more than the most minimal of governments.

ELECTORAL CONSENT

To the modern eye, there is a neat solution to Locke's reluctance to reopen the social contract for each generation: through the ballot box. In modern democracies, elections confer citizens' consent upon the government and generate the individual's obligation to obey. However, it might be argued that at elections, citizens only choose the make-up of a government; they do not give consent to its form.

By voting regularly in elections, citizens consent to being governed and reaffirm the social contract.

"One cannot just ... give people benefits and expect an obligation in return."

Robert Nozick

Participation and obligation

In Robert Nozick's hypothetical scenario, your neighborhood benefits from a community-run broadcast service. You are given no choice in the matter, but are expected to host the station for a day. Are you obliged to comply?

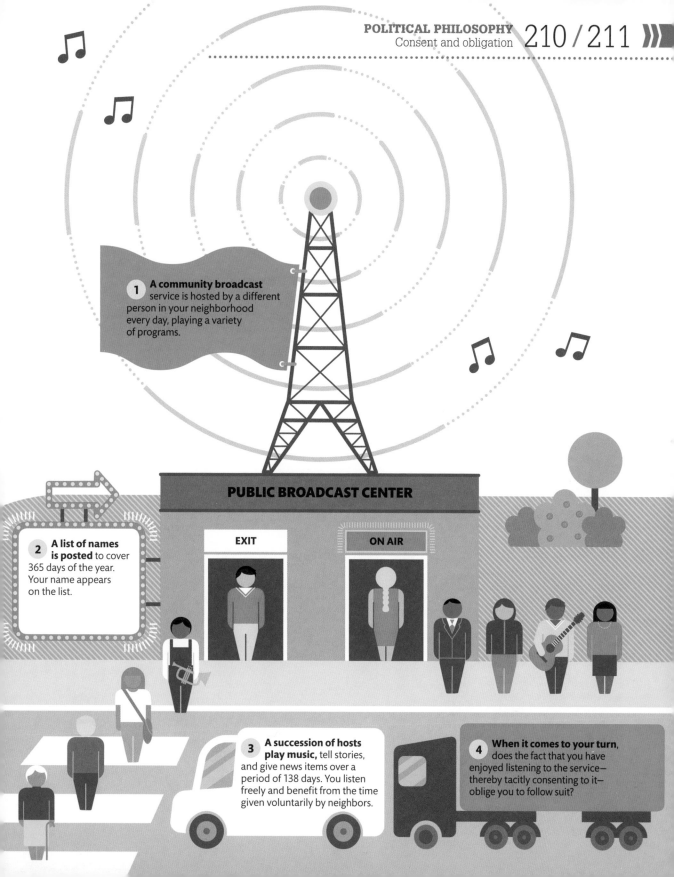

1 **A community broadcast** service is hosted by a different person in your neighborhood every day, playing a variety of programs.

PUBLIC BROADCAST CENTER

EXIT

ON AIR

2 **A list of names is posted** to cover 365 days of the year. Your name appears on the list.

3 **A succession of hosts play music,** tell stories, and give news items over a period of 138 days. You listen freely and benefit from the time given voluntarily by neighbors.

4 **When it comes to your turn,** does the fact that you have enjoyed listening to the service—thereby tacitly consenting to it—oblige you to follow suit?

What rights should people enjoy?

Most democracies guarantee their citizens a wide range of freedoms. One simple principle for deciding which rights states should permit was put forward by the Victorian philosopher John Stuart Mill.

Accommodating views

Mill (1806–1873) rejected the idea of democratically determined systems of rights, fearing a tyranny of the majority that represses those with minority views. Instead, he argued for extensive rights, determined by the "Principle of Harm," which asserts that limits should only be applied to freedoms that might harm others or cause a restriction i n their rights and freedoms. This liberal idea permits freedom of expression and religion and includes the right to consensual sex with a partner, among other things.

Mill was writing at a time when religious persecution was a recent memory and homosexuality was illegal. But his principle clearly defends any right or view—no matter how in the minority it is—so long as no one affected is harmed.

Principle of Harm

In Mill's "marketplace of ideas," people are welcome to express any view that does not cause harm. If a true view is suppressed, people lose the chance to exchange an erroneous viewpoint for truth. If a false view is suppressed, individuals are denied the opportunity to challenge or reaffirm an opinion they had considered true. However, it is possible that some freedoms that do not appear harmful may inadvertently cause or enable the hurting of others.

The right to offend

For Mill, the act of causing offense does not constitute "harm"; he expected points of view to be robust. However, this raises the question of hate speech and acts of racial provocation, and whether we should have the right to be gratuitously offensive to vulnerable groups. Even if we do not share in the offense, we can often see that the harm is genuine.

How far to tolerate the views of the intolerant—such as authoritarian extremists who would have no compunction in bringing all rights to an end—is a classic liberal dilemma. Some draw a line between views advocated as doctrine and views expressed in order to incite action that could cause measurable harm. But this neat distinction may fail to prevent harm in practical situations.

EXCESS LIBERTY
The marketplace of ideas is itself a contested notion. The right to express a false view—such as shouting "fire!" in a crowded theater—could have unintended consequences.

DAMAGING IDEAS
The only rights and beliefs that should be excluded from the marketplace of ideas are those that may cause harm to others.

SELF-REGARDING ACTIONS

The Principle of Harm applies to views and actions that affect other people, but Mill does not reveal his view of self-regarding actions, which affect only oneself. In principle, actions that only affect the individual can cause no harm to others and appear to be protected by the Principle of Harm. However, even private acts have the potential to do public harm. For instance, since it does no harm to regularly drink alcohol to excess in private at home, it could be claimed that this right is protected by the Harm Principle. However, if the majority of the population exercised this right, there could be a significant negative effect on society. Again, the question of harm arises, but it is difficult to pinpoint exactly when this harm, or the potential for harm, is reached.

FREEDOM OF SPEECH
What happens if fascists use freedom of speech for their own ends, such as curbing freedoms?

FREEDOM OF CHOICE
If brown shoes sell the most, is freedom of choice harming producers of black shoe polish?

FREEDOM OF RELIGION
Should religious tolerance include all beliefs, even those that persecute other faiths?

Marketplace of ideas

HARMFUL IDEAS NOT PERMITTED

"**All ideas** need to be heard, because **each idea** contains one aspect **of the** truth."

John Stuart Mill, *On Liberty* (1859)

Kinds of liberty

In the 20th century, philosophers and politicians redefined the traditional notion of liberty, stressing that freedom has both positive and negative meanings.

Defining freedom

Modern thinking about liberty has moved beyond Mill's definition of liberty as simply a lack of constraint on individuals (see pp.212–213). In the 20th century, politicians such as Franklin D. Roosevelt in the US and William Beveridge in Britain, as well as the Russian-British philosopher Isaiah Berlin, identified various problems with this idea. In his essay *Two Concepts of Freedom*, Berlin argued that, if pursued to its logical conclusion, liberty as a lack of constraint (that is, freedom to act, speak, and join associations without coercion from authorities) can easily become illiberal. As he wrote: "Men are largely interdependent, and no man's activity is so completely private as never to obstruct the lives of others." In other words, one man's liberty can also be another man's impoverishment—or, as Berlin puts it: "Freedom for the pike is death for the minnow." Freedom of expression, for example, can lead to hate speech, and so to the demonization of minorities.

Berlin's point is that "freedom" is a complex concept, and that in political discussion, it frequently leads to confusion. To help matters, he distinguished between "positive freedom" (freedom to live one's life) and "negative freedom" (freedom from constraint). He argued that a liberal society is

Four freedoms

In 1941, President Franklin D. Roosevelt proposed "four freedoms" that everyone in the world should enjoy. These included two positive liberties—freedom of speech and freedom of worship—and two negative liberties—freedom from poverty and freedom from fear (specifically fear of military aggression). Each type of liberty is insufficient in itself and needs to be balanced by the other.

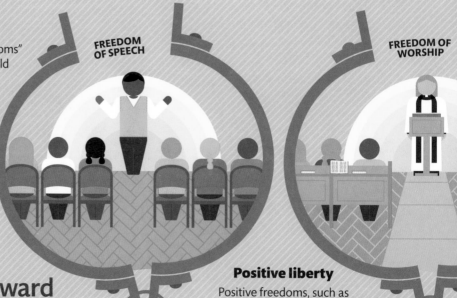

FREEDOM OF SPEECH

FREEDOM OF WORSHIP

Positive liberty
Positive freedoms, such as freedom of speech and freedom of worship, ensure that individuals can speak and practice religion without being obstructed by the state or other individuals.

"... we look forward to a world founded upon four essential freedoms."

Franklin D. Roosevelt, *State of the Union Address* (1941)

one in which both aspects of liberty should be satisfied, which inevitably leads to compromise.

The limits of liberty

Philosophers have since argued that although negative freedom may be a necessary condition for liberty, it is not sufficient to guarantee it. The reason for this is that freedom of expression, for example, is worthless to people who are half-naked, illiterate, or starving. As the Senator Henry Cabot Lodge once wrote: "A hungry man is more interested in sandwiches than freedoms." Philosophers have thus balanced freedom from constraint with other kinds of freedom—such as freedom from squalor, want, and disease. Such freedoms are effectively entitlements (to food, shelter, and so on), which require that others in society provide them.

A government may enforce this by raising taxes, which some may see as an infringement of liberty. Immanuel Kant (see pp.184–185) described such intervention as "the greatest despotism imaginable," which may sound exaggerated to modern ears. However, such measures could justifiably be called authoritarian and will always be argued by some to be illiberal.

NEED TO KNOW

> **Positive freedom** is freedom to live one's life without social and economic insecurity—specifically freedom from coercion by the state and other individuals.

> **Negative freedom** is freedom from constraints— particularly freedom from abject poverty.

> **Franklin D. Roosevelt** proposed his "four freedoms" only months before the Japanese Navy Air Service bombed Pearl Harbor, an event that highlighted the need for a right to be free from fear.

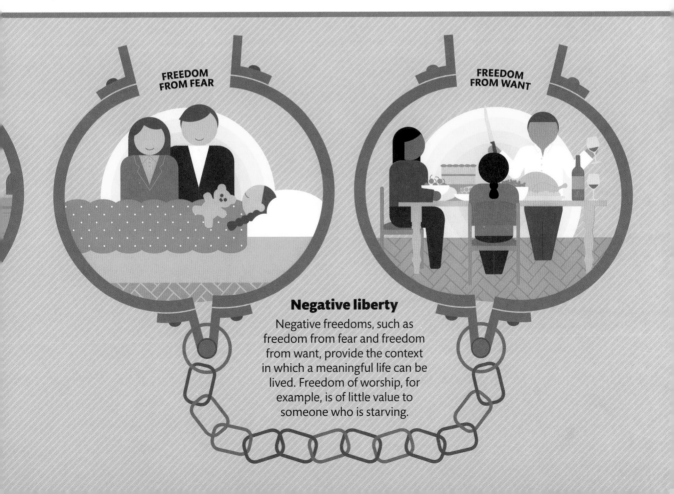

FREEDOM FROM FEAR

FREEDOM FROM WANT

Negative liberty

Negative freedoms, such as freedom from fear and freedom from want, provide the context in which a meaningful life can be lived. Freedom of worship, for example, is of little value to someone who is starving.

Should rights be limited?

Some philosophers argue that the rights of individuals, or even those of minority groups, should be limited when they come into conflict with the security and stability of society as a whole.

Extensive rights

People in Western democracies enjoy more rights than ever before. Many countries now guarantee full suffrage, protection against discrimination, freedom of speech, reproductive rights, the right to form groups such as trade unions, legal processes that ensure that the accused are treated fairly, and legal protections for the vulnerable. But are there grounds for limiting these rights? Benjamin Franklin wrote: "Those who would give up liberty to purchase a little safety deserve

Degrees of freedom

In practice, most people would reject the extremes of strictly limited rights (authoritarianism) and few or no limits to rights (libertarianism or anarchism). In real-world politics, curbs to freedoms can only be justified in the interests of the majority, but the specifics of those interests can be controversial. For example, many countries have restricted the right to freedom of speech by introducing laws against hate speech, but what gives offense to some may be regarded as harmless by others. The need for national security, particularly when many countries face a genuine threat of terrorism, might also override the rights of expression, privacy, and protest. Mass migration has made most developed countries increasingly multicultural, meaning that the right to free expression of religious and cultural practice also needs to be handled carefully. Liberal culturalists recommend an inclusive, permissive approach, whereas nostalgic communitarians argue that minorities should conform to the dominant cultural norms of the society that they live in.

EXTREME

2

1

LIMITED RIGHTS

1 Shackling individual rights

Authoritarian governments are primarily concerned with protecting the state and preserving order. They tend to place heavy limits on the rights of citizens in order to maintain the regime and to protect themselves against criticism or challenge.

2 Acting in the national interest

Many states justify the limiting of individual rights in the national interest. These states may, for example, seek to override privacy rights by extending powers of surveillance or ignore human rights by using torture in interrogations.

neither liberty nor safety," but some philosophers argue that to counter global threats, such as terrorism, people should sacrifice some of their rights in the interests of the wider community.

Justifiable limits

Thomas Hobbes argued that to enjoy the benefits of the state, citizens must surrender their rights (see pp.202–203). He believed that limiting the rights of individuals was the only way to impose order, and that a failure to do so would lead to civil war in what he called a "state of nature."

A classic philosophical example of individual rights threatening public security is when someone exercises their right to free speech by shouting "Fire!" in a crowded theater. It could be argued that the potentially dangerous consequences for members of the public justify limiting this right to free speech.

✓ NEED TO KNOW

❯ **Liberal culturalists** advocate protecting the identities and needs of minority groups.

❯ **Communitarians** emphasize the role of the community in defining and shaping moral concepts.

❯ **Libertarians** argue for a smaller state and greater personal liberty.

❯ **Anarchists** believe that people should live free of government.

MODERATE

3

"Freedom of speech is a central pillar of a free government."

Benjamin Franklin, *On Freedom of Speech and the Press* (1737)

Striking a balance
When deciding whether—and where—to place limits on people's rights, governments must balance individual freedoms against collective responsibilities within a framework of what society deems acceptable.

EXTREME

4

LIMITLESS RIGHTS

3 Protecting minority rights

Social changes have created increasingly diverse societies. A communitarian view suggests that rights should be kept broadly in line with the values and norms of the majority, while a liberal culturalist position aims to protect minority rights.

4 Dismantling limits on rights

Libertarians argue that people are rational enough to be self-governing and believe that state powers should be limited as much as possible. Anarchists believe that there should be no limits to human rights and that no one has dominion over another.

How should we manage change?

Political philosophy explores how to improve society and how change should be introduced. Edmund Burke and Karl Marx offered contrasting arguments for both steady reform from above, and radical revolution from below.

To conserve or overthrow

Although it might be assumed that a conservative approach to the question of change would be to resist it entirely, this is not exactly how most conservatives think. As Burke wrote in his classic defense of conservatism *Reflections on the Revolution in France* (1790), "a state without the means of some change is without the means of its conservation." Burke believed respect for institutions and traditions—"prejudices," as he called it—holds society together. Change is introduced by the elite and occurs slowly, steadily, and in the best interests of society as a whole.

Proponents of radical change argue instead that institutions serve elites who are unlikely to permit change that might erode their position. The only way to achieve change is through wholesale revolution.

MEASURED CHANGE FROM ABOVE

Burke (1729–1797) commended inherited governance—for instance, the British system of the crown, peerage, and inherited privileges—because it combines the principle of conservation with the possibility of improvement and change. In his view, the stability of a society is guaranteed by respect for institutions, which are justified by their longevity and their contribution to society in the past. A people "will not look forward to posterity who never look backward to their ancestors." Subversion of the state is no way to bring about reform; any change must be gradual and carry forward the tried and tested—those features known to work, which have lasted over time. In Burke's words, "Such a mode of reforming might take many years ... Circumspection and caution are a part of wisdom."

Conservative views of change

> **Society can be understood** as a contract between the living, their ancestors, and those not yet born.

> **The glue of society** is the sentiments or affections for its established constitution, processes, or institutions.

> **Reform of the state** should occur incrementally and slowly, not upsetting its existing structure and traditions.

> **The privileged elite** are the agents of change, overseeing improvements, such as state-sponsored education and democratic reform, that benefit society as a whole.

IDEOLOGIES IN PRACTICE

Conservative shortcomings

Burke's model allows a considered pace of change, but relies on the elite to recognize and bring about necessary reforms. However, where those changes might impact on the interests of the elite, change often stalls as a result.

Left-wing thinkers argue that rather than being a source of benevolent change, the state remains a mechanism for serving the interests of the elite—and that the working classes still labor in unpleasant employment, with few workers' rights, more than a century after Marx first championed their cause. In reality, it is hard to see how Burke's defense of the status quo and its mechanisms for reproducing itself can allow change, and Burke offers few practical examples of how it might do so.

Revolutionary flaws

Marx's model of revolutionary change involves the wholesale dismantling of society. This carries the risk foreseen by Burke: that we cannot anticipate or control what happens after the moorings of society have been cut.

Although it predated Marxism by a century, the popular uprising of the French Revolution ended with Napoleon Bonaparte's militaristic rule. The Russian Revolution of 1917 was directly inspired by Marxist thought and was followed by the brutal repression of Stalin's Soviet communism. Neither outcome was what most of the revolutionaries had hoped for. The end result in both cases supports the charge that revolutionary change is too often followed by a vacuum filled by tyrannical regimes.

REVOLUTION FROM BELOW

Karl Marx (1818–1883) called for a more radical form of change. In his many works, Marx claimed that history is marked by repeating cycles of class conflict. He argued that in capitalist societies, the state is simply an executive committee for managing the common affairs of the bourgeoisie, the predominant controlling (middle) class. In his view, this social group will not allow gradual change to challenge its position of power. Marx saw socialist revolution as an inevitable event—the product of increasing exploitation of the proletariat (working) class, who are pressed into ever more degrading and unfulfilling work. He regarded these working-class revolutionaries as vanguards of a new society, ushering in an era of new social relations between people.

Revolutionary views of change

> **Human history** is best characterized as a continuing process of class struggle, driven by inequality between the proletariat and the bourgeoisie.

> **Change to this cycle** will be effected through a socialist uprising of workers, who will overthrow the old order and establish a new form of society.

> **The workers** are at the forefront of the new social order, claiming what is rightfully theirs and collectively bringing about a more egalitarian, communist system.

To work is human nature

The philosopher Karl Marx believed that people are inclined to work cooperatively and creatively, but that this natural tendency is exploited by the capitalist system.

Understanding humanity

Marx's view of human nature and the role of the state was markedly different from that of his predecessors. Thomas Hobbes, for instance, considered humans to be selfish and aggressive, and so in need of a strong government to prevent civil war (see pp.202–203). John Locke, meanwhile, had a more generous view (see pp.204–205). Like Marx, Locke saw men and women as naturally cooperative, but he argued for a government to safeguard certain natural rights. For Marx, human nature—which he termed "species character"—is to

work: to collectively and creatively produce an outcome or item that belongs to the worker. This product is an externalization of the worker's character, and so the act of creating it through work is inherently satisfying. Governments, however, deny people this "natural condition"—the liberty and ability to express their human nature.

Capitalist exploitation

Marx believed that the entire capitalist economic system—of

which the political superstructure is merely the most visible part— oppresses workers in order to maximize profit. For Marx, the nature of most people's work in the capitalist system is not fulfilling.

Because of the division of labor, to increase efficiency, workers are more specialized and distanced from the finished product. As the development of capitalism accelerates, the workers become progressively more alienated from their activity, its output, and the

Marx's labor theory

Marx believed that the capitalist method of production alienates workers from the process and product of their work and from other people, with whom they no longer freely cooperate, but must compete with for employment.

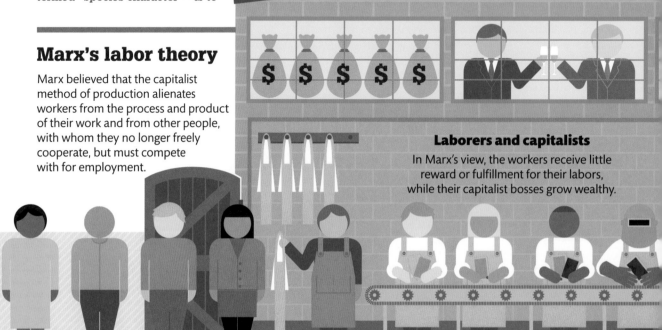

Laborers and capitalists
In Marx's view, the workers receive little reward or fulfillment for their labors, while their capitalist bosses grow wealthy.

people around them, degrading the social aspect of work. Workers no longer freely cooperate to produce something satisfying, but must instead compete for employment.

Labor as commodity

Under capitalism, workers possess only their labor—which becomes a commodity—rather than the product itself. What they make is no longer theirs, but belongs to capitalists. The harder they work, the more profit they make for their employers, who demand higher productivity, requiring yet more labor from the workers.

OVERTHROWING REPRESSION

According to Marx, to keep the capitalist system in place, the political superstructure—the state—must ensure that workers accept their position. The state has the ability to subdue workers by manipulating the media, public bodies, or prominent spokespersons to create a "false consciousness," such as the belief that capitalism is good or that it cannot be replaced by anything better. Should the persuasive abilities of the state falter, it has other powers of imprisonment, coercion, and force.

Marx advocates the overthrow of the capitalist system and the states that support it so that work can once again be a freely undertaken, social, and expressive activity. The state will lose its class character and no longer be an instrument of class domination. Ultimately, it will wither away to serve a purely administrative function. Marx joins many anarchists in thinking that in an ideal world, the state should be minimal or abolished altogether.

> "The production of too many useful things results in too many useless people."
>
> Karl Marx, *Economic and Philosophic Manuscripts of 1844*

State control

Under capitalism, the state uses powers of force and coercion such as the police to ensure that workers accept their position submissively.

Enslaved by products

Workers become victims of "commodity fetishism"—the more they put into their labor, the more they feel enthralled by the products they create.

Making more objective political decisions

Most people approach political questions—such as who to vote for or what policies to support—from their own subjective viewpoint. However, some philosophers have proposed more objective ways of answering political questions.

Claiming objectivity

People often judge political ideas by what they stand to gain from them: they ask "Is it good for me?" rather than "Is this party or policy good for everyone?" The disadvantaged may want to transform the political system, but privileged groups—those with decisive political power—are less likely to welcome change.

Karl Marx thought his philosophy was objective, since he thought communism was in the interests of the vast majority of people and felt that even those who stood to lose would understand once they saw that the new order was an "association in which the free development of each is the condition for the free development of all" (see pp.218–219). With its central tenet "the greatest happiness of the greatest number," utilitarianism also claims objectivity, arguing that individuals whose interests are not served by a policy can take comfort in the fact that it should still please the majority (see pp.186–187).

John Rawls (1921–2002) proposes an alternative form of objectivity. He asks us to imagine ourselves in an "Original Position"—a hypothetical situation before society has been created, when the distribution of wealth and property has yet to be made. Behind this "veil of ignorance," we cannot know our eventual place in the social or economic hierarchy. Nor do we know what our "natural assets"—our abilities and strengths in relation to others—will be, nor our gender or ethnicity. Rawls asks: if we were behind this "veil," what principles of justice would we choose for our society, and what wealth distribution would we favor? He suggests that we would decide on two principles: the Liberty Principle and the Difference Principle (see box).

Maximize the minimum

Rawls believes that we would "maximize the minimum," ensuring that the least well-off in society are not badly disadvantaged—precisely because, on lifting the "veil," we might find ourselves in this group. Rawls argues that this would result in a fairer distribution of wealth and resources. Rawls's argument makes a case for distributive justice. His thought experiment is an appeal to something beyond our subjective positions on justice. It is an attempt to arrive at a set of ideals that most people would subscribe to and give personal political decision-making a sound philosophical basis.

"Justice **denies that the loss** of freedom **for some is made** right **by a** greater good shared **by others.**"

John Rawls, *A Theory of Justice* (1971)

Sharing liberty and wealth

In Rawls's Original Position, the veil of ignorance prevents people from knowing their relative wealth, social standing, or natural assets. Rawls believes that in this position, individuals act in the interest of all in society, choosing principles of justice that ensure that liberty and wealth are distributed fairly.

1 I want to be free.

2 I should maximize my chances of a good life.

3 I don't know where I stand in the social hierarchy.

4 I must do all I can to stay off the bottom of the economic order.

5 I don't know where I might end up in an unequal society, so I should make society as equal as possible.

RAWLS'S PRINCIPLES OF JUSTICE

Rawls suggests that in an imagined Original Position, we would most likely use two principles to create just social and economic conditions: the Liberty Principle and the Difference Principle.

Liberty Principle

The Liberty Principle would advocate equal rights to an extensive system of basic liberties.

> **Freedom of conscience** to hold beliefs and views as we choose.

> **Freedom of association** to gather with others in public or in private.

> **Freedom of expression** to convey opinions freely without fear of censure.

> **Personal property**—the right to own private property.

> **Democracy**—the freedom to exercise the right to vote.

Difference Principle

The Difference Principle would allow social or economic inequalities only on the basis of certain conditions.

> **Inequality should benefit the poorest**, so that any imbalance in wealth and opportunity positively affects those who have less.

> **Anyone can increase their wealth**, regardless of social standing, because wealth is attached to positions of power that are open to all.

Perspectivism and politics

Some philosophers have argued that perspectivism—the view that objective truth does not exist—can help us reach a consensus. For others, perspectivism risks making us ignore expert opinions.

Subjective truths

Friedrich Nietzsche (see pp.78–79) was the first to develop a version of perspectivist philosophy, arguing that there is no objective truth, only subjective interpretations that are all equally valid. This view was revived in the latter part of the 20th century, when several philosophers, including Jean-François Lyotard (1924–1998), reached similar conclusions to Nietzsche. In *The Post-Modern Condition*, Lyotard discredited what he calls Grand Narratives—attempts at any broad, sweeping narrative that claims to offer a single true account of history or civilization. He said that these Grand Narratives all claim to have at their center a Truth (with a capital T), which we should reject, and instead view the world in terms of little narratives, each based around a particular context, and all equally valid.

In *Contingency, Irony, Solidarity*, Richard Rorty (1931–2007) argued that we should "look after freedom, and truth will look after itself." He believed that a broad consensus of subjective truth is preferable to a sole, predefined objective truth. For Rorty, reaching this consensus enables us to have a greater, better-educated involvement in making political choices.

NIETZSCHE
There is no such thing as objective truth. There are only subjective, individual perspectives.

SCIENCE

LIBERALISM

Objective truth is dead

Nietzsche's perspectivism was a reaction against religion and Enlightenment ideals such as emancipation and progress. For Nietzsche, these ideals demanded the same moral standards from everyone without taking into account their individual perspectives. Lyotard also rejected Enlightenment ideals, science, and religion, seeing these as old-fashioned, oppressive Grand Narratives. Richard Rorty dismissed the idea of absolute objective truths, arguing that instead we should listen to each other and embrace the idea that truths can be expressed in different ways.

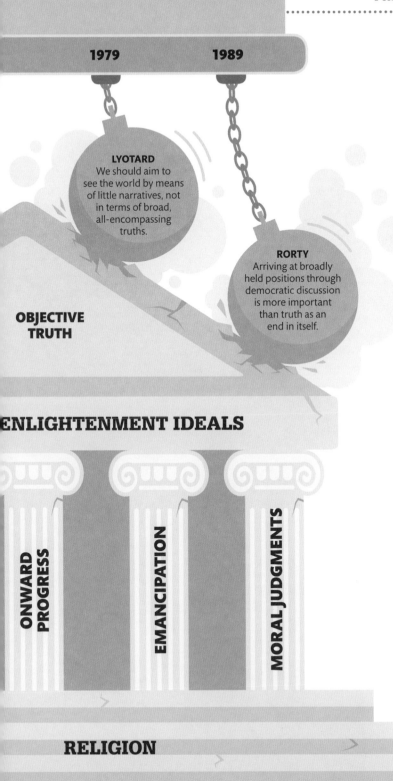

1979   1989

LYOTARD
We should aim to see the world by means of little narratives, not in terms of broad, all-encompassing truths.

RORTY
Arriving at broadly held positions through democratic discussion is more important than truth as an end in itself.

OBJECTIVE
TRUTH

ENLIGHTENMENT IDEALS

ONWARD PROGRESS

EMANCIPATION

MORAL JUDGMENTS

RELIGION

THE DANGERS OF PERSPECTIVISM

Many commentators believe that Rorty's view of individuals respecting each other's opinions and reaching a consensus of subjective truth is overly optimistic, and that perspectivism actually has dangerous implications for politics. In the absence of objective truth, individuals lose the ability to make good historical and electoral judgments. If there are no objective reference points, individuals may choose the message that suits them and believe their own interpretation of events, becoming further entrenched in their own point of view. This makes them less likely to listen to expert opinions or expose themselves to views that challenge their own. They may therefore make poor electoral choices based on insufficient information or populist appeals to simplistic solutions.

Perspectivism may also undermine political philosophy itself—without objective truth, there can be no ideal standards to aspire to. Furthermore, perspectivism is philosophically self-defeating. It claims that all points of view are equally valid, but perspectivism itself is just a point of view. It cannot assert itself as being more valid than other views.

"There are
no facts, only
interpretations."
Friedrich Nietzsche

A just war?

For centuries, political philosophers have debated the idea of whether war can ever be justified on a moral or religious basis, and if there is a moral way to fight or behave during warfare.

War and morality

Can war ever be justified? How can it be justified? How should it be conducted? Just war theory addresses these three fundamental questions about war. It mainly originated in the thinking of Christian theologians such as St. Augustine (in *The City of God*) and Thomas Aquinas (in *Summa Theologica*), who asked if war and bloodshed could ever be reconciled with morality and Christian faith.

Aquinas argued that an act of war should be a last resort, after all peaceful means of resolving a dispute between nations have been exhausted. An act of war should also have a justifiable cause. Finally, a just war should be winnable because it would be wrong to cause suffering and death with no chance of success.

In addition to these criteria for judging whether and how war can be justified (*jus ad bellum*), Aquinas provided a set of principles for how war should be conducted (*jus in bello*). The harm caused by war should not outweigh any potential gains from it; there should be a distinction between combatants and civilians; and the losers of the war should not be humiliated.

These principles offer a set of criteria by which a political power or a combatant can judge a war that they might declare or take part in, or a critic or

> ## "We do not seek peace in order to be at war, but we go to war that we may have peace."
>
> St. Augustine

Pacifism and realism

Some versions of both pacifism and realism are more extreme than others. The most extreme pacifists believe that war is always morally wrong; the most extreme realists believe that we can never make moral judgments about war. However, moderate pacifists argue that wars of self-defense are justified. Moderate realists broadly accept just war theory.

Limited engagement
Many pacifists argue that reaction to aggression must be limited and nonviolent if possible

Total nonviolence
The most committed pacifists believe that all wars are violent and therefore can never be justified.

Pacifism

historian can make retrospective judgments about whether it was right to go to war.

Modern views on war

Just war theory has faced challenges over the last century from the opposing philosophies of pacifism and realism. Pacifists reject war wherever possible, the most extreme pacifist view being that war is never justified. Realists argue that morality has no place in the judgment of conflicts and that war should instead be judged according to the national interest.

APPLYING JUST WAR PRINCIPLES

> **Geneva Conventions** These set out the international rules for the conduct of war, including rights for prisoners of war and the protection of civilians.

> **UN Charter** This says that member states may only go to war as a means of self-defense or to maintain international security when all other options for resolving conflict have been exhausted.

> **War crimes** These are dealt with by the International Criminal Court and are judged according to just war principles.

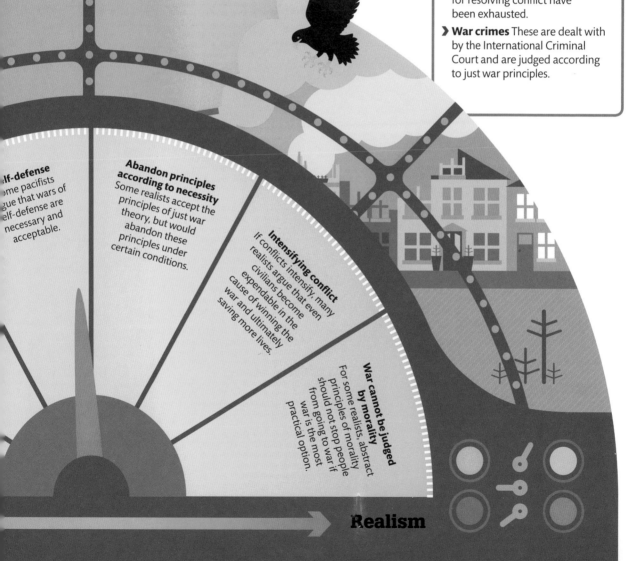

Self-defense
Some pacifists argue that wars of self-defense are necessary and acceptable.

Abandon principles according to necessity
Some realists accept the principles of just war theory, but would abandon these principles under certain conditions.

Intensifying conflict
If conflicts intensify, many realists argue that even civilians become expendable in the cause of winning the war and ultimately saving more lives.

War cannot be judged by morality
For some realists, abstract principles of morality should not stop people from going to war if war is the most practical option.

Realism

Women and patriarchy

All feminists believe that women should have the same rights as men, but many still debate the best way to achieve this when men hold most of the power.

The patriarchy problem

Patriarchy is a social system in which men are more powerful than women, and women struggle to gain the same employment and political rights as men. It is prevalent in both the workplace and the home, with women still expected to be largely responsible for domestic chores and childcare. The feminist movement aims to dismantle patriarchy and bring about equality between men and women. But feminists do not all agree on what the most effective way of dismantling patriarchy might be.

What can feminists do?

One of the first feminist tracts was *A Vindication of the Rights of Women* (1792) by Mary Wollstonecraft. In it, she argues that society is patriarchal because women have been taught to accept their submission to men, and that reeducating women is therefore one way to create a fairer and more equal society.

The philosopher and liberal politician John Stuart Mill (see pp.186–187) supported equal rights for women, but argued that men, as well as women, needed to be educated to question patriarchy.

However, education on its own has not been enough to dismantle patriarchy, which is still very much in evidence today. Some feminists propose more controversial methods of combatting patriarchy, such as positive discrimination in the workplace. Even more controversially, the sociologist Catherine Hakim suggests that in order to survive within a patriarchal system, women should use their erotic appeal to gain advantage over men.

Treatments

There are advantages and disadvantages to many of the proposed ways to dismantle patriarchy. Education is still important, but it has failed to completely solve the problem. Positive discrimination is a means of correcting the legacy of workplace discrimination against women. However, it is still discrimination, and appointing a woman over a better-qualified male candidate could stigmatize her or leave her feeling patronized. Many people would argue that self-criticism is vital for anyone who wants to combat patriarchy. If women are self-critical, they are more likely to question the ways in which they have been conditioned to submit to men. If men are self-critical, they will be able to discern their privilege and be more empathetic toward women.

SELF REEDUCATION

Girls and women should be taught not to accept their submission to men.

PUBLIC EDUCATION

Educating women alone is not enough. Men must be taught to accept women as their equals.

Antidotes

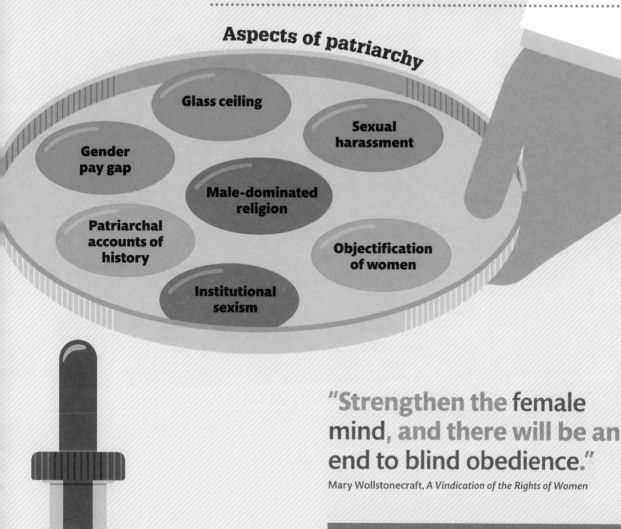

Aspects of patriarchy

- Glass ceiling
- Sexual harassment
- Gender pay gap
- Male-dominated religion
- Patriarchal accounts of history
- Objectification of women
- Institutional sexism

"Strengthen the female mind, and there will be an end to blind obedience."

Mary Wollstonecraft, *A Vindication of the Rights of Women*

POSITIVE DISCRIMINATION

There should be preferential hiring, higher pay, and generous admissions policies for women.

FEMINIST PHILOSOPHY

Before the rise of the women's movement in the 1960s and '70s (see pp.128–129; 138–141), philosophy was itself patriarchal, with the vast majority of philosophical arguments put forward by men. Feminist philosophy addresses this problem by asking three main questions:

❯ **The role of gender** What role has gender played in the formation of traditional philosophical problems and concepts?

❯ **Bias** How does traditional philosophy reflect and reinforce bias against women?

❯ **Equality** What is the best way to defend philosophical concepts and theories that presume women's equality?

LOGIC

Philosophers offer arguments to defend their particular
views. However, they also have views on the nature of
argument itself. This is the field of logic, which asks:
What makes a good argument compelling?

LOGIC

Aristotle thought that humans are the only rational animals. Other philosophers disagree with this, but human reason is certainly unlike that of any other animal. It has taken us to the Moon, helped us to understand the workings of our own planet, and enabled us to create societies in which cooperation has replaced competition.

On a smaller scale, reason enables individuals to form plans and therefore achieve their goals. No matter what our goals are, we need to decide how best to achieve them. So reasoning takes two forms: theoretical reasoning, by which we determine truth, and practical reasoning, by which we determine success. Bad theoretical reasoning usually leads to falsehood, and bad practical reasoning usually leads to failure. Aristotle attempted to describe reasoning in such a way as to distinguish good from bad reasoning. This is the discipline of logic, the subject matter of which is argument—that is, the process of reaching true conclusions from true premises.

Arguments fall into two broad categories: deductive arguments and inductive arguments. Deductions move from general premises to specific conclusions about particular states of affairs. For example, the argument "All dogs are brown. Fido is a dog. Therefore, Fido is brown," draws a specific conclusion about Fido based on a general premise about the nature of dogs. This is an example of a "syllogism"— a type of argument that was identified by Aristotle and takes the form "All As are X. B is an A. Therefore, B is X." It is important to note that the conclusion about Fido is valid whether or not it is true that all dogs are brown in reality. Inductions, on the other hand, draw general conclusions from specific states of affairs—such as "All the swans I have seen have been white; therefore, all swans are white." Here, it is important to note that the conclusion is not valid— it is little more than a speculation based on the premises. Nevertheless, induction is the method of science—it is the way in which theories are constructed and revised.

Aristotle focused on deductive logic, producing a system of formal syllogisms that are still in use over two millennia later. In the 19th century, the German mathematician Gottlob Frege brought logic into the modern age. He created a system of formal notation into which sentences in ordinary language can be translated, thus revealing their logical structure.

However, there are limitations to the usefulness of formal logic. Not all deductive arguments can be shown to be conclusive, and there is no logical justification for the process of induction. The conclusion of even the best inductive argument is only made probable by the truth of its premises. Nevertheless, both forms of argument are immensely useful to practical reasoning, and logical language governs everything we do with computers. Logic thus offers a glimpse into the potential, and limits, of our cognitive abilities.

Rationality

Aristotle believed that human beings are the only rational animals. He argued that we are rational because we are capable of acting for reasons and using rational thought to acquire new beliefs from old.

Acting for reasons

To act for reasons is to have in our mind, as we act, a description of our act, and to perform it in the hope of achieving some goal, even if that goal is not achieved. For instance, I might reach out my hand for my coffee cup and, in doing so, knock over a vase of flowers. I may not have intended to knock over the vase. However, the act of knocking it over was identical to the act of reaching for my coffee—an act that was intentional: I was choosing to perform it in the hope of satisfying my desire for coffee.

We know that normal human beings are generally rational in that we usually act for specific reasons. This means that many of our actions are informed by processes of reasoning—strings of rationally related beliefs. So one belief might include a reason that supports another belief (in that, if the first belief is true, the second belief is more likely to be true). Or two beliefs might entail a third (so if the first two beliefs are true, then the third must be true). Or one belief might contradict another (so that if the first is true, then the second is false, or vice versa). All these rational relations are useful for determining the extent to which we should—or should not—accept a given belief as true.

What is logic?

Logic is the study of argument, which means that logic is also the study of reasoning, since reasoning is based on arguments (see pp.236–237). In the same way that arguments can be good or bad, reasoning, too, can be good or bad. In this way, logic sets standards for behavior. It is interesting to note that it would not be possible to be irrational if we were not rational beings. Our capacity to act for reasons means that we are capable of acting for either good or bad reasons. When we act for a bad reason, we are being irrational.

But many actions cannot be said to be either rational or irrational. Such actions are not performed for a reason and are described as "nonrational." Nonrational actions may, for example, include instinctive or emotional reactions to things or events.

Two ways of thinking

Modern psychologists have embraced the "dual process" theory of mind, which suggests that our minds use two processes or systems. The first, known as system one, generates fast, automatic responses to stimuli; the second, system two, provides a slow, reasoned, and conscious response to problems.

SYSTEM ONE

If someone sees a snowball flying at their face and ducks, it might seem as if they acted for a reason—that is, ducking to avoid the snowball. However, it is more likely that there were no beliefs and desires involved in the action— it was simply automatic, like a reflex. This is "system one" thinking.

REASON IN ANIMALS

Do nonhuman animals act for specific reasons? Those of us who have pets or watch nature shows on television will probably believe that a great deal of animals' behavior suggests that they are rational—that they do act for reasons. But we have to be careful: animals cannot tell us why they behave in the way they do, while humans can, because we use language. The fact that animals cannot tell us whether they act for reasons does not mean that animals do not act for reasons, of course. But it does mean that, in order to be certain, we need to conduct careful experiments. What we do know is that understanding language is essential to understanding logic.

ALTHOUGH SOME ANIMALS can make speechlike sounds, they cannot use language to explain their actions.

"Nothing in life is as important as you think it is, while you are thinking about it."

Daniel Kahneman, *Thinking, Fast and Slow* (2011)

SYSTEM TWO

If someone has to engage in the kind of thinking and problem-solving that requires quite a lot of effort and attention, then they are using "system two" thinking. An example of a system two problem was posed by the psychologist Daniel Kahneman: gloves and a hat cost $1.10. The hat costs $1 more than the gloves. How much are the gloves? (System one thinking would offer 10 cents as an easy answer, but the correct answer is 5 cents.)

Recognizing arguments

In logic, if we make a claim, we will be expected to justify it and to show that there is no counterargument to that claim. To do this, we must first be able to recognize an argument.

What is an argument?

In order to reason well—to put forward an argument in support of a claim and address arguments against that claim—we must be able to distinguish arguments from the other ways we use language (see below). An argument is a set of sentences, or a complex single sentence that can be broken down into smaller "atomic" sentences, in which one sentence is being asserted on the basis of one or more others. (An atomic sentence is a sentence, all the constituents of which are less than sentences.)

Premises and conclusion

In any set of sentences that makes up an argument, the sentences must be related as premises (the reasons given) and a conclusion (the assertion made). Here is an example of an argument made up of three atomic sentences: "All men are mortal [premise 1], and since Socrates is a man [premise 2], Socrates is mortal [conclusion]." Arguments structured like this are called syllogisms.

Many sets of sentences are not arguments. For a set of sentences to be an argument, one sentence must assert something and the others must give reasons for that assertion.

Language line-up

People use language in many ways other than constructing arguments. For example, they make assertions ("It's Tuesday"), they ask questions ("Is it Tuesday?"), they issue commands ("Close the door!"), they make predictions ("It'll be behind the door"), and they offer explanations ("Because that is where she put it"). A philosopher must be able to pick out an argument from among these other uses of language.

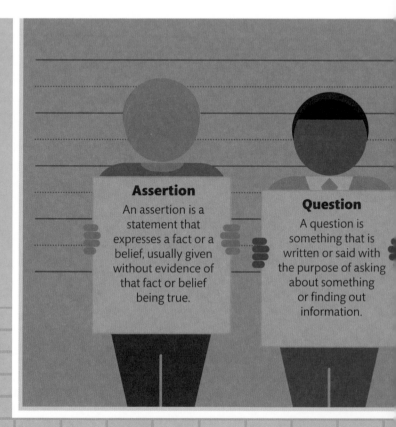

Assertion
An assertion is a statement that expresses a fact or a belief, usually given without evidence of that fact or belief being true.

Question
A question is something that is written or said with the purpose of asking about something or finding out information.

HOW TO SPOT A NONARGUMENT

An argument must include a conclusion (the assertion made) and premises (the reasons given for the conclusion). If no assertion is made, no reasons can be given, so there is no argument. Here are two examples of nonarguments.

No conclusion

"Socrates went to the library. While Socrates was out, there was a storm. The storm frightened Socrates' parrot." None of these sentences is being asserted in such a way that the others are being offered as reasons. This is not, therefore, an argument.

Conditional

"If Socrates is a man, then he is mortal." This is not an argument because neither of its atomic parts ("Socrates is a man", "He is mortal") is being asserted on the basis of the other. It is a conditional—the whole sentence is being asserted.

✓ NEED TO KNOW

> **The conclusion** of an argument is the assertion or claim being made on the basis of the premises given.

> **The premises** of an argument are the reasons given for the assertion being made (the conclusion). A premise may be contained within another premise.

> **A syllogism** is a form of logical argument first defined by Aristotle. An example would be "All dogs are four-legged. Rover is a dog. Therefore, Rover is four-legged." The first premise is a general statement; the second premise is specific; and the conclusion is necessarily true.

"Truth springs from argument amongst friends."

David Hume

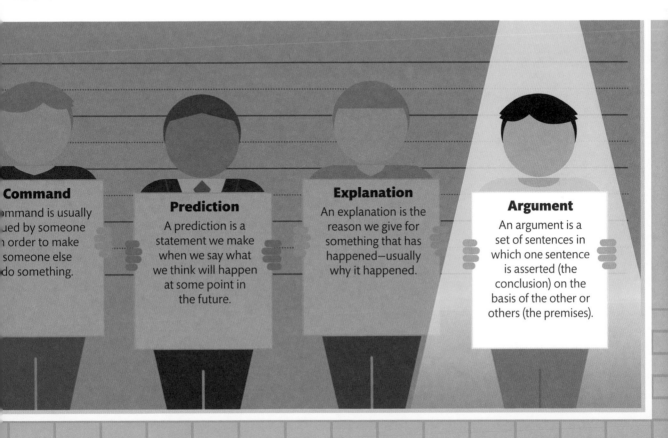

Command
A command is usually issued by someone in order to make someone else do something.

Prediction
A prediction is a statement we make when we say what we think will happen at some point in the future.

Explanation
An explanation is the reason we give for something that has happened—usually why it happened.

Argument
An argument is a set of sentences in which one sentence is asserted (the conclusion) on the basis of the other or others (the premises).

Analyzing arguments

Analyzing an argument involves identifying its premises and its conclusion and eliminating anything irrelevant or unclear that makes it more difficult to identify the premises and conclusion.

Simple and complex arguments

Having recognized an argument (see pp.236–237), the next step in testing if its conclusion is true or false is to analyze it. To analyze an argument, we must identify its premises and conclusion and set these out "logic-book style" (see box, opposite). Some arguments are so simple that it can seem pointless to analyze them.

But many of the arguments we encounter in everyday life are more complex. For example, they may contain information that has no relevance to the conclusion or words whose meaning is unclear. Analyzing these complex arguments enables us to remove any irrelevant or confusing details and to understand what the premises and conclusion of the argument really are.

Analyzing a complex argument

Most of the arguments that we come across in everyday life are very complex. They may contain irrelevant details or ambiguities, and it can be difficult to identify their premises and conclusion. The argument below is so complex that it is not easy to make sense of it until we analyze it logic-book style.

① **Red will only succeed in avoiding elimination** ⑤ **if** ④ **they beat blue, and furthermore** ④ **they will not succeed without losing to green along the way.** ③ **For as a quick look at the table will show, they** ④ **cannot avoid** ⑤ **going down unless** ④ **they beat** ② **green or blue, and** ③ **even then, green will have to** ② **beat yellow. It is** ③ **certain that if green beat** ② **yellow,** ④ **they will not fail against red.**

Suppressed premises

An argument might leave out, or suppress, a premise. This may be because a premise is obvious. For example, if someone says that it is raining and they are going out with an umbrella, they do not have to add "because I don't want to get wet." However, if a premise has been suppressed because it is controversial, when we analyze the argument, we should supply that premise. For example, if someone argues that they have no children, so they should pay less tax than people who do, they have suppressed the controversial premise that people should only have to pay for services if they use them.

LOGIC-BOOK STYLE

Setting out an argument logic-book style involves listing its premises in a logical order that shows how they lead to the conclusion. For example, the argument "The red team will go through if the blue team loses, and blue have lost, so red will go through" can be set out as follows:

❯ **Premise 1** The red team will go through to the next round if the blue team lose their next match.

❯ **Premise 2** The blue team have lost their next match.

❯ **Conclusion** Therefore, the red team will go through.

Six steps to analyzing an argument

To analyze an argument logic-book style, first identify the conclusion and premises. Next, eliminate any confusing factors, such as irrelevancies, words that refer back to something, and inconsistent terminology. Finally, make sure that any controversial premises (those which we might not agree with) have not been left out of the argument.

(1) Identify the conclusion
The conclusion is the claim being made. We may be able to identify it by spotting words such as "so" or "therefore." In this argument, the conclusion is "Red will only avoid elimination if red beat blue and lose to green."

☐ CONCLUSION

(2) Identify the premises
There are three premises (reasons for the conclusion): red will not avoid elimination unless red beat blue or green; red will not avoid elimination unless green beat yellow; and if green beat yellow, green will also beat red.

——— PREMISE 1
·········· PREMISE 2
▬ ▬ ▬ PREMISE 3

(3) Eliminate irrelevancies
An irrelevancy may be a reason (e.g., "as a quick look at the table will show") for a premise but not a premise itself, or just a turn of phrase (e.g., "it is certain that"). They have no bearing on the conclusion, so should be removed.

IRRELEVANT WORDS OR INFORMATION

(4) Remove cross-references
If we replace cross-references with the words that they refer back to, the argument will be easier for us to understand. Here, the last "they" refers to green, while the other "they" refers to red.

⬭ "THEY" = RED
 "THEY" = GREEN

(5) Remove inconsistent terminology
In this argument, "elimination" and "going down" mean the same thing. To make the argument clearer, we should use one term or the other, but not both terms.

DIFFERENT WORDS THAT MEAN EXACTLY THE SAME THING

(6) Supply controversial suppressed premises
In many arguments (not the one here), one or more premises may have been left out, or suppressed. Suppressing controversial premises can give the impression that an argument is stronger than it actually is, so we should identify and supply these premises.

Evaluating arguments

Evaluating an argument involves establishing whether or not it is sound—that is, whether or not the conclusion follows from the premises and whether or not those premises are true.

A good argument

If an argument's conclusion follows from its premises (see pp.236–237), that argument is "good." This is true whether or not the premises are true. So some—or all—of the premises of a good argument might be false. For example: "All women are immortal [premise 1]. Socrates is a woman [premise 2]. Socrates is immortal [conclusion]." Both premises here are false. However, the conclusion follows from the premises in that if the premises were true, the conclusion would also be true—so the argument itself is good. When a conclusion does not follow from the premises, the argument is "bad."

If a conclusion follows from a set of premises, then accepting that the premises are true gives us good reason to believe the conclusion. In a good deductive argument (see pp.242–243), we can be sure that if the premises are true, the conclusion is true. In a good inductive argument (see pp.244–245), if the premises are true, the conclusion is likely (though not, as with deductive arguments, certain) to be true.

A sound argument

Once we have established that an argument is good, the next stage is to question whether or not its

How to evaluate an argument

Evaluating an argument is a two-stage process. Only once the argument has been found to be good (by confirming that its conclusion follows from its premises—that is, if its premises are all true, its conclusion is certain or likely to be true) can the truth of its premises be assessed. If the argument is good and all of its premises are true, it is a sound argument—the ideal argument.

> "[Logic] provides a mastery of invention and judgment."
>
> John of Salisbury, *Metalogicon* (1159)

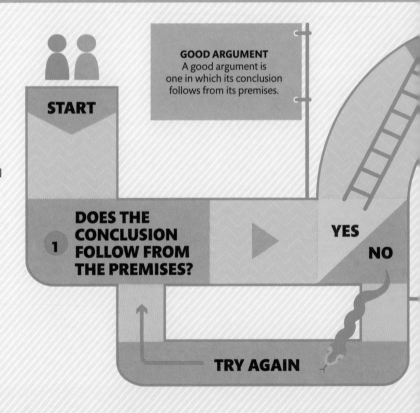

START

GOOD ARGUMENT
A good argument is one in which its conclusion follows from its premises.

1 DOES THE CONCLUSION FOLLOW FROM THE PREMISES?

YES

NO

TRY AGAIN

premises are true or false. However, it is often difficult to know if a premise is true or false. This is why it is so important that arguments are good.

If a deductive argument is good and its conclusion turns out to be false, then we know that at least one of its premises must be false (see pp.242–43). A good deductive argument with a false conclusion can therefore be extremely useful in identifying one or more false premises. Inductive arguments are not quite so useful, as the conclusion might follow from true premises and still be false (see pp.244–45).

Philosophers are experts on whether or not arguments are good, but it is scientists who tend to be experts on whether or not the premises of an argument are true (see box). The ideal argument is good, and all of its premises are true. This is what we call a "sound" argument. All sound arguments are good, but not all good arguments are sound, because a good argument can still have false premises.

THE SCIENTIFIC METHOD

The scientific method uses good deductive arguments to determine whether a hypothesis (commonly reached by inductive argument) is false. For example, in 1859, the mathematician Urbain Le Verrier discovered that the conclusion of the good argument below is false:

Premise one: If Newton's Laws of Motion are correct, Mercury's orbit will be regular.

Premise two: Newton's Laws of Motion are correct.

Conclusion: Mercury's orbit is regular.

Le Verrier observed that Mercury's orbit is not regular (so the conclusion of this deductive argument is false). This meant at least one of the premises of this good argument must be false. So either we have misunderstood Newton's Laws of Motion (they do not imply that Mercury's orbit will be regular) or Newton's Laws of Motion are not correct. Einstein later proved that the mass of the Sun affects Mercury's orbit (and that Newton's Laws of Motion are not always and everywhere correct).

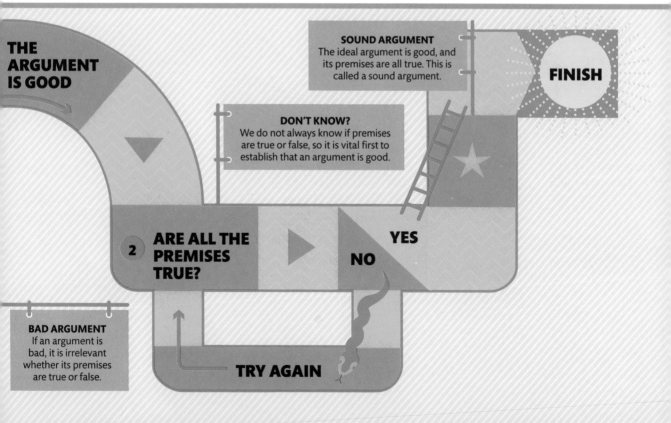

THE ARGUMENT IS GOOD

SOUND ARGUMENT
The ideal argument is good, and its premises are all true. This is called a sound argument.

FINISH

DON'T KNOW?
We do not always know if premises are true or false, so it is vital first to establish that an argument is good.

2 ARE ALL THE PREMISES TRUE?

YES

NO

BAD ARGUMENT
If an argument is bad, it is irrelevant whether its premises are true or false.

TRY AGAIN

Deductive arguments

Aristotle was the first philosopher to study the principles of deduction. Deductive arguments are constructed in such a way that, if they are valid and their premises are true, the conclusion must also be true.

Valid is good

In a good argument, the conclusion (the assertion made) follows from the premises (the reasons given), regardless of whether the premises are true or false (see pp.240–241). A good deductive argument is called a "valid" argument. An argument is valid if and only if there is no logically possible situation in which its premises are true and its conclusion is false.

The notion of validity is often misunderstood. We may think, for example, that a deductive argument with false premises cannot be valid. But as long as we can work out (deduce) the argument's conclusion from the premises given—whether the premises are true or false—that argument is valid.

False but still valid

Just as a deductive argument with false premises can be valid, so can a deductive argument with a false conclusion. For example: "Tigers always have stripes [premise 1].

Domestic cats are little tigers [premise 2]. Domestic cats always have stripes [conclusion]." This is a valid (good) deductive argument because if the premises were true, the conclusion would also be true. But the conclusion isn't true, so the argument is not sound—at least one of its premises is false. (Even if premise 2 is metaphorically true, it isn't literally so.) In a sound argument, the premises must be true, and the conclusion must follow from those premises.

Validity and truth

If we know that the conclusion of a deductive argument is false but that the argument is valid, we can deduce that a premise must be false. So validity and truth are not the same thing. Validity preserves truth; it does not generate it. If the premises of a valid argument are true, then the conclusion of that argument is guaranteed by logic also to be true. This is an extremely useful property for an argument to have.

1

VALID OR INVALID
The question of whether a deductive argument is valid is an either/or question: either the argument is valid or it is not. There are no degrees of validity.

Evaluating a deductive argument

As with any argument, when it comes to evaluating a deductive argument, the first question to ask is whether or not the conclusion follows from the premises. This can be answered by trying to imagine a counterexample—a possible situation in which the premises are all true but the conclusion is false. The argument is valid if and only if there is no counterexample. The second question to ask is whether the premises themselves are true or false. A sound deductive argument has true premises and a conclusion that, given the truth of the premises, is guaranteed to be true by logic.

"Every good philosopher is at least half a mathematician."

Gottlob Frege, mathematician

2 TRUTH AND CERTAINTY

If the premises of a deductively valid argument are true, we can be certain that the conclusion will be true. Deductive validity gives us certainty (based on the truth of the premises).

DETECTING DEDUCTION

There are three characteristics of deductive arguments. These enable us to distinguish deductive arguments from inductive arguments (see pp.244–245).

3 EVALUABLE *A PRIORI*

We can work out whether or not a deductive argument is valid using only the words that make up that argument. We need no background knowledge other than our understanding of these words (our *a priori* knowledge) to evaluate it.

✓ NEED TO KNOW

❯ **A counterexample** is a possible situation in which the premises are true and the conclusion is false. An argument is valid if there is no counterexample.

❯ **A priori knowledge** (see pp.68–9) does not rest on experience of the world. Deductive arguments can be evaluated *a priori*, and in doing so, established as valid or invalid.

❯ **A sound deductive argument** is valid and its premises are true. This means that its conclusion is also true.

Inductive arguments

Unlike deductive arguments (see pp.242–243), inductive arguments can never be valid (see pp.240–241). This is because the conclusion of an inductive argument may not be true even if its premises are true.

The nature of induction

Deduction and induction are two different kinds of arguments. Deduction gives us certainty because a good (valid) deductive argument is always such that if its premises are true, its conclusion must be true. For example, if all men are mortal, and Socrates is a man, then Socrates is mortal. This is not true for inductive arguments, which can have false conclusions even when their premises are true. Determining a good inductive argument, therefore, cannot involve deciding whether or not it is valid. However, we can still assess an inductive argument's strength or weakness by evaluating how likely it is that its conclusion will be true if its premises are true.

Types of inductive argument

Unlike deductive arguments, whose conclusions follow logically from their premises, inductive arguments (see box) are based on assumptions. An inductive generalization assumes that something is always the case because it has happened in the past. A causal generalization assumes that one thing always causes another. An argument from authority assumes that the opinion of a perceived authority figure is correct. An argument from analogy makes a claim about one thing on the basis of its perceived similarity to something else. Finally, an abductive argument is an attempt to find the best explanation for something given the available evidence.

Evaluating inductions

Although all inductive arguments are invalid, we can still evaluate an inductive argument according to how strong or weak it is. The stronger an inductive argument is, the more likely its conclusion is to follow from its premises. Unlike deductive arguments, inductive arguments cannot be evaluated *a priori*, or on the basis of the premises and conclusion alone. To evaluate an inductive argument, we need background information about its subject matter. Take the argument "The traffic on this road is bad every time I drive on it, so it will be bad tomorrow." To evaluate the argument, we would need to know how many times the speaker had driven on the road and whether any temporary conditions that had made the traffic worse might no longer apply. If we had this information, we would be far better placed to assess whether the argument is weak or strong.

Weak argument
"It was sunny on June 30 this year. Therefore, it will be sunny on June 30 next year." The weather is so difficult to predict that the conclusion is very unlikely to follow from the premise.

CONCLUSION UNLIKELY

TYPES OF INDUCTIVE ARGUMENT

There are many different types of inductive argument. Each type of argument is associated with one or more questions that someone who wants to evaluate the argument would ask.

TYPE	EXAMPLE	QUESTION(S)
INDUCTIVE GENERALIZATION	Sue's voicemail is on whenever I call her, so it must always be on.	How many times have I tried to call Sue? Does she want to avoid me?
CAUSAL GENERALIZATION	When I call Sue, I feel nervous, so calling Sue makes me nervous.	Does it always make me nervous? Does anything else make me nervous?
ARGUMENT FROM AUTHORITY	Sue told me that philosophy is dead. Therefore, philosophy is dead.	Is Sue an expert on the history of philosophy?
ARGUMENT FROM ANALOGY	Philosophy is like math. Math is easy. Therefore, philosophy is easy.	Is there any way in which philosophy is not like math? Is all math easy?
ABDUCTIVE ARGUMENT	The phone is ringing. Sue may have got my message. Therefore, Sue is calling.	Could there be anyone else trying to call me?

Moderate argument
"Leo predicts that it will be sunny tomorrow. Therefore, it will be sunny tomorrow." The strength of this argument depends on the reliability of Leo's forecasts—which may be reliable.

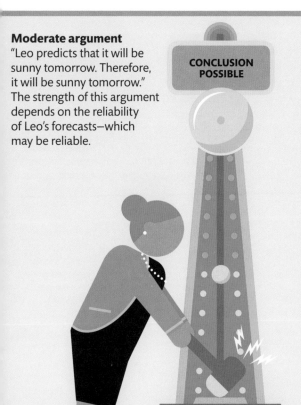

CONCLUSION POSSIBLE

Strong argument
"Leo's weather forecasts have always been reliable, so his present forecast is reliable." The premise of this argument gives enough evidence to make its conclusion likely.

CONCLUSION PROBABLE

Fallacies

A fallacy is a bad argument (one that depends on faulty reasoning) that can easily be mistaken for a good argument. Recognizing the various types of fallacy helps us to identify bad arguments and reason well.

Fallacies, not false beliefs

In everyday language, people often talk about fallacies as being false beliefs, but this is not the case. A fallacy is in fact an argument that depends on bad reasoning but that appears to depend on good reasoning. Sometimes people argue fallaciously on purpose to manipulate an opponent. But arguments can be unintentionally fallacious.

There are many different types of fallacious argument. Some are fallacious because of the way in which the argument is structured; others are fallacious because of the content of the argument. It is easy to mistake a fallacy for a good argument, so anyone who wants to reason well and avoid using fallacies must be able to recognize the most common types of fallacy.

FORMAL
Formal fallacies depend on the form, structure, or logical order of an argument. They do not relate to its content.

INFORMAL
Informal fallacies depend on the content of an argument. The argument would still be a fallacy even if its content was arranged in a different order.

GOOD VS. BAD ARGUMENT

Modus ponens is a form of good argument. Its first premise (see pp.236–237) is a conditional ("if ... then") sentence. Its second premise is the "if" clause (the "antecedent") of the first premise. Its conclusion is the "then" clause (the "consequent") of the first premise. If its premises are true, its conclusion must also be true.

The fallacy of affirming the consequent can easily be mistaken for a *modus ponens* argument. In this fallacy, the second premise is not the antecedent but the consequent. It is a bad argument because its conclusion can be false even if its premises are true. See the example below: the shirt does not fit, but this is not necessarily because it is too small. It could be too big.

Modus ponens argument	Fallacy of affirming the consequent
Premise one: If this shirt is too small, it will not fit.	**Premise one:** If this shirt is too small, it won't fit.
Premise two: This shirt is too small.	**Premise two:** This shirt doesn't fit.
Conclusion: This shirt does not fit.	**Conclusion:** This shirt is too small.

Categorizing fallacies

Aristotle identified 13 fallacies, which he divided into two categories: fallacies outside language, which have become known as formal fallacies, and fallacies that depend on language, which have become known as informal fallacies. This broad categorization is still used today.

AFFIRMING THE CONSEQUENT

In this fallacy (see box), it is assumed that if the "then" clause of a conditional sentence (the consequent) is true, the "if" clause must also be true. This is a bad argument because it can be disproved with counterexamples (see pp.242–243).

DENYING THE ANTECEDENT

This fallacy assumes that if the "if" of a sentence is not true, the "then" cannot be true. For example: "If this shirt is too small, it will not fit. The shirt is not too small, therefore the shirt fits." This can have a counterexample: the shirt might not be too small, but not fit because it is too big.

CONJUNCTION FALLACY

This fallacy means mistakenly thinking that two states of affairs occurring at the same time is more probable than either one occurring in isolation. However, one event is always more likely to occur on its event than two events in conjunction, no matter how much they might seem to be linked.

EQUIVOCATION

This fallacy is committed whenever a single word (or phrase) with two different meanings is used within an argument. For example: "I wear cool clothes in hot weather and fashionable clothes are cool, so I wear fashionable clothes in hot weather." "Cool" does not have the same meaning throughout this argument.

STRAW MAN

The straw man fallacy involves misrepresenting or distorting an opponent's argument. For example, if Joe says children should wear school uniforms, Mia might accuse him of saying children should not express themselves. Mia would be creating a straw man argument that could distract Joe into an attempt to defend himself.

CIRCULAR ARGUMENT

In a circular argument, the conclusion is the same as the premise (or one of the premises). For example: "All sandals are shoes, therefore all sandals are shoes." This argument is valid (see pp.242–243) but not useful because anyone who accepted the premise would already accept the conclusion.

Formal logic

One of the best ways to evaluate an argument is to translate it into a string of symbols called formulae. This removes any ambiguity in the argument and reveals its logical structure.

Translating natural language

Converting an argument from natural, everyday language into its logical form entails replacing its words with symbols. These symbols represent the various elements of the argument and show how they relate to each other.

Having formalized an argument, we can then use a purely "mechanical" system for evaluating it and comparing it with other arguments. Replacing words with symbols in this way allows us to focus on an argument's formal structure.

The simplest branch of formal logic is called the propositional

calculus. This breaks an argument down into the simplest statements possible—its propositions. However, many arguments cannot be broken down into the propositional calculus because their validity relies on sub-propositional form. In these cases, we can sometimes use the predicate

Formalizing and testing arguments

If an argument can be translated into its logical form using the propositional or the predicate calculus, we are able to follow a set of simple rules to help us evaluate it. These rules can only be applied once an argument has been formalized.

Propositional calculus
This simple deductive argument can be translated into propositional calculus.

PREMISE 1: IF THE SUNFLOWERS ARE OUT, THEN THE SUN WILL BE SHINING.
PREMISE 2: THE SUNFLOWERS ARE OUT.
CONCLUSION: THE SUN WILL BE SHINING.

Assign "sentence letters" to the propositions
To apply propositional calculus, identify the propositions that constitute the argument and assign a "sentence letter" to each proposition. Here, the sentence letters are P and Q.

P: THE SUNFLOWERS ARE OUT.
Q: THE SUN WILL BE SHINING.

Replace the propositions with the sentence letters
By using sentence letters instead of words, we reveal the logical structure of the argument. Here, the argument depends on the conditional, or the logical constant "if ... then" (see box).

LOGICAL CONSTANT
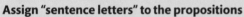
PREMISE 1: IF P THEN Q
PREMISE 2: P
CONCLUSION: Q

Insert the logical constant symbol and brackets
The next step is to replace the logical words "if" and "then" (see box) with the logical constant that symbolizes them (an arrow) and insert brackets to make it clear which sentence letters the arrow relates to.

PREMISE 1: $(P \rightarrow Q)$
PREMISE 2: P
CONCLUSION: Q

Formalize the argument as a sequent
We use the double turnstile ($\vDash$) symbol to specify that there is no situation in which the formulae to the left of the symbol are true and the formulae to the right are false. This formalizes the relationship between the premises and the conclusion.

$(P \rightarrow Q), P \vDash Q$

calculus to analyze the arguments. The predicate calculus is the second simplest branch of formal logic.

Limits to formal logic

Many arguments cannot be converted into formal language. It is not possible to formalize any inductive argument (see pp.244–245), and many deductive arguments (see pp.242–243) cannot be formalized into the simple languages of the propositional or the predicate calculus.

LOGICAL CONSTANTS

Logical constants are words that have a constant meaning. In formal logic, they are represented by symbols. There are different sets of symbols (notational variants). The one used here is the most common set.

CONSTANT	MEANING	SYMBOL
Negation	"it is not the case that"	~
Conjunction	"and"	&
Disjunction	"or"	v
Conditional	"if ... then"	→
Biconditional	"if and only if"	⟷

PREMISE 1: ALL DAFFODILS ARE YELLOW.
PREMISE 2: THAT FLOWER IS A DAFFODIL.
CONCLUSION: THAT FLOWER IS YELLOW.

Predicate calculus
Some arguments, such as the one on the left, cannot be translated into propositional calculus—their formal structure would be lost. They have to be translated into predicate calculus.

Dx: x IS A DAFFODIL.
Yx: x IS YELLOW.
A: THAT FLOWER.

Assign letters
Assign letters to each element of the argument. Here, Y means "is yellow," D means "is a daffodil," A means "that flower," and x represents an unknown thing that is both Y (yellow) and D (a daffodil).

PREMISE 1: ∀x (Dx → Yx)
PREMISE 2: Da
CONCLUSION: Ya

Display the logical structure
To reveal the logical structure of an argument, we must once again formalize it. In the conclusion, ∀x means "everything, x, is such that" and (Dx → Yx) means "if x is yellow, x is a daffodil."

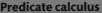 ∀x (Dx → Yx), Da⊢ Fa

Formalize the argument as a "sequent"
Finally, we must express the argument as a "sequent" of predicate calculus. This formalizes the relationship between premises and conclusion. To do this, we use the single turnstile symbol (⊢). This symbol tells us that the formulae to the right of the symbol can be proved by the formulae to the left of the symbol.

Index

Acknowledgments

Dorling Kindersley would like to thank Hugo Wilkinson for editorial assistance; Phil Gamble for design assistance; Alexandra Beeden and Katie John for proofreading; and Helen Peters for indexing.

The publisher would like to thank the following for their kind permission to reproduce their photographs:

(Key: a-above; b-below/bottom; c-center; f-far; l-left; r-right; t-top)

65 123RF.com: loganban (br). **86 123RF. com:** Panagiotis Karapanagiotis / karapas (b). **100 Alamy Stock Photo:** Geoff Marshall (b). **131 Alamy Stock Photo:** PhotoAlto (tr). **137 Getty Images:** Underwood Archives (br). **141 123RF.com:** Francesco Gustincich / develop (tr). **171 Alamy Stock Photo:** Michael Kemp (br). **191 123RF.com:** Andor Bujdoso / nd3000 (br). **195 Alamy Stock Photo:** ilpo musto (tr). **210 Getty Images:** Hill Street Studios (bl). **235 Getty Images:** Mike Powell (tc).

All other images © Dorling Kindersley
For further information see:
www.dkimages.com